RADICAL PHILOSOPHY

2.18
Series 2 / Autumn 2023

Civilising through food **Hourya Bentouhami**	3
Interpassive students in interactive classrooms **Alan Bradshaw and Mikael Andehn**	16
Development as national liberation **Martín Arboleda**	23
The canonisation of the Frankfurt School as 'permanent exiles' **Ryan Crawford**	39
Grammars of the figure in the Iranian Uprising **Austin Gross**	57
Aijaz Ahmad (1941–2022) in memoriam **Ammar Ali Jan, Rafeef Ziadah and Rashmi Varma**	64

REVIEWS

Mark Bould, *The Anthropocene Unconscious: Climate Catastrophe Culture* The Salvage Collective, *The Tragedy of the Worker: Towards the Proletarocene* **Chris Wilbert**	77
Roberto Esposito, *Institution* **Matt Phull**	80
Oishik Sircar, *Violent Modernities: Cultural Lives of Law in the New India* **Ntina Tzouvala**	83
Terry Pinkard, *Practice, Power, and Forms of Life* **Ethan Linehan**	86
Emmanuel Alloa, *Looking Through Images* **Tullio Viola**	89
Lorenzo Kom'boa Ervin, *Anarchism and the Black Revolution* **Christopher J. Lee**	93
Alexander Kluge, *Russia Container* **Marina Gerber**	96
Raphaël Fèvre, *A Political Economy of Power* **Isabel Oakes**	99
Drucilla Cornell, 1950-2022 **Chiara Bottici**	102
Bruno Latour, 1947–2022 **Patrice Maniglier**	104
Maria Mies, 1931-2023 **Alessandra Mezzadri**	111

Editorial collective
Brenna Bhandar
Victoria Browne
David Cunningham
Isabell Dahms
Peter Hallward
Lucie Mercier
Daniel Nemenyi
Hannah Proctor
Rahul Rao
Martina Tazzioli
Chris Wilbert

Engineers
Daniel Nemenyi

CC BY-NC-ND
RP, Autumn 2023

ISSN 0300-211X
ISBN 978-1-914099-04-5

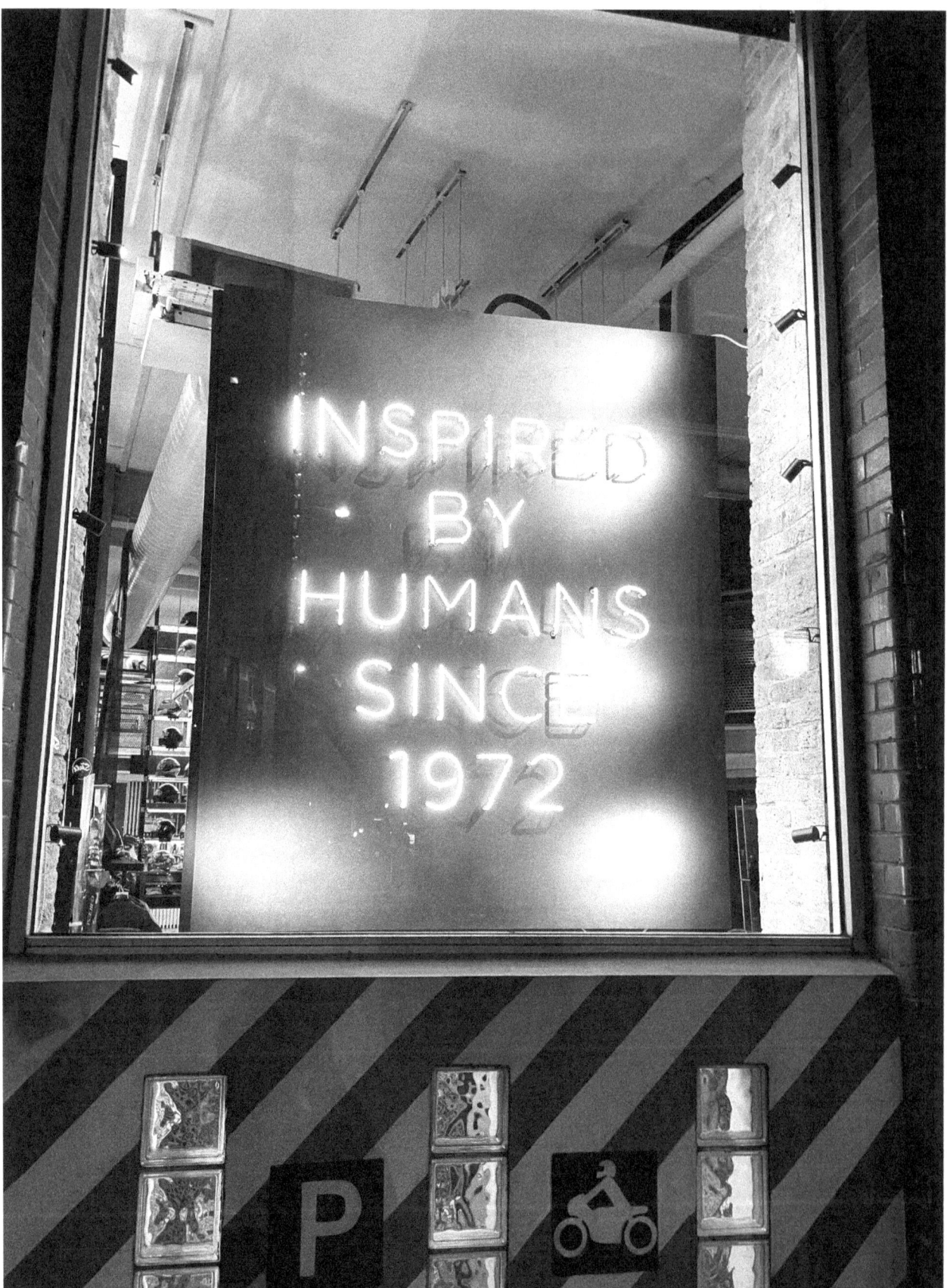

Civilising through food
French fantasies about gastronomy and Muslim diet
Hourya Bentouhami

In January 2022, Fabien Roussel – a leader of the French Communist Party – urged the French public not to be ashamed of eating meat, drinking fine wine and eating good cheese because 'it's French gastronomy'.[1] The remark was made following a polemic around the introduction of a meat-free menu in school canteens during the pandemic.[2] There is nothing surprising about this attachment to a fetishised version of French gastronomy.[3] This discourse has been audible for several years across the political spectrum from the far Right to the institutional Left and in what is now called the New Right in France, which has recomposed itself through an ethnicisation of French identity, now constructed mainly as Christian, European, secular and anti-Muslim. Food tropes and a focus on food as an identity and racial marker are clearly visible in the media production of far-Right YouTubers and identity foodistas whose cooking blogs are suffused with colonial sentiments: 'It's not a steak that votes Green or La France Insoumise, it's a steak that votes Eternal France. If we send it to Indochina, it wins'.[4] All this is part of a desire to counter a so-called bourgeois bohemian culture in a language shot through with nostalgia and colonial racial melancholy. In addition, this discourse takes on a gendered logic in its stigmatisation of the eating habits of Muslims, with practices such as fasting during Ramadan or abstaining from eating pork or non-halal meat considered feminine ways of relating to food. We thus have a discourse which racialises through food in terms of its composition (especially in respect of animal and dairy products), preparation (in particular its method of cutting and cooking) and its ingestion and assimilation.

This poses philosophical and phenomenological questions about what it feels like to see those who do not belong to the community in the act of eating. Contemporary discourses, which are often premised on the idea that Islam is a foreign religion, are rooted in the colonial history of France and the colonisation of North Africa especially from the nineteenth century. In this article, I examine these sedimented layers to offer an archaeology of a white French gaze that is fixated on the mouths of Muslims in a manner that is deeply sexualised and that has its own economic and political rationality, never ceasing to produce deadly racialising effects. This gaze is constituted by fantasies of penetrating Muslim bodies to consume their difference, abuse their exceptionality and eventually either assimilate them into one's own corporeality/identity or reject them as waste. I do not address the question of the religious and anthropological status of the inedible in Islam[5] or analyse the historical or religious justification of food prohibitions. Rather, I offer a philosophical reflection on the political meaning of watching others eat and producing a discourse on this eating that is rooted in the materiality of social relations: in such a perspective, it is Islam that is considered inedible. I will demonstrate the 'racial indigestion' of Muslim populations in the French context.[6] Racial indigestion is understood here in a double sense: first, as the racialisation produced through the stomach, the palate and the sense of taste; and second, as the inassimilability and unmanageability of Muslims in the nation and in the space of gastronomy as it is constituted in the colonial nineteenth and twentieth centuries. As Lauren Janes has shown, '[t]he anxiety about eating the food of others – of incorporating aspects of the colonized into one's body – stemmed, at least in some part, from the understanding of diet as a key marker of racial difference'.[7] This makes it possible to account for a disgust that is noted in texts by observers, travellers and the nascent profession of food critics in the colonial period who construct the racial inedibility of Islam.

Embedded in this symbolic aspect of cultural depreciation is the economic and political profitability of gastronomic and/or dietetic racism. Civilisational discourses that focus centrally on food and the anxiety of ingestion are part of a racial capitalism premised on a denial of the politics of reproduction and subsistence in an international commodity market and an international division of labour that has tracked a global colour line since colonisation and slavery in overseas territories. This article begins with an analysis of the contemporary symptoms of racial indigestion vis-à-vis Muslims and concludes with a colonial archaeology of this phenomenon.

Masculinity, animal slaughter and the abstraction of violence in industrial food processing

The ideological focus on meat and dairy products (notably with an affective and semiotic overinvestment in pork) to signify an attachment to republican civility is particularly pronounced in France in the European context.[8] See *Mythologies* (New York: Hill and Wang, 1972), 62–63. In contrast, in Germany, part of the far Right defends veganism.[9] Nonetheless, a masculinist attachment to meat and a concomitant association of culinary exoticism with effeminacy and 'sexual inversion' or 'perversion' seems to be fairly pervasive in Europe. This contemporary anti-Muslim discourse resonates with colonial representations. In the colonial era, Muslim men (typically ethnicised as Arabs) were constructed in the western imagination as sodomites imagined to feed on sperm and indulge in the pleasures of hashish and opium.[10] Muslim women were imagined as 'fricatrices' or rubbing addicts, practicing lesbianism as compensation for their lack of access to men;[11] sapphic consolation would also be expressed by the fact that these women are often represented as being in harems, and then able only to indulge in sex and gustatory enjoyment.[12] This demonstrates how racial difference is articulated in a fantasy of sexual inversion. The appetite for orality as a sexual practice is itself represented as a passive, feminine and oriental practice. Today these fantasies are expressed through a deployment of a homophobic masculinity that seeks to recuperate a martiality supposedly lost due to the feminist and queer ideologies which invaded France and engendered overly tolerant attitudes towards migrants, the putative invasion of Muslims and their 'great replacement' of the white population.[13]

In northern European societies, the sexualisation of food orality and the gendered moralisation of food habits focuses specifically on meat. This sexual politics of meat is based on a paradox.[14] First, the act of devouring meat is valued as an act of power and domination, a taming of the beast. In addition, the process of preparing meat is premised on a heterosexual order of the kitchen, a sexual division of labour in the preparation of food whereby the collective social cooking of meat is considered a male duty – recycling clichés about the mastery of fire and technique by men – while women, because they supposedly use their hands alone, are considered technologically under-equipped in culinary practices. Second, this paradox of the sexual politics of meat rests on a process of abstraction, of negation of living animality that is nonetheless put to death, cut up and prepared as edible matter. The idea of a modern, techno-industrial masculinity is attested to by converting the executed animal into an 'absent referent' – a process of abstraction necessary for the edibility of the animal, for its ingestion to defuse the triggers of disgust, in particular the conscious representation of having to ingest another bloody living being.[15] The disgust over slaughtering is indeed widely shared. These days, the death of animals, as Noélie Vialles notes in her survey of slaughterhouses, is euphemised. We do not kill: 'we slaughter ... Slaughterhouses are also located outside cities, on the outskirts. In the organization of the work, a kind of dilution of responsibility is maintained which is based on a double requirement: all animals must be obligatorily desensitized before being bled. In France, currently, this desensitization is carried out by perforating the cranial box with a slaughter gun'.[16] Eating meat therefore entails quite considerable symbolic work to reconstruct the lethal act.

As far as Muslims are concerned, it is taken for granted that they subscribe to this negation/abstraction of lethal labour at the heart of the killing of meat.[17] In the banlieues – where (post-)migratory neighbourhoods are located and which are wrongly thought to be predominantly Muslim – the lethal act in ritual slaughter (above all the practice of butchering in the streets) is considered

too visible. Even the far Right in its anti-Islam rhetoric occasionally deploys the bourgeois ethos of the necessary abstraction of the lethal act in animal meat processing for it to be considered modern. What is reproached in Muslims then is their non-observance of this abstraction of blood and animality. They are considered unable to enter into food modernity, particularly where ritual slaughter according to the rules of halal are concerned: cutting an animal's throat and letting it bleed completely without stunning it is regularly described as a shameful disregard for animal welfare. Muslims are accused by the far Right, but also by the traditional Right and parts of the Left, to be incapable of this modernity which is performed through a defence of animal welfare considered solely from the angle of the minimisation of the suffering of the animal during its industrial slaughter. In fact, the noisy valorisation of both the imaginary evacuation of violent death and the devouring of bloody cooked or even raw meat as well as the consumption of dairy products and wine, is part of a fantasy of complete control in the formation of the perceived Self: we seek to control the conditions of its public appearance during shared or public meals. Roussel made no secret of this as he went to visit apprentice butchers on a slaughtering site, to reconnect with a fantasy of a popular Left whose virility is indexed by the meat that we chop and eat, underscored by the amnesic injunction to forget the ecological disaster of meat production. These discourses and communicative practices are thus part of the rituals of a patriarchal and ecocidal mandate.

Similarly, practices of food abstention are understood as existential threats to others. Not drinking alcohol, and even more, not eating during the month of Ramadan are considered a cultural and ideological aberration. Hence the fact that a good Muslim is one who disavows Islam by drinking alcohol and eating pork.[18] In contrast, Muslims who observe dietary restrictions prevent others from enjoying their food. They are the opposite of the figure of *le bon vivant* (good living). Their abstemiousness effectively imposes their rules on everyone, disrupting the implicit rule of the universality of meals which presupposes, for instance, not taking religious beliefs into account in the planning of children's meals or collective catering arrangements in private or public settings. Meals based on 'republican' appetisers such as *saucisson* and *pinard* (sausages and wine) have become a way of excluding through food people considered to be *allophage*, that is to say whose diet is based on the fact of abstaining from prohibited foods for personal, philosophical or religious reasons, such as Muslims, but also Jews, vegetarians, vegans and teetotallers.

It is, then, worth adding to the analysis of patriarchy in food practices what Afro-veganism has clearly shown: the presence of a racial policy of meat, alcohol and dairy products that is attested to by the obsession with the food that Muslims do and do not eat.[19] By racialisation, we mean the description in moral and political terms of a Muslim population's food habits as intrinsically other and unable to comply both with the universality of Republican commensality and with the ethnic singularity of the national meal. Dietic discourse, and in particular xenophobic and Islamophobic assertions about 'good food', have thus been central to the recomposition of the far Right.

Studying food practices and their logics of racialisation makes it possible to understand the phenomenology of race in a different way by moving its display scenes beyond an 'epidermal ontology of race', often concerned only with the symbolic and material investments of the surface of bodies, in particular the skin.[20] Instead it allows us to look at the banal modalities by which the nation and its ethnicised and racialised identity are represented through metabolic devices internal to the body. But this metabolic materiality is also the object of denial. The nation's account of what it eats is premised on the denial of not only social reproduction and the sexual division of labour but also of the extractive and polluting methods through which food is produced. One pretends to see in Muslim eating an existential identity threat even as there is a very real threat to the means of subsistence and access to drinking water and edible, local food given the realities of climate change and the burning of fossil fuels in the Anthropocene. The ethnicisation of Land is also a way of denying the material reality of ecological devastation and energy depletion.[21] The indexing of the right to feed on the land to national attachment and the injunction to disavow one's religion is actually, and paradoxically, a way of denying one's earthly condition, because French national cuisine – the ethnicisation of French gastronomy inscribed in a policy of civility – is also a marketing emblem in the global techno-industrial circuits of large-scale food production.[22] To be exported, French cuisine must be ethnicised. Foreigners must be able to taste the 'real' French meal, rid of the influence of postcolonial cuisines but also of the migrant labour that produces it. Who will see, for example, who produces the strawberries from the fields that are the greenhouses of southern Europe?[23] North African women are asked to leave their children behind to come and work in precarious migratory conditions, to exhaust the land so that Europe has strawberries all year round at low prices. Their status as women identified as Muslim is seen as an advantage in the regulation of labour since it is the guarantee that they will return to their country of origin and to their duty as good Muslim mothers once their seasonal contract is over.[24] The ideological depreciation of Muslims' mouths in European countries is the counterpart of the functioning of racial capitalism, which consists in creating different racialised subjects endowed with differential values, whose hands and legs are exploitable and disposable in labour-intensive agricultural fields and fast food delivery. The question of who can eat with the national 'us' is therefore inseparable from the denial of the social reproduction of food workers, and the invitation to eat at the same table as this national 'us' is often accompanied by an injunction to renounce being Muslim in order to be able to have the right to food.[25]

The pig, the Muslim and the Jew: how to convert to food 'normalcy'

In 2015, former French President Nicolas Sarkozy claimed that eating pork was a value of the Republic that needed to be taught in French schools. Not eating pork is apparently to withdraw from the universal claim of the Republic emblematised in sharing the 'pig', which is elevated as a totem, a universal equivalent of all meals.[26] The reproduction of the nation requires an assimilation, understood literally as a common eating which is also an identical eating, where the ingredients and preparation of food follow the same phagic scenario. It is worth noting that the remark was made in response to the demand for substitutions in school canteen menus. The idea that one could eat something else instead of meat, and in particular pork, was inconceivable. In the contemporary symbolic economy of food, substitutes become the subject of disproportionate emotional and regnal investment enabling an expulsion of Muslims from the bounds of acceptability, civility and nation. Outrage at gastronomic substitution expresses deeper anxieties harboured by the far Right and the new Right in France about the 'Great Replacement' of White Christian Europeans by Muslims. The deprivation of meat, and more specifically pork, is seen as a form of de-masculinisation associated with Muslims and Jews. The attachment to the pig in the reproduction of the nation is a fundamental factor in understanding this disqualification of Muslims. To refuse to eat pork would be to refuse to share: because flesh is first and foremost what we are made of and eating it involves resolving the question of the distinction between the same and the other. Flesh in the second place implies the sharing of remains: it brings into play cooperation and altruism and therefore raises fundamental questions for the social order. 'To eat meat, unlike many other types of food, you have to share. And the sharing of meat is a fundamental, if not founding, act of social life'.[27] We should add that sharing pig meat entails also sharing the responsibility for its killing, recycling it symbolically and transforming it into a social bond. What we would thus reproach Muslims for is a commensal secessionism and a refusal to be part of the social bond. In this sense, it is articulated with anti-Judaism.

Pork has a fundamental place in the racial imagination because it has already played a major role in French and southern European anti-Judaism and anti-Semitism.[28] Without conflating historical shifts and geo-cultural contexts too abruptly, we can nevertheless register this knot between anti-Semitism and anti-Muslim racism in the culinary field at the time of the so-called Spanish Reconquest which sought to inspect what went into mouths to identify the culinary and confessional disloyalty of lay-Jews and Moriscos: eating couscous and cooking with olive oil (rather than pork fat) opened oneself to the suspicion of crypto-Judaism or crypto-Islam. The purchase of certain ingredients such as eggplants and chickpeas or spices such as coriander and saffron, or the aroma of a dish cooked in olive oil, were enough to alert neighbours to possible heresy. This resonance between anti-Semitism and anti-Muslim racism allows us to see how disgust vis-à-vis Muslim and Jewish foods in particular has been permanently embedded in an imagination that makes these cuisines not only foreign but potentially dangerous because of their supposed power of identity conversion. Culinary anxiety around Jewish food is still palpable in contemporary antisemitism in Western societies to the extent that the Jewish diet is reduced to the 'abstinence of pork' as it is with Muslims.

Likewise, the proximity between 'Jewish food' and 'Muslim food' triggered a common repulsion from colonial travellers to North Africa in the nineteenth century. When François Bournand, a journalist and historian, described a feast in Tunisia in the late nineteenth century, he did so in terms that identified spicy cuisine as being both Muslim and Jewish, racialising what he saw as a dirty culinary otherness and demonstrating how antisemitism and Islamophobia were articulated through culinary xenophobia.

> The spicy dishes and the lack of cleanliness of the culinary preparations among the natives have always, despite the habit [i.e. his familiarity with life in Tunisia], inspired an invincible repugnance in me, which has never allowed me to eat much either among the Muslims or among the Israelites.[29]

There is indeed a form of antisemitism in contemporary Islamophobia in the sense that the same rhetorical repertoires of tracking down the enemy within are reactivated to try to ascertain who is Muslim from names and culinary practices at a time when Muslims are no longer migrants. Such measures are necessitated by the conundrum of needing to distinguish what has been partly assimilated – a conundrum that is addressed by identifying and differentiating the dietary processes that bear the residual mark of allophagy, of a different 'ethnic' communal eating, given that, as food and migration studies have shown, community food is often what remains of a culture of origin long after migration, conversion or assimilation.[30] Spurred by such intuitions, the far-Right Mayor of Béziers from the Rassemblement National party sought to identify Muslim children through their last names and dietary prescriptions registered in school canteens. The notion that names announce religious affiliation and diet drove Eric Zemmour, a far Right leader and current presidential candidate to call for a banning of names that do not sound Republican and French (read: African and Muslim-sounding names). At stake in this relationship between names and eating is nothing less than a disciplining of republican orality. We can now ask ourselves, how is it possible to be a Muslim in France in terms of food? Or in Montesquieu's formulation in the Persian letters, how can one wish to be a Muslim, that is to say not drink alcohol and, even worse, not drink wine or eat pork in a country devoted to good living and renowned for its sausages and wines?

Food disgust and the ambivalence of Republican appetite

What do we do when we worry about what Muslims eat? If food is an object of anxiety it is because eating is a process of incorporation, erasing the boundary between the world and our bodily interiority. It occurs through ingestion and metabolisation, a process that promises a regeneration of the body or threatens its disintegration depending on the quality of the food and its ability to correspond to our internal arrangement. The act of incorporation thus implicates issues that are both vital and symbolic, accounting for the deep anxieties associated with it. The life and health of the eater are at stake every time the decision to incorporate is made. As Claude Fischler puts it, borrowing a term from Kleinian psychoanalysis, the body fears 'incorporation of the bad object'. 'The incorporated object can contaminate it, transform it from within, possess it, and therefore dispossess it of itself'.[31]

Ironically, the anxiety about one's identity in discourses of civilisational decline in food habits relies on what was usually described as a primitive or primal fear. It recalls the belief reported by J. Frazer according to which 'the savage commonly believes that by eating the flesh of an animal or man, he acquires the qualities – not only the physical but even the moral and intellectual qualities – which were characteristic of that animal or that man'.[32] In fact it is almost always food of animal origin that arouses disgust, the affect of which seems to emanate from a shared carnal condition. Moreover, our relationship to animal flesh constantly references sexuality. Fantasies of the incorporation of the bad object also raise fears of desexualisation, that is to say the loss of markers of sexual difference, so that eating food from another culture that is considered not to conform to norms of gender difference would be to lose one's civilisational rank, gender and race.[33] At the level of the unconscious, there is a profound continuity between the table and the bed, between edible and desirable flesh. Lévi Strauss stressed the 'very profound analogy which people throughout the world seem to find between copulating and eating. In Yoruba, "to eat" and "to marry" are expressed by a single verb the general sense of which is "to win, to acquire", usage which has its French parallel where the verb "consommer" applies both to marriage and to meals.'[34] From this perspective, cannibalism, which consists of eating individuals of one's own human flesh, would be the hyperbolic form of sexual union; hence the prohibition on eating individuals of one's own family and sex.

By the same token, the taboo of culinary exogamy may carry the risk of organic and spiritual corruption and loss of identity, unless the class marker of an exotic cook or kitchen maid unlocks the taboo of 'Muslim' inedibility. Culinary miscegenation might revive nostalgia for a colonial bourgeois way of life: to have a 'dada' for instance (kitchen maid in Morocco) preparing briouats, chicken pastilla or eggplant zaalouk can be a useful marker of social distinction among wealthy French elites. Similarly, the heterosexual order is also expressed by positions in the order of what is edible. 'The equivalence most familiar to us and undoubtedly also the most widespread in the world', says Lévi Strauss, 'poses the male as eater and the female as eaten'.[35] These structuralist pronouncements are problematic if we take them as normative assertions, but if they describe the logic of a gendered and racialised unconscious, they seem to correspond to familiar ways of naming foodways and our relation to food.[36] Nonetheless, this approach tends to stick to the level of description of the production of sexual difference without considering that the material historicity of the myth around this difference might offer a way to criticise the difference in itself, structured as it is around binaries such as cooked/raw, civilised/savage, masculine/feminine and anchored as it is in a social stratification in which the 'eaten' are in reality the ones who prepare, clean, cook and serve the food. The 'eaten' refers then to a subordinated group that is disadvantaged in the division of labour and capital.[37]

This is why we must also take into account other anthropologies and cosmogonic explanations that do not necessarily ratify sexual difference inscribed in a food order, but which on the contrary highlight food tropes that do not gender the social order, allowing us to see how the production of sexual difference through diet and the food order is also historical, contingent and rooted in social antagonisms. I would rather subscribe to the view of Mary Douglas, for whom the symbolic aspect of food is the expression of social relations. Then food or commensal prohibition are seen also as a social prophylaxis, a way of organising power and social relations by forming a community 'against': 'dirt offends against order'.[38] By eliminating it, gestures of purification are positive gestures of prophylaxis, which give unity and meaning to the experience and this gesture of purification is carried by the belief that 'it is only by exaggerating the difference between within and without, above and below, male and female' that one can reconstitute a sense of self immune to defilement.[39]

In this critical perspective where the symbolic is rooted in the materiality of power distribution in a given society, how can we explain what we do when we worry about what Muslims eat? Two things are striking. First, by expressing this anxiety, we worry about the nourishment of our food. Muslims eat but are also eaten symbolically. This is a position of inferiority from which we clearly want exemption. We refuse to eat with Muslims but also, occasionally, like them since they are a subordinated group endowed with the power of contamination. In 2012, far Right leader Marine Le Pen insinuated that all Parisian butchers were now halal and that people ate their products without knowing it. At work here is the idea that we ingest 'Muslim', and in doing so are ourselves converted and denationalised. For Muslim women, it is often their food hygiene and in particular the sugar that they incorporate that is often called into question, the fat produced by sugar threatening sexual dimorphism and the eroticisation of dominated bodies. Such representations can also lead to denial of care as evidenced by the persistent trope of the Fatma in the medical clinic, which we can observe for example through the blog of a doctor who fears the arrival in her office of the 50-year-old Arab woman, fat and diabetic, asking for clinical attention.[40] In these examples, the eater not only worries about the food that they incorporate but also about how the absorption of a food incorporates the eater into a culinary system and therefore into the group who practices it, unless they are explicitly excluded: 'The classifications, practices and representations that characterize a cuisine incorporate the individual into the group, situate the whole in relation to the universe and incorporate it in turn: they therefore have a fundamentally religious dimension in the etymological sense of the term, in the sense of re-ligare, to link.'[41]

Second, attention to what Muslims eat is also the vector and the product of the sexualisation of Muslim bodies, which are repelled and desired both by their putatively disordered use of phagic and sexual orality but also by their supposedly anti-erotic behaviour and their lack of taste in food (as apparently evidenced by their favoured halal junk food of kebabs). Thus, Muslims are also those who do not have or no longer have the ability to savour pleasure, to taste.[42] It should be noted that theoretically in the material act of eating, there is a prior desexualisation which makes animal meat suitable for consumption. We often eat young or castrated animals, that is to say animals excluded from reproductive activity on the principle that the flesh of an uncastrated animal tastes less good. Animal flesh is often either destined for reproductive or food purposes but not both at the same time. So we only consume 'desexualised' flesh, flesh whose use and nature is exclusively food.[43] Eating desexualised animals, then, is to desexualise the phagic act. But here, on the contrary, it would seem that the assimilation of Muslims, their consumption, digestion, and symbolic assimilation into the national republican order is subject to their prior sexualisation, possible eroticisation and waste transformation.[44]

Disgust is then related to eroticisation since it is strongly linked to the fact that it is the mouth which incorporates, tastes and mixes with itself, through sensorial acts such as chewing and smelling. This orality is profoundly sexual, or at least erotic in its symbolic and material dimension. It is not only a question of analogy with the fantasy of penetration, where the question of who has the right to penetrate – to cross the threshold of the body – is central, but rather of a mixed representation between race, gender and class insofar as the desire for devouring is a desire for the material appropriation of subordinated bodies.[45] It is symptomatic of this correlation between the eroticisation of otherness and disgust at the presence of Muslims on 'national' territory that Nadine Morano – a French politician – evoked a nostalgia for white gastronomy in her neighbourhood, where one could supposedly no longer find ham, while also affirming that she loved couscous and brik with egg. Disgust is not always expressed clearly in an attitude of rejection and is also palpable in practices of erotic predation. It participates in an affective economy that combines forms of ingestion, assimilation, devouring, appropriation. This is precisely the sense in which I suggest reading contemporary instances of 'republican' disgust towards Muslim diets as a symptom of a colonial remainder.

A colonial politics of digestion: gastric fatigue, civilisation and inedible Islam

We find the concern about food in Muslim countries in colonial medicine, which sought to understand both what was good to eat in the colonies and what ought to be 'rationalised'. Thus, Georges Treille's *Principes d'Hygiene Coloniale*, published in 1899, aims to 'outline the general rules which seem to me the most appropriate to facilitate their establishment for Europeans in hot countries', noting that 'the fundamental principle which Europeans in hot countries must observe is to spare all fatigue in the stomach'.[46] Digestibility, thought to be a function more of the method of preparation and cooking than of the foodstuffs themselves, is considered to be the priority: 'food must pass through without gastric fatigue … supplying the stomach with food that is both easily digestible and restorative'.[47] Gastric sensitivity is often racialised in this archive, which seeks to acclimatise European stomachs to the food available in 'hot' countries. We find this same concern at the beginning of the twentieth century in the first specialised gastronomic journals which are interested in the 'ethnic' or even racial conditions of digestion, not to prevent digestive diseases but to keep at bay the experience of bad taste. Thus, F. Barthelemy, instructor at the Cordon Bleu School and for a time editor in chief of *Le Cordon Bleu*, wrote about Morocco after the Treaty of Fez in 1912 and its 'repugnant foodways'. In his description of couscous, he describes the preserved butter that flavours Moroccan dishes as very often 'rancid'. Rottenness and evidence of decay is a central elicitor of disgust, especially when connected to food:

We hope that French civilisation will bring to the Moroccans not only her benefits from economic and social point of view, but also from the culinary and alimentary points of view and that the modest couscous can soon be, transformed by the French culinary art, present on the table of our gourmets.[48]

Seen in this historical perspective, we can see how a dish like couscous occupies a special place in the racialisation of foodways since it was seen as Muslim and Arab for a time and, after decolonisation, as French because it was a favourite dish of the *pieds-noirs* – French settlers in North Africa, many of whom chose to depart for France alongside a Maghreb Jewish population who also left after Algeria gained its independence.[49] Considered a 'Muslim' dish to mark racial difference in the nineteenth and first half of the twentieth century, couscous is today detached from its putative Muslimness. What is striking in the historical mutation of couscous representation is that racial difference is represented as not only cultural – as a difference of cuisine and foodways – but also as biological, with racial/religious belonging marked by different stomachs, metabolisms and palates.

Colonial observers were also disgusted by the fact of eating with the hands, which was seen as a sign of intellectual and civilisational backwardness. A 1905 article by the gastronomic critic Myrh in *Le Cordon Bleu* describes couscous as the dish of the Arabs, eaten with the hands in the same dish and on the floor (or almost), all elements that marked the ontological distance between the French and the Arabs. Difference thus passes through both the utensil and table manners. The civilisational imperative of eating at a table, distant from the floor, reflects the normative ideal contained in the distanciation between the hand and the mouth, the body and the floor. These distances from bodily markers partake in a broader narrative of civilisation and food progress. Erasmus's *On Civility in Children* had prepared the ground. Contrasting human habits to those of animals, he regarded eating with the fork, the maintenance of distance between the body and the ground and from food, and the consumption of food from a seated position at a table as marks of humanisation, access to adulthood and above all to civilisation. But how to elevate and civilise a Muslim population through food? Along with the incitation to eat 'properly' with forks, in separate dishes and at a high table, sitting on a proper chair, was the idea that food itself should be civilised. As Lauren Janes writes, the 1930s culinary critic Gauducheau asserted that 'eating more bread, meat, dairy, and wine would help French colonial subjects evolve to become more like Frenchmen.'[50] Indeed as Roland Barthes explains, abstaining from wine is not without consequences in France:

> The universality principle fully applies here, inasmuch as society calls anyone who does not believe in wine by *names* such as sick, disabled or depraved: it does not *comprehend* him (in both senses, intellectual and spatial, of the word). Conversely, an award of good integration is given to whoever is a practising wine-drinker: knowing how to drink is a national technique which serves to qualify the Frenchman, to demonstrate at once his performance, his control and his sociability. Wine gives thus a foundation for a collective morality, within which everything is redeemed: true, excesses, misfortunes and crimes are possible with wine, but never viciousness, treachery or baseness…[51]

Similarly, the relationship between the symbolisation of wine and the denial of its imperial capitalist production in 'Muslim' land in Algeria, raises the question of the obsessive reference to the mouths of Muslims which obscures the hands that cultivate their land and the depletion of that land by an aberrant monoculture:

> … the mythology of wine can in fact help us to understand the usual ambiguity of our daily life. For it is true that wine is a good and fine substance, but it is no less true that its production is deeply involved in French capitalism, whether it is that of the private distillers or that of the big settlers in Algeria who impose on the Muslims, on the very land of which they have been dispossessed, a crop of which they have no need, while they lack even bread.[52]

The Islamisation of the dietary habits and foods of Arabs has not always been at the heart of colonial practices. On the contrary, agricultural policies during the colonial period attempted to de-Islamise representations of what came from Algeria to emphasise its assimilation into the French nation. For this it was necessary to represent it as a wine power. Thus in 1931 during the colonial exhibition in Paris, the Algerian pavilion presented a replica of the Sidi-Abderrahmane Mosque in Algiers, but it was the only reference to Muslim culture and Islam. Instead, Algeria was portrayed as a kingdom of wine and biblical food such as olives and dates in an exoticisation of the desert and 'wild' nature, but also as a cultivated, prolific, bucolic paradise of vineyards.

Night view of the Algerian Pavilion at the International Colonial Exhibition, Vincennes, 1931

As Janes explains, thanks to colonial development, Algeria had become a 'huge vineyard', with the pavilion considered a 'triumph of Bacchus' as a result of the considerable efforts of chambers of commerce and the Confederation of Wine Makers. There is a significant material dimension to the representations of food produced in 'Islamic' lands. Algeria became a significant locus of wine production following the phylloxera crisis of 1870 in France which ravaged metropolitan vineyards. This required breaking with the notion of 'terroir' – the idea that the taste of wine is a function of a unique combination of factors including soil, climate, topography and the 'soul' of the wine producer, which could not be reproduced elsewhere. The pavilion insisted on the possibility of the export and recomposition of terroir in a land as hostile and contradictory, on account of its Muslimness, as Algeria by underscoring the French character of Algeria and the familiarity of its soil and products. In contrast, the other North African pavilions were given over to an exoticisation of difference with their emphasis on souks, spices and snake charmers. The Moroccan restaurant in particular sought maximum authenticity with its Moroccan chef and alcohol-free menu.[53]

In our own time, 'foreign' food when eaten or cooked by groups external to this culture, becomes a gastronomic delight, a socially valued element on a gustatory journey, whereas when cooked by migrant minorities or people with a migratory past, is considered poor, low quality and cheap. Hence the injunction to minoritised groups to eat such food at home and to consume the 'national' food of the host country in public. This process of ethnicising the food of others, disqualifying others as competent to cook their own cuisine, or conversely the exotic idea of authenticity achieved through a chef belonging to the relevant 'culture', combined with the injunction to eat national food, is the expression in France of the coloniality of diet normativity in public space, which reproduces whiteness through food, excludes Islam from the regime of the edible and 'Muslims' from the regime of gastronomic desirability.[54]

Is it possible to decolonise food? Muslims, real or alleged, are not passive objects of racial discourses on food. It is important to note that it is precisely when they resist gastronomic disciplining that they are reduced to their religion through the medium of their food habits. Yet food is also a terrain of solidarity and insurgence. There is no shortage of examples to illustrate this. Through their conviviality around food in the so-called 'Jungle of Calais', where restaurants run by refugees offered spaces of survival and friendship, migrants reconstituted sociality in a place demonised and attacked by their opponents.[55] On the border with Italy, farmer and pro-migrant activist Cédric Herrou defies French authorities to assist migrants seeking to enter the country who – excluded from the labour market – work on his organic farm under the aegis of the international solidarity movement

Emmaus.⁵⁶ The Front de Mères (the Mothers' Front), a parents' union which fights against discrimination and violence suffered by children in working-class neighbourhoods, demands healthy food in school canteens.⁵⁷ Marginalised communities thus build their own commons by way of culinary disobedience and an eroticisation of food that resists gastronomic domination, thereby rediscovering a forbidden or devalued commensality and a popular gastronomic creativity, especially among recent migrants who are often prevented from eating at all. These ways of being, cooking and eating resist the reactionary performativity of public authorities who claim that there is a republican way of eating, but also struggle against food deprivation and towards a vision of food justice that entails an ecologically sensitive access to nutritious food for all.

Hourya Bentouhami is Lecturer in Social and Political Philosophy at the University of Toulouse Jean Jaurès. She recently published Judith Butler. Race, genre et mélancolie *(Paris: Editions Amsterdam, 2022).*

Notes

1. Fabien Roussel, 'Un bon vin, une bonne viande, un bon fromage, c'est la gastronomie française', *Franceinfo*, https://www.dailymotion.com/video/x87beam. The following article was first presented as a lecture at the International Consortium of Critical Theory, University of California, Berkeley, where it benefited from feedback from Natalia Brizuela, Samira Esmeir, Lucie Mercier, Stefania Pandolfo, and Leti Volpp. It was also discussed as a work in progress at the seminar 'Food and Race: A Transatlantic Conversation', that I co-organised with Mathilde Cohen at the Institute of French Studies, New York University, where I had stimulating feedback from Sylvie Durmelat, Julie Kleinman, Tao Leigh, Ann Morning, Krishnendu Ray, Frédéric Viguier and Lionel Zevounou. I am also thankful to Lewis Gordon and Elena Comay del Junco, at the Department of Philosophy at the University of Connecticut, where I wrote the first version of this article as a Fulbright Visiting Scholar.
2. 'Menu sans viande dans les cantines scolaires: la polémique en cinq actes', *Franceinfo*, 22 February 2021, https://www.francetvinfo.fr/politique/eelv/menu-sans-viande-dans-les-cantines-scolaires-la-polemique-entre-le-gouvernement-et-le-maire-de-lyon-en-quatre-actes_4306571.html.
3. Mathilde Cohen, 'The Whiteness of French Food: Law, Race, and Eating Culture in France', *French Politics, Culture, and Society* 39:2 (2021), 26–52.
4. 'Le steak qui vote France éternelle', https://www.tiktok.com/@leconservateur.tv/video/7217097126055103750. Both the Greens and La France Insoumise are leftwing political parties.
5. Mohamed Benkheira, *Islâm et interdits alimentaires – Juguler l'animalité* (Paris : PUF, 2000).
6. Kyla Wazana Tompkins, *Racial Indigestion: Eating Bodies in the 19th Century* (New York: New York University Press, 2012).
7. Lauren Janes, *Colonial Food in Interwar Paris: The Taste of Empire* (London: Bloomsbury, 2016).
8. As Roland Barthes notes in his essay 'Steak and Chips' the steak tartare conveys the mythology of a masculine primacy in sexual reproduction proper both to Frenchness and its universal claim to its own food: 'There are to be found, in this preparation, all the germinating states of matter: the blood mash and the glair of eggs, a whole harmony of soft and life-giving substances, a sort of meaningful compendium of the images of pre-parturition.'
9. Bernhard Forchtner and Ana Tominc, 'Kalashnikov and Cooking-spoon: Neo-Nazism, Veganism and a Lifestyle Cooking Show on YouTube', *Food, Culture and Society: An International Journal of Multidisciplinary Research* 20:3 (July 2017), 415–441.
10. Joseph Massad, *Desiring Arabs* (Chicago: Chicago University Press, 2007); Todd Shepard, *Sex, France, and Arab Men, 1962–1979* (Chicago: Chicago University Press, 2018).
11. Jocelyne Dakhlia, 'Harem: ce que les femmes, recluses, font entre elles', *Clio: Femmes, Genre, Histoire* 26 (2007), 61–88.
12. Massad, *Desiring Arabs*, 236–237.
13. Sarah Bracke and Luis Manuel Hernández Aguilar, 'Thinking Europe's "Muslim Question": On Trojan Horses and the Problematization of Muslims', *Critical Research on Religion* 10:2 (2022), 200–220; Sara R. Farris, 'From the Jewish Question to the Muslim Question: Republican Rigorism, Culturalist Differentialism and Antinom-

ies of Enforced Emancipation', *Constellations* 21:2 (2014), 296–307.

14. Carol Adams, *The Sexual Politics of Meat: A Feminist-Vegetarian Critical Theory* (London: Bloomsbury, 1990).

15. Adams, *The Sexual Politics of Meat*, 66.

16. Noëlie Vialles, *Animal to Edible* (Cambridge: Cambridge University Press, 1994).

17. Nilüfer Göle, *The Daily Lives of Muslims: Islam and Public Confrontation in Contemporary Europe* (London: Zed Books, 2017), 215–242.

18. In the summer of 2009, Minister of the Interior Brice Hortefeux, while posing for a photograph with an Arab grassroots activist said 'It's ok when there is only one, it is when they are many that it becomes a problem.' In the amused audience, a woman yelled 'He's Catholic, he eats pork and drink alcohol', to which the minister replied 'Oh but this is not right, it does not correspond to the prototype'. 'Ce que Brice Hortefeux a vraiment dit', *Le Monde*, 11 September 2009, https://www.lemonde.fr/politique/article/2009/09/11/qu-a-vraiment-dit-brice-hortefeux_1238863_823448.html.

19. Afro or Black veganism argues that in a white supremacist political and cultural system, Black beings in slave-holding America were dehumanised just as animals were reduced to the rank of body-labour, made killable, edible and used as an instrument of terror against Blacks to control and hunt them down. During segregation, both people of colour and pets were prohibited from entering restaurants run by whites. Rather than an identity, Black veganism is an intellectual and philosophical posture which seeks to understand the human/animal dualism as a racial dualism which refers both to the racialisation of animals and the animalisation (which is in fact the dehumanisation) of humans. Therefore the process of animalisation at the heart of racialisation must be investigated in critical studies of race, especially when considering food; and the notion of humanity itself must be understood in its historical context as an oppressive category. See Tier-Autonomie, 'An interview with Syl Ko', *Jahrgang* 6:1 (2019), 1–22; A. Breeze Harper, ed., *Sistah Vegan: Black Female Vegans Speak on Food, Identity, Health, and Society* (Brooklyn: Lantern Publishing and Media, 2020). The dynamics of racialisation have largely been studied in Anglophone literature. See Hanna Garth and Ashanté M. Reese, eds., *Black Food Matters: Racial Justice in the Wake of Food Justice* (Minneapolis: University of Minnesota Press, 2020); Psyche A. Williams-Forson, *Building Houses out of Chicken Legs: Black Women, Food, and Power* (Chapel Hill: University of North Carolina Press, 2006); Rachel Slocum, 'Race in the Study of Food', *Progress in Human Geography* 35:3 (2011), 303–327. In general in France, food has not been considered much in critical race and gender studies despite an important article on the question: see Tristan Fournier, Julie Jarty, Nathalie Lapeyre, Priscille Touraille, 'L'alimentation, arme du genre', *Journal des anthropologues* 140-141:1-2 (2015), 19–49.

20. Kyla Wazana Tompkins, *Racial Indigestion: Eating Bodies in the 19th Century* (New York: New York University Press, 2012).

21. Stéphane François, 'L'extrême droite française et l'écologie. Retour sur une polémique', *Revue Française d'Histoire des Idées Politiques* 44:2 (2016), 187–208.

22. Rick Fantasia, *French Gastronomy and the Magic of Americanism* (Philadelphia: Temple University Press, 2018).

23. Arab Chadia, *Dames de fraises, doigts de fée, les invisibles de la migration saisonnière marocaine en Espagne* (Casablanca: En toutes Lettres, 2018).

24. Emmanuelle Hellio, 'Importing Women to Export Strawberries (Huelva, Spain)', *Etudes Rurales* 182: 2 (2008), 185–200.

25. Sara Farris, 'Social Reproduction and Racialized Surplus Populations', in Peter Osborne, Eric Alliez, and Eric-John Russell, eds., *Capitalism: Concept, Idea, Image: Aspects of Marx's* Capital *Today* (Kingston Upon Thames: CRMEP Books, 2019), 121–134.

26. Both the far Right and the New Right converge in the totemisation of pig meat. Sarkozy's comment was prefigured by The Identity Bloc, a far Right collective which regularly tried to distribute its 'pig soup' to homeless people in Paris, reaffirming the virilist 'gaulois' spirit. In order to be served, visitors to their mobile soup kitchen were required to eat the pork soup. In 2007, their website proclaimed 'cheese, dessert, coffee, clothing and candy go with the pork soup. No soup, no dessert' (Janes, *Colonial Food in Interwar Paris*, 165). More recently, as Judith Butler was receiving a doctorate honoris causa from the University of Bordeaux, some far Right 'pro-family' demonstrators distributed an invitation to share 'pig soup'. The obsession with the preservation of the putative naturalness of sexuality and gender and with food as a national marker are thoroughly entangled.

27. Claude Fischler, *L'Homnivore: Le Goût, la Cuisine et le Corps* (Paris: Odile Jacob, 2001), 138.

28. Claudine Fabre-Vassas, *The Singular Beast: Jews, Christians, & the Pig* (New York: Columbia University Press, 1997).

29. François Bournand, *Tunisie et Tunisiens* (Paris: J. Lefort, 1893), 325. See also Nina S. Studer, 'Too Spicy for the French: Medical Descriptions of Sexuality, Masculinity and Spices in the Colonial Maghreb', *Anthropology of Food* 16 (2022), doi.org/10.4000/aof.13668. More generally, on the intertwining of Jewish and Muslim racial categorisations in the understanding of *limpieza de san-*

gre (blood purity), see Reza Zia-Ebrahimi, *Antisémitisme et islamophobie. Une histoire croisée* (Paris: Amsterdam, 2021).

30. Krishnendu Ray, *The Ethnic Restaurateur* (London: Bloomsbury, 2016).

31. Fischler, *L'Homnivore*, 69.

32. James George Frazer, *The Golden Bough: A Study in Magic and Religion*, vol. 8 (Frankfurt: Outlook VerlagsGmbH, 1890), 100.

33. After recalling the idea formulated by Clastres of a correspondence between the prohibition of incest, the production of social bonds and food restrictions in the Guayaki population in Brazil, Fischler brings together the 'modern' fear of chickens injected with hormones with the fear that hormonal transformation induced by the pill would erase sexual dimorphism.

34. Claude Lévi-Strauss, *The Savage Mind* (Chicago: Chicago University Press, 1966), 105.

35. Lévi-Strauss, *The Savage Mind*, 136.

36. See Françoise Héritier-Augé, 'Semen and Blood: Some Ancient Theories Concerning their Genesis and Relationship', in *Fragments for a History of the Human Body*, eds. Michel Feher, Ramona Naddaff and Nadia Tazi (New York: Zone, 1989), 159–175, who considers the difference between the feminine and the masculine, female and male, through the ontological difference between the raw and the cooked.

37. Marilyn Strathern, *The Gender of the Gift: Problems with Women and Problems with Society in Melanesia* (Berkeley: University of California Press, 1988).

38. Mary Douglas, *Purity and Danger: An Analysis of the Concepts of Pollution and Taboo* (London: Routledge, 2001 [1966]), 2.

39. Douglas, *Purity and Danger*, 4.

40. 'Chauderie hémicorporelle gauche', 29 April 2008, http://www.jaddo.fr/2008/04/29/chauderie-hemicorporelle-gauche/.

41. Fischler, *L'Homnivore*, 69.

42. For a story of two veiled Muslim women who were chased out of a gourmet restaurant, see 'Deux femmes musulmanes voiles chassées d'un restaurant de Seine-Saint-Denis', *La Croix*, 29 August 2016, https://www.la-croix.com/France/Justice/Deux-femmes-musulmanes-voilees-chassees-restaurant-Seine-Saint-Denis-2016-08-29-1200785134

43. Vialles, *Animal to Edible*.

44. See the veiled Muslim woman as sexual prey in my article on eroticisation and the prohibition of the veil: Bentouhami, 'The Veil, Race and Appearance. A Political Phenomenology', in Emily Lee, ed., *Race as Phenomena: Between Phenomenology and Philosophy of Race* (Lanham: Rowman and Littlefield, 2019) 55–68.

45. As Nassima Mekaoui has shown, there was a passion for the appropriation of the bodies of cooks in the colonial era in overseas France and in Algeria with the production of a generic body (that of Fatma), a surplus body also subjected to rape as were many working class maids and domestic servants. Nassima Mekaoui, 'Les domestiques dans l'Algérie coloniale à l'épreuve des relations de classe, d'altérité et de domination (1830-1962), unpublished PhD Thesis, École des Hautes Études en Sciences Sociales, 27 November 2014.

46. Georges Treille, *Principes D'Hygiene Coloniale* (Paris: Georges Carré et C. Naud, 1899), foreword.

47. Treille, *Principes*, 184–185.

48. Cited in Janes, *Colonial Food in Interwar Paris*, 112.

49. Sylvie Durmelat, 'Making Couscous French? Digesting the Loss of Empire', *Contemporary French Civilisation* 42:3-4 (2017), 391–407.

50. Cited in Janes, *Colonial Food in Interwar Paris*, 165.

51. Barthes, *Mythologies*, 59.

52. Barthes, *Mythologies*, 61. It is worth noting that *Mythologies* was published in 1957, during the Algerian War of Independence.

53. Janes, *Colonial Food in Interwar Paris*, 145.

54. Cohen, 'The Whiteness of French Food'.

55. Myrtille Plotain, 'In the Restaurants of the Calais Jungle', *Vice*, 13 March 2016, https://www.vice.com/en/article/8qe79k/dans-les-restaurants-de-la-jungle.

56. Charlotte Oberti, '"Rebel valley" farmer starts France's first Emmaus-backed farming community for refugees and homeless people', *Info Migrants*, 19 July 2019, https://www.infomigrants.net/en/post/18262/rebel-valley-farmer-starts-frances-first-emmausbacked-/-farming-community-for-refugees-and-homeless-people.

57. See their intersectional manifesto for a vegetarian alternative in school canteens: Front de Mères, 'Manifeste pour une alternative végétarienne à la cantine', 30 November 2017, https://www.front2meres.org/manifeste-pour-une-alternative-vegetarienne-a-la-cantine/.

Interpassive students in interactive classrooms

Alan Bradshaw and Mikael Andehn

A lecturer will ask the audience 'and can anybody tell me what this is?' And she or he is met by an everlasting silence, with people refusing to look her in the eye … Now the thing is, I'm a very confident person … I'm very outgoing. I usually volunteer to do presentations but even I felt too awkward to even speak. The atmosphere was toxic silence, which turned into pain when the lecturer would probe the audience … 'anyone?' I distinctly remember one lecture where the 'anyone?' continued for around two minutes in desperation for the audience to provide her with any confidence and truthfully, it was the most painful two minutes of my life. Half of the audience were already on their phones because they had already given up or were just bored mindless. The other half don't want to speak.[1]

The above description from a London university will be recognisable to students and faculty everywhere because it reflects the ever-expanding norm of universities today: student disengagement and failed desperate attempts at interactivity. The *Chronicle of Higher Education* reported that we are now amid a 'stunning level of student disconnection'.[2] Something is going seriously wrong. Despite enormous investment in the 'student experience' – ranging from campus architecture that looks like airport terminals and 'flipped classroom' platforms to the requirement for all university teachers to be certified by professional associations – the reality is that lecture theatres today are increasingly dysfunctional spaces in which teaching and learning does not, and often *cannot*, take place. Ironically, despite the chorus of indignation lamenting the rise of the student as consumer, today the student is all too often precisely the person who *refuses to consume* their education.

Rather than lapse into despair and indignation, or embrace fetishised and overblown claims about the new realities of Gen Z brains or their consumerism, we seek an alternative interpretation of this mass phenomenon of disengagement. To do so we return to critiques of 1990s ideology that embraced the *a priori* virtue of interactivity, and mine concepts of 'interpassivity' and 'flat affect' for their strategic potential. Given widespread acknowledgement that universities are today captured by neoliberalism, we refuse to accept that student disengagement is the problem. Just maybe, we suggest, it is the antidote.

1990s ideology

Indicative of 1990s web boosterism was David Bowie's famous BBC interview with Jeremy Paxman.[3] Bowie, sparkling with excitement, promised that in the twenty-first century all content would be incomplete until the audience actively engaged and transformed it. This was the era of the famous 'dotcom' bubble, where finance rushed investment into anything internet related, until, inevitably, the bubble 'burst'. 'Interactivity' was understood as a general experience rather than a function associated with specific technologies. It was expected to herald a new era of empowerment and democratisation that would flatten and transform fields of media, education, politics and art.[4]

Henry Jenkins influentially theorised that media were becoming driven by a participatory culture wherein consumers desired to have the media they want, where they want it, when they want it, and in the format they want, leading to what he termed a *convergence culture* where what might be traditionally understood as media producers and consumers become transformed into participants expected to interact with each other.[5] As

Turner recounts, the era was understood as pointing towards peer-to-peer adhocracy and a levelled market: 'In the mid-1990s, as first the Internet and then the World Wide Web swung into public view, talk of revolution filled the air. Politics, economics, the nature of the self – all seemed to teeter on the edge of transformation'.[6]

'Interactivity' became understood by some as indicative of postmodernism, or as Jacques Rancière put it, a disguised postmodernism.[7] For example, the rise of 'postmodern museums' abandoned 'traditional display cases, silent contemplation and the aura of priceless authenticity', to be replaced with 'an anti-elitist emphasis on participation, involvement, sound and lighting effects, performance, and the creation of spectacular multimedia "experiences"'.[8] In this moment we see a broad paradigm shift across multiple fields. Inasmuch as the promise of interactivity was held to be positive, traditional modes of delivery came to be regarded as unacceptably arcane and predicated upon passive consumption. According to Žižek, what was being celebrated was the *democratic potential* of interactive media that would emancipate users from the role of passive observer, not only to participate actively in the spectacle, but increasingly to establish its very rules.[9]

Rancière had long questioned the purpose of public education in terms of equality of intelligence and the power dynamics between students and teachers, most notably in his influential *Ignorant Schoolmaster*.[10] In 2008 he returned to this question, now transplanting the teacher-student dynamic to one of theatre performer and audience in order to reassess at a time when it was fashionable to celebrate the notionally *a priori* virtues of interactivity and denigrate passivity. Rancière parodied the popular discourse as follows: Spectatorship is a bad thing because to be a spectator means being passive and separated from the possibility of doing. Instead we must aspire to activate the spectator towards action and to do so, theatre must be transformed into a place where action is actually performed by living bodies in front of living bodies. 'What is required', he noted, 'is a theatre without spectators, where those in attendance learn from as opposed to being seduced by images; where they become active participants as opposed to passive voyeurs'.[11] Theatres, like universities, have been guilty

of making spectators passive and must seek redemption through giving back to the spectators their collective energy.

Interactivity and pedagogy

For Rancière, the issue was primarily knowledge transmission and indeed, during the 1990s, pedagogy became subjected to media innovations around classroom interactivity, with didactic modes of lecturing increasingly critiqued as outdated because they were said to be predicated on student passivity. In 1997, for example, the British government commissioned the Dearing Report which concluded that the effectiveness of university teaching and learning needed to be improved and that universities must take full advantage of the advances in communications and information technology to radically alter the shape and delivery of learning, while emphasising the importance of interactive teaching and learning.[12] The Dearing Report recommended a professional accreditation programme for university teachers to oversee these improvements, leading to the formation of the Higher Education Academy. Today almost all British university faculty must formally be certified in pedagogical methods and gain a 'fellowship' at the Higher Education Academy, and this typically entails learning to embrace interactive teaching as best practice, and subsequently propagating this style to attain higher levels of 'fellowship'. The 1990s' preferences for pedagogical interactivity have become institutionalised.

Yet despite the professional commitment to developing vibrant interactive pedagogy, the reality of the classroom today is often one of malaise. The late Mark Fisher noted that students are now more immobilised than ever:

> During lessons at our college ... students will be found slumped on desks talking almost constantly, snacking incessantly (or even, on occasions, eating full meals) ... The lack of an effective disciplinary system has not, to say the least, been compensated for by an increase in student self-motivation ... They typically respond to this freedom not by pursuing projects but by falling into hedonic (or anhedonic) lassitude: the soft narcosis, the comfort food oblivion of Playstation, all-night TV and marijuana.[13]

Across university schools, faculty will describe the struggle to generate rare sparks of life in classrooms. During lockdown, a common reprise was students turning off cameras during online lectures, leaving the lecturer unclear if anybody was listening at all. Fisher's supposition is that young people are struggling to concentrate in the contemporary attention economy – a common refrain. According to pedagogy theorist James Lang, the problem is that the *distractability* of devices is not properly managed in classrooms and we fail to harness those devices' potential for pedagogy, nor do we sufficiently appreciate how young people's capacities have been transformed by technology.[14] Similarly, Michel Serres regards any indignation over how younger people do not concentrate as marking an insufficient appreciation of just how different the lives of young people are today.[15] The entire premise of pedagogy as knowledge transmission is, he claims, an anachronistic misnomer inasmuch as the knowledge is already distributed online. A further popular view is that students have been absorbed by a consumerist subjectivity that is not conducive to education. Perhaps most notably, Bernard Stiegler theorises how this consumerism is a form of proletariatisation that has transformed students into demanding clients who are impossible to satisfy, but also into people so absorbed and libidinally captured by media devices that they are unable to concentrate or engage in any properly transformative education.[16] The result is to leave their lecturers in a completely impossible position.

The general conclusion from these popular analyses is that the 'solution' for learners struggling to concentrate must be grounded in lecturers rejecting didactic teaching methods and a greater push towards more interactive modes of pedagogy cognisant of the changed features of the Gen Z brain and a more enlightened embrace of technology in the classroom – a doubling down without ever wondering if the interactivity itself might be the problem's source. In this sense, the tone of discussion has hardly altered since the 1990s when, as Robert Pfaller observed, 'a vast audience of believers' reading 'euphoric texts' presented 'a discourse of interactivity, facilitated mainly by new media'.[17] The discourse of interactivity, he contended, was grounded on unquestioned facts and therefore constituted more of an ideology than a theory.

In the *Emancipated Spectator*, Rancière argued that the distance between the performer and spectator should not be understood as an evil to be abolished but as the normal condition of communication. Rancière asked the pertinent question: what if 'it is precisely the attempt at suppressing the distance that constitutes the distance itself?'[18] Rancière argued that it is the act of looking, of being a spectator, that confirms or modifies distribution and that interpreting the world is already a means of transforming or reconfiguring the world. His point, therefore, is that the spectator was always already active: observing, selecting, comparing and interpreting. Further, Rancière rejected any normative principle that dramaturgy should aggregate an audience into a community, but rather claims that the collective power of spectators is not to be found in their propensity for interactivity, but rather in their power to translate, in their own way, what they are looking at. At stake in this idiosyncrasy, he believed, was our power to make our own way in the world and it is precisely that capacity, Rancière argued, that works through the very unpredictable and irreducible distances that the discourse of interactivity now seeks to eliminate. Correspondingly, we advocate scepticism towards any claim that 'didactic' lecturing produces student passivity or that teachers must strive to 'activate' their students.

Interpassivity

Robert Pfaller reads radical possibility into dysfunctional phenomena like disengaged students slumped over desks, and he does so by regarding the disengagement itself as a strategy of escape and potentiality. The name of the strategy is *interpassivity*.[19] To that end, it is important to note how the supposedly disengaged student will nonetheless go through formal practices of engagement: dutifully turning up for lectures, submitting term papers and sitting exams. Rather than see the act of turning up to a lecture but then not listening as contradictory, Pfaller might regard this as typically interpassive behaviour. His examples of interpassivity include a student who purposefully spends hours in a library photocopying course literature that they will never read. Or a person recording movies but never watching them. Or a person who watches a comedy show yet never laughs. In each case the pleasure is delegated onto an external object, as though it is the photocopier that studies the texts, the Tivo box that watches the movies and the canned laughter that is amused by the comedy. This delegation of enjoyment is the basis of interpassive behaviour and, Pfaller argues, is a widespread but largely unacknowledged form of cultural behaviour today.

For Žižek, this belief in the subjectivity of commodities is an instance of Marx's commodity fetish whereby we perversely have object relations between people but subject relations between commodities. Such thinking is clearly present in marketing theory via influential concepts like the 'brand personality' or the 'consumer identity project' that inherently assume it isn't people who have identities or personalities but, rather, that it is done for them by the brands they consume. As Žižek notes, advertising conventionally performs the pleasure of consumption: 'Coke cans bearing the inscription "Ooh! Ooh! What taste!" emulate in advance the ideal customer's reaction'.[20] The crucial ideological moment for Žižek is to be found in consumer culture's injunction that we must enjoy ourselves. His example is of a family holiday; 'a father who works hard to organize a family holiday and, after a series of postponements, tired of it all, shouts at his children: "Now you'd better enjoy it!" On a holiday trip, it is quite common to feel a superego compulsion to enjoy: one "must have fun", and one feels guilty if one doesn't enjoy it'.[21] In such a circumstance, any external object that we might delegate our obligation to enjoy the holiday to, would be very useful.

For Pfaller, the interpassive moment is marked by two stages. First, pleasure must be transferred to a representative agent or object. Second, we must transfer belief in the illusion they have staged to an undefined and naïve other. To return to the example of a family who feel obliged to enjoy their holiday even though they are all fed up – the family might take photographs in which they all smile as though they are having great fun. The photograph will be to prove to some external person that it was, in fact, a magnificent holiday after all. The possibility that this person might believe in the illusion of the magnificent holiday is enough. Both Pfaller and Žižek argue that we engage in such behaviour routinely.

The interpassive classroom

The radical possibility of interpassivity lies in its ability to oppose interpellation – the ideological moment theorised by Althusser in which we recognise ourselves as the subject of a hail and become interpellated within a power order.[22] (Althusser's famous example is when a police officer shouts 'hey you there!' and you turn around.) Pfaller's argument is that interpassivity may be interpreted as anti-ideological behaviour: a strategy of escaping identification and the consequent interpellation.

With this in mind, we can return to the phenomenon of disengaged students. Rather than view disengagement as an absolute negative, we might instead interpret the students as opposing their interpellation by the obviously corrupted ideology of the contemporary university. The formal performance of studying and learning, then, is staged for the naïve other (the external examiner or perhaps the university chancellor who presents graduands with parchment, apparently highly impressed by the magnificent work the students have done). To paraphrase a Soviet joke, 'we pretend to teach, and they pretend to learn'. In this regard, the greatest threat to the contemporary ideologically saturated university is not that the students are passive, but as Žižek warns, 'the real threat of new media is that they deprive us of our passivity, of our authentic passive experience, and thus prepare us for mindless frenetic activity – for endless work'.[23]

And there's no denying the depth of frenetic ideology permeating contemporary universities where students are, to give one example, told to identify the 'twelve meta skills required by employers, and to build those skills throughout your own academic journey'.[24] These instructions are typical of how university life is today defined by injunctions of optimisation. At stake is a system that seeks to impose 'total education', requiring a full transformation of each individual through a constant regulatory and (e)valuative determination.[25] Stefano Harney and Fred Moten draw from Paulo Freire's *Pedagogy of the Oppressed* which argues that the prevailing 'banking model' of education dehumanises students.[26] Instead, Freire wanted education to be a forum whereby teacher and student discuss together to achieve equality based on understanding present forms of domination. The term Harney and Moten use to describe this process of coming together to arrive at a mode of being not grounded in oppression is *study*, and they argue that the contemporary university is not only itself non-conducive to the possibility of study but also that there is an active preclusion or prevention of study by university administration and an apparent disavowal of study from students themselves.[27] Their argument is that the university has become alienated from its own capacity to study, and that prevailing pedagogical methods only manifest that exploitation of our capacity to study.

And why shouldn't students disavow their education when, drawing from Jodi Dean's analysis, the promises of interactivity are typically a lie?[28] Media users, she tells us, who are interested in politics don't really actively contribute to content but are led to believe that they are making a difference by clicking a button, adding their name to a petition or commenting on a blog. For Dean these interactive practices are fetishes: we think we are being active but are actually being displaced from any 'real' action. The same goes, we might say, for interactive classrooms. For example, as part of the professionalisation of pedagogy, 'learning outcomes' and class content are mediated and predetermined months – and often years – in advance by faculty committees and do not arise organically from class discussion. Therefore the interactivity is a fetish: the lecturer doesn't really want to hear what students have to say, rather they just want the students to participate in order to boost the session's affective intensity as a goal in its own right. Student participation, therefore, is not creating nor impacting content and should be regarded as inauthentic dialogue. Accordingly, we should not think it is weird that students prefer to remain silent. A common reprise is for classroom technology to boost the possibilities for interactivity, yet as Dean might argue, technology then becomes the fetish whose actual role is to stand in for the disengaged student and to keep alive the fantasy of an active, engaged student subject. Moreover, to focus on student participation is to overlook the grim economics that defines the student experience as increasingly grounded in debt and anxiety – what Peter Fleming terms the 'student hellscapes' that are never measured or accounted for in student satisfaction surveys.[29]

The interactive classroom therefore constantly demands students to be highly expressive of affect, perhaps to the point of excess, and for their faces to provide a constant feedback loop of enthusiastic reinforcement for neurotic lecturers. By contrast, a facial expression of unavailability might be read as offering a degree of protection from the depletion demanded by the neoliberal university. This recourse is, according to Lauren Berlant, 'flat affect': an expressionless presentation, or an emotional opacity, in which affective display, in the face in particular, has little range, intensity and mobility, and feelings become unclear.[30] Berlant reads these moments as offering a degree of reserve from situational injunctions. Berlant resists any implication that flat affect occurs in lieu of the subject taking responsibility for their feelings and perceptions. In other words, flat affect might serve as a passive-aggressive mode of affective agency, rather than a substitute for it. Perhaps the most notable example of flat affect as strategy was JG Ballard's *High Rise*, in which female characters wander the building in an apparently catatonic state, passively disengaged from the violent behaviour of the male occupants.[31] But the women are actually meeting in private and eventually kill or enslave the men and seize the building. The women's performative withdrawal allows them to both escape much of the men's violence, but also to bide their time while leading their enemy to underestimate them. Berlant warns, however, that flat affect is an ambivalent strategy, creating the possibility of self-erasure and therefore must be understood as a sort of final and desperate recourse for the profoundly disempowered.

An ambivalent antidote

The significance of 'flat affect' for ideology is important to consider. Within the neoliberal university – certainly as determined by the Browne Report, which led to the trebling of British tuition fees – students are mobilised as the agent that will push for and demand university reform. Implicit in the all-important UK National Student Survey, for example, is the idea that the 'student experience' must be constantly measured and responded to as the engine that will drive university reform towards its predetermined neoliberal endpoint. Student affect, therefore, becomes a form of capital that a university seeks to build. In this regard, the students' affective response is not just pre-determined ('the students *want* more employability content') but also the key point of legitimation and the primary alibi for the neoliberal reterritorialisation of the university. The student subjectivity they are expected to inhabit, therefore, is one that is not just predetermined but also overdetermined, making excessive affective demands. In this context, the withdrawal into flat affect jams the juggernaut, leaving an excruciating absent centre.

What is most interesting about the disengaged student, then, is precisely their refusal to enjoy their education in the manner it is intended to be enjoyed. This is to reject analyses by Fisher and others who see a laziness or failure to concentrate at stake. Rather, we argue that what the students are refusing is precisely the real pleasure of being educated and instead prefer to commit themselves to only the drudgery of sitting uncomfortably in lectures or not turning up at all. It is as though the imagined 'other' is being delegated the quality experience of education, leaving the students to take on the misery and the expense, leaving the ideal of education intact. But it is also in this delegation that the interpellation towards the prescribed subjectivation can be circumvented. Pfaller notes that this situation results in a certain 'mischievous pleasure' of inhabiting an alternative subjectivity: a *rebellious* mode of learning outside of the subjectivation demanded from interactive engagement.

It is now over a decade since British universities experienced a wave of protest and occupation, led by militant student activists. Since then, Student Unions have been largely rationalised and integrated into the managerial infrastructure, with the radical University of London Union shut down permanently. Pushed to the edge, we might say – as Todd McGowan and Ryan Engley do – that the interpassive student *stands in for* the missing revolutionary impulse, leaving them with what Fisher called 'reflexive impotence'.[32] But rather than see passivity as an absolutely negative symptom of malaise, we argue for the interpassive as an ambivalent antidote for the narcissist age. In other words, in our students' gesture of refusing to see themselves enjoying their education, they are not resisting their own education but rather refusing its commodified and alienated form, leaving a gap which we, as their teachers, must work to interpret as carrying the possibility of a more authentic pedagogical encounter. Knowing as we do that resistance becomes co-opted, interpassivity marks the premise that 'resistance is not enough' just as it rejects the ideology that activity is good and passivity is bad.

Interpassive withdrawal is ambivalent because, as Berlant argues, flat affect is the final recourse of the profoundly disempowered that carries the risk of self-negation. As educators, our role must be to comprehend how we might positively respond to student disengagement, accepting its radical potential as a form of anti-ideological behaviour and not just lamenting its destructiveness. We must learn how this can be done because the alternative is to exhaust ourselves reproducing the interactive fetish, or, worse, to allow this ambivalent strategy of interpassivity to lead to mutual self-negation.

Alan Bradshaw and Mikael Andehn teach in the School of Business and Management at Royal Holloway, University of London.

Notes

1. 'UK universities are scamming us all: my time at Goldsmiths', *Youtube* (accessed July 2022), *https://www.youtube.com/watch?v=2Xrw4ClFi9w*.
2. Beth McMurtrie, 'A Stunning Level of Student Disconnection', *The Chronicle of Higher Education*, April 5, 2022, https://www.chronicle.com/article/a-stunning-level-of-student-disconnection
3. David Bowie speaks to Jeremy Paxman on Newsnight (1999), Youtube (accessed October 2022), https://www.youtube.com/watch?v=FiK7s_0tGsg.
4. Margerite Barry and Gavin Doherty, 'What We Talk About When We Talk About Interactivity: Empowerment in Public Discourse', *New Media & Society* 19:7 (2017).
5. Henry Jenkins, *Convergence Culture: Where Old and New Media Collide* (New York: New York University Press, 2006).
6. Fred Turner, *From Counterculture to Cyberculture: Stewart Brand, the Whole Earth Network, and the Rise of Digital Utopianism* (Chicago: University of Chicago Press, 2009), 1.
7. Jacques Rancière, *The Emancipated Spectator*, trans. Gregory Elliott (London: Verso, 2009).
8. Stephen Brown, *Postmodern Marketing* (London: Routledge, 1995), 74.
9. Slavoj Žižek, 'The Interpassive Subject' (accessed October 2022), https://www.lacan.com/zizek-pompidou.htm.
10. Jacques Rancière, *The Ignorant Schoolmaster: Five Lessons in Intellectual Emancipation*, trans. Kristin Ross (Stanford: Stanford University Press, 1991).
11. Rancière, *The Emancipated Spectator*, 4.
12. The Dearing Report (accessed October 2022), http://www.educationengland.org.uk/documents/dearing1997/dearing1997.html.
13. Mark Fisher, *Capitalist Realism: Is There No Alternative?* (London: Zero Books, 2012), 28.
14. James Lang, *Distracted: Why Students Can't Focus and What We Can Do About It* (New York: Basic Books, 2020).
15. Michel Serres, *Thumbelina: The Culture and Technology of Millennials* (London: Rowman & Littlefield, 2014).
16. See Bernard Stiegler, *States of Shock* (Cambridge: Polity, 2015); *Taking Care of Youth and the Generations* (California: Stanford University Press, 2010). For a helpful summary see also Kristy Forrest, 'The Problem of Now: Bernard Stiegler and the Student as Consumer', *Educational Philosophy and Theory* 52:4 (2019), 337–47.
17. Robert Pfaller, *Interpassivity: The Aesthetics of Delegated Enjoyment* (Edinburgh: Edinburgh University Press, 2017), 2–3.
18. Rancière, *Emanciptated Spectator*, 134–35.
19. Pfaller, *Interpassivity*.
20. Žižek, *The Interpassive Subject*.
21. Žižek, *The Interpassive Subject*.
22. Louis Althusser, *On Ideology*, trans. Ben Brewster (London: Verso, 2008).
23. Žižek, *The Interpassive Subject*.
24. This is taken from a newsletter sent to students in a London business school.
25. Stefano Harney and Fred Moten, *All Incomplete* (New York: Minor Compositions, 2021).
26. Paulo Freire, *Pedagogy of the Oppressed* [1970], trans. Myra Bergman Ramos (London: Penguin, 2006).
27. Stefano Harney and Fred Moten, *The Undercommons: Fugitive Planning & Black Study* (New York: Minor Compositions, 2013).
28. Jodi Dean, *Democracy and Other Neoliberal Fantasies: Communicative Capitalism and Left Politics* (Durham: Duke University Press, 2009).
29. Peter Fleming, *Dark Academia: How Universities Die* (London: Pluto Press, 2021).
30. Robbie Duschinsky and Emma Wilson, 'Flat Affect, Joyful Politics and Enthralled Attachments: Engaging with the Work of Lauren Berlant', *International Journal of Politics, Culture, and Society* 28 (2015). See also Lauren Berlant, 'Structures of Unfeeling: Mysterious Skin', *International Journal of Politics, Culture and Society* 28 (2015).
31. JG Ballard, *High Rise* (London: Harper Perennial, 2006).
32. Todd MaGowan and Ryan Engley, *Interpassivity* (accessed October 2022), https://soundcloud.com/whytheory/interpassivity.

Development as national liberation

The experience of the Popular Unity government in Chile

Martín Arboleda

During the twentieth century, the concept of development galvanised a wide variety of popular struggles for democratisation, agrarian reform, socialism, and economic sovereignty across the global South. In social theory, the question of development also sparked major intellectual debates that shed new light on the nature of power and liberation in the interstate system.

At some point, however, this ideal waned as an emancipatory horizon for social thought. Since the publication of Wolfgang Sachs and of Arturo Escobar's seminal critiques of the (Western) development project, the idea of development has generally been dismissed by poststructuralist social theory merely as a neocolonial discourse of power.[1] These texts, it has been argued, marked the emergence of a new intellectual consensus that no longer sought alternative paths to development but rather alternatives to development *tout court*.[2] Also, the consolidation of the Human Development approach as an overarching framework for policymaking across the wide spectrum of multilateral institutions and NGOs would seem to have reduced development to the allocation of aid and social policy. In a similar way, Latin American neostructuralism has been said to strip the tenets of classical developmentalism of their democratic and political content and reframed development as nothing more than a quest for 'growth with equity'.[3]

In short, it would seem as if this once-contested idiom of power and struggle had reached an impasse. However, the dynamics of extreme social inequality – both between and within countries – and ecosystem collapse that have followed from recent world crises have opened new forays for reflexive engagements with the concept of development. It has become increasingly evident that any viable solution to the intertwined threats of fascism and an escalating climate emergency is unthinkable in the absence of a political movement that is able to wrest control of the economy from the domestic oligarchies, large transnational corporations, and imperialistic interests that hinder the possibility for real human and ecological flourishing. How to attain authentic national independence from the disruptive, polarising forces of a hierarchically-structured world economy, it should be noted, was precisely the underlying question that animated the radical theories of development that emerged from the Third World – and especially from Latin America – during a considerable part of the twentieth century. In this sense, it is unsurprising that recent years have brought renewed attempts to uncover some of the key principles that informed these traditions of thought, which have since been eclipsed by either poststructuralist or liberal approaches to development.[4]

This article argues that development can be mobilised as an emancipatory ideal for democratic struggles, especially when positioned within current efforts to place freedom firmly once again on the agenda of the political left and of critical social theory. In recent years, an emerging tradition of socialist republicanism has expanded the normative ideal of freedom by pointing out that the most blatant forms of tyranny and domination are in fact manifested in the despotic organisation of work, assets, and production in the capitalist economy.[5] In Latin America, an emerging scholarly discussion on the lineages of this tradition has also unfolded alongside historical explorations of the ways in which tropes of republican freedom underpinned the design and implementation of novel anti-oligarchic, anti-imperialist, and anti-racist institutions that advanced the frontier of democratic experimentation into unforeseen realms. Although revolutionary movements for national independence in the nineteenth century have been a core focus of inquiry,[6] the era of development and of national liberation struggles in the twentieth century also looms large as an instance of conceptual and political intensification within the long historical arc of this intellectual tradition. As José Miguel Ahumada shows, Latin American theories of development were informed by an eminently republican understanding of the free state as that which not only ensured material wellbeing but could also assert its own self-determination against the complex framework of domination that is the capitalist interstate system.[7]

In light of the above, this article explores the links between development theory and national liberation struggles in Latin America. It does so by unearthing the case of economic planning under the Popular Unity government in Chile during the 1970-1973 period. The case of Popular Unity [*Unidad Popular*] is noteworthy not only as a historically-unique experiment in the design of an intricate institutional infrastructure for a model of socialism that was avowedly anti-imperialist, libertarian, and pluralistic; crucially for the purpose of this paper, it was also where development and dependency theories became more directly interwoven with the decision-making fabric of the state.[8] Specifically, the article looks at the Popular Unity project through the lens of two of its most emblematic figures: Jacques Chonchol and Pedro Vuskovic, both of whom were organic intellectuals formed in the tradition of dependency theory and also served as ministers of agriculture and economy, respectively, during the Allende government. In the same way that the Haitian Revolution advanced an immanent critique of Enlightenment ideals that enlarged the content of freedom, economic planners working with Popular Unity unmasked the nature of capitalist progress as *faux* progress, and advocated for '*a popular option for development*' that could deliver real human progress in its stead.[9] Consequently, Chonchol and Vuskovic embarked on an ambitious set of transformations that not only sought to reconfigure the structure of production but to redistribute wealth and power in society through mass worker empowerment and through the implementation of pluralistic property forms.

Conventional understandings of the origins of development are rooted in a diffusionist narrative that considers political idioms and ideas to originate in the global North, and to later flow to the global South where they become adopted and reproduced.[10] My article contributes to recent efforts to supersede this diffusionist narrative and reconstruct the era of development as one where Latin America emerged as a key site of theoretical and institutional innovation.[11] Specifically, it takes forward Luciana Cadahia and Valeria Coronel's lucid invitation to 'return to the archive' of the republican imagination and put into focus the role that the region has performed in shaping global debates over the nature of democracy, power, and political modernity.[12]

Salvador Allende, 1 May 1971. Photo by Armindo Cardoso. Archivo Memoria Chilena.

In its first section, the article reassesses the question of national liberation by framing the contributions of Latin American theories of development and underdevelopment. The second section begins by highlighting the specificity of development theory marshalled by Popular Unity, and then goes on to explore the specific modalities of development planning devised by Jacques Chonchol and Pedro Vuskovic. In the third section, the article discusses the reactionary forces that the reforms implemented by Chonchol and Vuskovic unleashed. To the extent that they challenged the vested interests of oligarchic groups and of US imperialism, these reforms were met with trenchant forms of economic sabotage that eventually became apotheosised into a ferocious reactionary retaliation by the military in September of 1973. In this way, the article also intends to shed light into the high political and social stakes that development as national liberation entails.

Reopening the archive of development

During a considerable part of the twentieth century, development became one of the most contested and polysemic concepts in the political vocabulary. On the one hand, it provided an entire policy rationale to theories of modernisation that conceived history in stagist and unilinear terms, and where Europe was deemed the *telos* or most advanced stage of human civilisation. Economies were considered 'underdeveloped' (i.e. backward) to the extent that they deviated from specific features of European societies, in turn considered the yardstick by which human progress was measured. On the other, development also became asserted as an idiom of emancipation by plebeian and popular struggles that sought to challenge unilinear understandings of progress and break free from imperialist and oligarchic forms of domination. It was during the 1980s that this concept underwent a process of theoretical closure as it was severed from its radical and emancipatory interpretations. Especially, it was the Latin American School of Development – which encompasses the traditions of structuralism as well as dependency – which most systematically advanced a normative and methodological concern for economic sovereignty within the context of a stratified yet interdependent capitalist world-system.[13] This focus – itself the 'rational kernel' of the Latin American School – in turn presupposes a specific understanding of freedom (i.e. republican freedom as non-domination) that today seems to have been eclipsed.

Some of the key theoretical principles of international authority and stratification that gave rise to the Latin American School emerged after the creation of the UN's Economic Commission for Latin America (CEPAL) in 1948, and especially by the formative contributions of Argentinean economist Raúl Prebisch.[14]

Tropes of national liberation in the twentieth-century, on the other hand, became widespread in the aftermath of emblematic historical events such as the 1910 Mexican Revolution – whose rallying cry was 'land and freedom' – and subsequent processes of anti-oligarchic nation-building.[15] However, it was not until the Cuban Revolution in 1959 that development and national liberation became more systematically intertwined, especially on the basis of a political program that sought to advance human emancipation through conscious economic planning. As one of the leading public figures of the new revolutionary government, Che Guevara in particular helped to forge links between these political and normative ideals.[16] In a 1964 address to the General Assembly of the United Nations, titled 'On Development', Guevara denounced a system of international trade that had become weaponised into a mechanism for enforcing the subordination of underdeveloped economies. He insisted that the principle of self-determination included in the Charter of the UN should be fully implemented, to encompass the sovereign right of nations to choose their own strategies of development and economic specialisation without incurring reprisals of any kind.[17] These ideas were not only influential for national liberation struggles in the region, but also for the epistemic circuits and intellectual milieus that would later lead to the emergence of dependency theories.[18]

Despite the various nuances and disagreements between the traditions that comprise the Latin American School of Development, the literature suggests that they share a set of common features that make them distinctive vis-à-vis other competing approaches. First, they share the assumption that the global economy is hierarchically structured into cores and peripheries. This not only means that the level of analysis is the interstate system as such, but that the latter is woven together by relations of domination between its internal elements (i.e. national economies).[19] A crucial implication that emerges from this assumption, according to Cristóbal Kay,[20] is that the Latin American School of Development presupposes a counterpoint to major theories of modernisation insofar as the development of the core is premised on the underdevelopment of the periphery. Originally introduced by authors in the tradition of structuralist economics during the 1950s, the core-periphery model had mainly revolved around questions of unequal exchange and bilateral economic relations. It was with the emergence of Marxist dependency theory in the late 1960s and 1970s that the framework for understanding international subordination advanced towards a more deliberate concern with the structure of production and the regimes of labour exploitation. This enabled Marxist readings of dependency to lay bare the forms of impersonal and systemic economic domination that ensued from large-scale industrialisation under an international division of labour. A landmark moment in this second phase of theoretical elaboration was the publication of Ruy Mauro Marini's book *The Dialectics of Dependency* in 1973.[21]

Second, these approaches also shared a methodological emphasis on the vexing problem of the distribution and appropriation of the economic surplus. This means that underdevelopment was seen as a concrete result of the changing forms in which socio-political actors appropriated rents, profits, and interests at the national and international levels.[22] Consequently, the historical-structural method became harnessed as a research technique designed to grasp the concrete forms in which the economic surplus became extracted and mobilised.[23] Third, and as framed by Cardoso and Faletto's classic statement on the topic, the program of development is ultimately concerned with *the social control of production and consumption at the national level* – that is, the logical corollary of development is the transformation of the productive and technological structure of the national economy through conscious planning.[24]

Proponents of Marxist dependency theory considered that the question of planning also brought to the fore the eminently international and *internationalist* nature of socialism – as a distinct framework of relations between free and equals in the world system. Because the intensive utilisation of national wealth through science and technology would demand considerable material and economic resources, Vânia Bambirra stressed that robust mechanisms for international economic solidarity between socialist nations would need to be put into place. Under a consciously planned economy, Bambirra argued, 'industrialisation would continue to depend on foreign inputs even though it would no longer be dependent accumulation.' Rather, the author concluded, 'it would be essentially a particular form of socialist reproduction underpinned by relations of exchange and cooperation between free nations.'[25]

It was the particular form to be assumed by development planning, in fact, which marked the major point of contention within the Latin American School broadly considered. Structuralist authors (who favoured a reformist approach to public intervention and social change) considered that development was possible under capitalism, whilst dependency theorists (who espoused a more avowedly revolutionary stance) considered that the development of the periphery could only be achieved by means of a particularly socialist form of economic planning.[26]

These theoretical and methodological principles, it should be pointed out, bear a striking resemblance to those that inform recent scholarly efforts to reconstruct the normative ideal of republican freedom as non-domination. It was the traditions of political theory and intellectual history that gravitate around what is commonly referred to as the Cambridge School that first sought to recover an understanding of freedom that departs from the liberal emphasis on methodological individualism and mere non-interference. According to the programmatic interventions of Philip Pettit and Quentin Skinner, the liberal idea of interference is confined to contingent practices of individual coercion and brackets out more insidious, institutionally-mediated and prolonged practices of domination and dependence that place both individuals and states at the mercy of others.[27] Another key tenet of this approach has to do with the fact that individual freedom can only be achieved within the framework of a free state, understood as a political arrangement where citizens govern themselves according to laws of their own making.[28]

In recent years, an emerging tradition of socialist republicanism has questioned the contributions of the Cambridge School insofar as its understanding of freedom has been said to elide dynamics of *economic* domination, and especially those that result from the undemocratic and oppressive organisation of work, production, and property systems in the capitalist economy. The original blueprints for this understanding of domination, as authors such as William Clare Roberts and Antoni Domènech point out, are to be found in Marx's own framing of socialism in terms of a 'society of free and associated producers.' Marx's idea of *free* or *combined* association, it has been argued, presupposes a mode of economic interdependence that is free from external barriers – and therefore a political and normative commitment towards freedom in its republican guise.[29] For Marx, these barriers were not reduced to the exertion of direct force but included the blind, external coercive laws of the capitalist market and their institutional manifestation in the bourgeois state. From this, it follows that for Marx, democracy was not to be understood exclusively as a mode of collective self-legislation or self-expression, but also as a means for checking and controlling the powerful.[30]

The ideas of power and domination laid out in the tradition of socialist republicanism, however, have remained circumscribed to the realm of the national economy and are yet to include a more systematic theorisation of the ways in which capitalist power also becomes manifested and reproduced in the interstate system.

In Latin America, by contrast, the rediscovery of this tradition has unfolded alongside a more deliberate attempt to problematise the evolving forms of international subordination that first originated with colonialism, and later morphed into more complex and advanced configurations.[31] Even though abolitionist movements, anti-colonial struggles, and wars of national independence have been central objects of concern for reconstructing a distinctively republican understanding of freedom in the region,[32] the socio-political processes that encompass the era of development and of twentieth-century socialism, however, are yet to be fully elucidated. In a 1978 book written from her second exile in Mexico, Vânia Bambirra, for example, suggests that the idea of national liberation would only acquire full theoretical and discursive consistency when anchored to the instrumental task of overcoming the class basis of international economic subordination as expressed in dependent capitalism.[33]

In this way, and according to José Miguel Ahumada,[34] Latin American theories of development raised the conceptual and political stakes of republicanism by positing the normative problem of freedom at the level of the interstate system. For Latin American developmentalism, the capitalist world economy is an intricate system of domination based on an industrial monopoly that enables hegemonic nations to submit peripheries to relations of economic servitude. In this way, Ahumada shows that core-periphery relations of dependency in the interstate system are often theorised as analogous to the forms of peonage that are usually found in the debtor/creditor relation, or in other elementary forms of bondage such as chattel slavery or feudal serfdom. This insight also leads Kay to suggest that a major preoccupation for these traditions was 'to uncover the external and internal mechanisms of exploitation and domination in order to elaborate a path of development free from exploitation and oppression.'[35] When viewed through the prism of republican freedom, Ahumada thereby concludes,[36] underdevelopment no longer refers to 'economic backwardness' but is rather more accurately conceptualised as *economic domination*.

Although Amartya Sen is internationally renowned for linking development to the question of freedom, his own understanding of the latter concept departs from a civic, republican emphasis on *non-domination* and is more closely aligned with a liberal reading that posits freedom more narrowly in terms of methodological individualism and self-realisation – an approach that he, in dialogue with Martha Nussbaum, has framed in terms of building *capabilities*. Although Sen's approach is noteworthy for having disentangled development from macroeconomic performance – especially as expressed in GDP growth – his reading of freedom is premised on a methodological emphasis on poverty, not wealth or the dislocations that result from its deregulation.[37]

Unsurprisingly, the framework of Human Development, largely inspired by Sen, has been espoused by the multilateral policymaking apparatus of the UN constellation in order to craft a technocratic approach to development that abandons any aspiration to planning and economic self-government, and is instead centred on the governance of poverty – regardless of how multidimensional its conceptualisation.

As Wolfgang Sachs rightly admits,[38] the Western development project therefore shifted from one that during the postwar period aimed at fostering growth, to one that came to foreground questions of social aid and welfarism. In a similar vein, Ha-Joon Chang claims that the mainstream understanding of development is that of an *ersatz* developmentalism of atomistic individuals and uncoordinated efforts that has nothing to say about organisational transformation through industrial and technological change.[39] The origin of this rationale, however, can be traced further back in time to the 1961 Punta del Este Summit in Uruguay, when the US administration under John F. Kennedy introduced the Alliance for Progress, an initiative that sought to purge development of the political content it had acquired in Latin America at the time. The Punta del Este meeting was attended by many experts and political leaders of the region, including Che Guevara and also Raúl Prebisch, who were critical about the vision that inspired the Alliance for Progress.

As Margarita Fajardo points out, rather than 'propounding the industrialisation of Latin America as the path to development, the Alliance for Progress's experts privileged 'the construction of aqueducts, houses, sewers, and the like', fomenting what [Che] Guevara called 'the planning for latrines'.[40] At this meeting, Prebisch – who was the head of CEPAL at the time – also warned about the perils of narrowing down the scope of development to the mere deployment of aid and philanthropy. In the years that followed, and as Michael Löwy recounts, Guevara would expand on some of these insights to probe further into the relationship between development planning and freedom. Guevara's notion of the plan is closely bound up with a philosophic problematic of the conscious transition to communism and his notion of freedom as the supersession of forms of alienation. In Guevara's view, Löwy concludes, 'planning is the path that leads socialist society toward the realm of liberty'.[41]

More recently, however, the various strands of post-development theory and cognate approaches have largely surrendered the ideas of freedom, progress, and development to the political right and to the neoliberal policymaking intelligentsia. Instead they have retreated to a vernacular and conservative language of anti-modern critique that only seems to speak to the concerns and anxieties of the professional classes. In this way, the commitments of the Latin American School of Development for a libertarian vision of democracy and social change seem to have fallen into historical oblivion. The remaining sections are devoted to recovering the memory of this radical tradition.

Popular Unity's libertarian strategy for development

It is not coincidental that the political history of twentieth century Chile and the intellectual history of the Latin American School of Development seem to overlap in important ways. Chilean socialism emerged from a vibrant militant culture that resulted from a motley variety of artisan federations, women's groups, *campesino* movements, labour unions, and mass political organisations.[42] Theoretically, the idea of socialism in Chile was fashioned in terms of an anti-oligarchic democracy anchored on a Marxist understanding of history *and* on the democratic principles of political freedom, social equality, and economic justice that informed nineteenth-century revolutions on both sides of the Atlantic.[43] Moreover, the influx of grassroots anarchism and also of liberation theology in Chilean political life enabled the crystallisation of a distinct ethos of 'libertarian socialism' that would later prove to be foundational for the political program of the Popular Unity coalition (hereafter UP for its Spanish acronym).[44] The concept of freedom that emerges from this political tradition becomes starkly opposed to the moral solipsism of liberal individualism and places the emphasis on militant organisation for the emancipation of society (from both capitalist *and* bureaucratic domination), and for the elevation of the human condition. This dual concern for economic sovereignty and humanism, according to Julio Pinto,[45] would later mark the world-historical uniqueness of UP as a pioneering model of democratic socialism, one that was clearly distinct both from liberal democracy and from state socialism.

It was the vibrancy of this socio-political environment that attracted the intellectuals who, during the 1950s and 1960s, settled in Santiago, taking positions in its universities and research centres. Some of these scholars and intellectuals would eventually become key proponents of structuralism and dependency theory, and would also eventually provide key policy and theoretical insights for UP after the electoral victory of Salvador Allende in November of 1970.[46] Accordingly, Sergio Bitar – an intellectual who also served as a minister in the Allende government – frames the specificity of UP's development strategy as one whose central objective was the satisfaction of the essential needs of the population and the achievement of greater social equality.[47] This objective, according to Bitar, presupposed a systematic reconfiguration of the structure of production, the dynamics of consumption, and the framework of international economic relations. The realisation of this program, he argued, demanded 'the displacement of dominant groups – both domestic and foreign – from the strategic sectors of the national economy, and through the concerted efforts of mass worker participation and state intervention'.[48]

Pedro Vuskovic and Jacques Chonchol were two of the organic intellectuals who would eventually establish a direct nexus between development planning and some of the insights that emerged from the energetic intellectual atmosphere that gravitated around the research centres in the dependency tradition. Before being appointed as a minister of the Popular Unity government in 1970, Vuskovic had worked as an economist at the UN's Economic Commission for Latin America (CEPAL) and had also been a member of the Centre for Socioeconomic Studies at Universidad de Chile (CESO); Chonchol, in turn, had worked as an agronomist and international consultant for the Food and Agriculture Organisation (FAO), and had been the director of the Centre for the Study of National Reality at Universidad Católica (CEREN). Because Pedro Vuskovic was a militant of the Socialist Party and a practicing economist and lecturer on economic planning at CEPAL and Universidad de Chile, his writings reflect a deliberate determination to connect theories of development to some of the most pressing problems of Chilean reality. During the 1964-1971 period, Vuskovic authored several articles and working papers that reflected on the political and policy implications of Chile's dependent and subordinate insertion into the international division of labour.

An important feature of these writings is that they depart from the methodological nationalism that was common to mainstream variants of structuralism and dependency. Inspired by the work of Theotônio Dos Santos and Ruy Mauro Marini, Vuskovic sought to uncover both the external *and* internal mechanisms that rendered the Chilean economy unable to meet the basic needs of the population. According to Vuskovic,[49] Chile was underpinned by a pattern of economic development that was both 'exclusionary' and 'monopolistic'. These two features, according to Vuskovic, contributed to a highly uneven pattern of income distribution, as well as to a limited rate of scientific and technological dissemination. Because capital-intensive production had become concentrated in 'enclaves' oriented either towards primary-commodity exports or towards luxurious items of consumption, Vuskovic considered that the under-utilisation of resources was one of the most pressing problems faced by the Chilean economy. A situation of 'structural heterogeneity' in which wealthy and globally-integrated enclaves coexisted with an impoverished and underperforming traditional sector, according to Vuskovic,[50] led to high unemployment rates as well as to major deficits for basic consumer goods.

For Vuskovic,[51] it was the traditional or informal – in his words, 'vegetative' – sector which had lower capital and investment requirements, as well as a larger potential to absorb the idle workforce. Accordingly, he advocated for an industrial policy that was able to channel resources towards the traditional sector as the potential lever for a more robust import-substitution strategy. This, for Vuskovic, was justified on the basis that it would not only combat high unemployment rates, but would expand the macroeconomic savings ratio whilst also increasing the production of staples and basic consumer goods – an urgent task in its own right given the high rates of hunger and undernourishment in the population. This 'popular option for development', as economists Sergio Bitar and Eduardo Moyano termed it, sought to create an internal market that could reconcile an ethical commitment for redistributive justice with a technical concern for sound macroeconomic performance.[52] However, Vuskovic was adamant that the implementation of such an industrial policy did not rest on the mere allocation of government subsidies. This kind of sectoral design, according to Vuskovic, was unthinkable in the absence of a broader, more political project to combat the disruptive forces of oligarchic power, largely embodied in the landholding aristocracy, the banking system, and commercial monopolies, that were increasingly dependent on export-oriented and exclusionary enclave economies.[53]

Because of its eminently political nature, the industrial policy proposed by Vuskovic therefore departed from structuralist authors that favoured alliances with the national bourgeoisie as a means to achieve economic development. Instead, he sided with more avowedly Marxist readings of dependency – such as that of Marini, Frank, and Dos Santos – that deemed domestic oligarchies and capitalist classes incapable of advancing the national interest given their own relations of dependency with foreign capital. It was for this reason that Vuskovic considered the working class to be the historical subject of development, and mass political organisation (i.e.

poder popular) a precondition for the successful implementation of the development strategy of a popular government.[54] The broadening and consolidation of popular power, according to Vuskovic, would stimulate mass support for the structural reforms of the UP's development strategy.

Known as the *Plan Vuskovic*, this strategy encompassed four core targets: First, the creation of a Social Property Sector (*Área de Propiedad Social* or APS) of nationalised and public firms that were deemed strategic for economic development; second, the implementation of a robust program for income redistribution that could democratise access to consumer goods and social security for the vast majority of the population; third, the creation of a state-owned banking sector and foreign trade company that could boost small and medium-sized companies by giving them access to credit and to international markets; fourth, an agrarian reform that could redistribute land away from the inherently inefficient and authoritarian *hacienda* system.[55]

Jacques Chonchol (left), 1 May 1971. Photo by Armindo Cardoso. Archivo fotográfico Biblioteca Nacional de Chile.

Because hunger was one of the most urgent problems in the agenda, and the landholding aristocracy had come increasingly to be considered a major obstacle for efficient agricultural production, the agrarian reform was deemed one of the most emblematic elements in the political program of Popular Unity. Jacques Chonchol would eventually emerge as one of the leading experts behind UP's ambitious plan to overhaul the entire structure of agrarian relations in Chile. Trained as an agronomist, Chonchol acquired vast empirical knowledge of Latin American agrarian systems during his time as a consultant for the FAO and CEPAL. After leading missions to Mexico, Peru, Colombia, Bolivia, and revolutionary Cuba in the early 1960s, Chonchol learned about the various dimensions of the *hacienda* system in the region and also about the different visions and experiences of agrarian reform.[56] A 'revolutionary Christian', as Claudio Robles refers to him, Chonchol began his political career as a militant of the Christian Democratic Party (PDC) but eventually grew dissatisfied with the party's reformist stance. In 1967, Chonchol began to espouse a more distinctly socialist orientation when he and other PDC militants drafted a manifesto titled 'A Non-Capitalist Path to Development.' This document aroused a heated polemic with the party leadership that eventually led Chonchol to split from the PDC and to become the cofounder of *Izquierda Cristiana* [Christian Left], one of the organisations that entered the UP coalition after 1970.[57]

It was perhaps because of his intellectual affinity with liberation theology and other humanist currents within Christian thought – especially the communitarian tradition of Jacques Maritain and Louis Joseph Lebret – that Chonchol reflected systematically on the relationship between freedom and development. In his 1964 book titled *Desarrollo sin capitalismo* [Development without Capitalism], which he wrote with Julio Silva Solar, Chonchol suggests that the profit imperatives of capitalist accumulation not only thwart the flourishing of the poor, they also put the wealthy in a position of unfreedom that is inimical to the common good. Hinting at the ways in which the unregulated concentration of wealth hinders the possibility for real social and human development, the authors hint at a more expansive understanding of freedom than that of Amartya Sen – one primarily concerned with the (un)freedom of the poor. A communitarian or non-capitalist path to development, according to Chonchol and Silva Solar, would then not only be concerned with the liberation of the poor but also with the liberation of the rich from the abstract compulsions of capitalist reproduction. The only way to free the rich from their submission to the disciplinary force of market allocation, the authors considered, was to reconfigure the structure of property relations, a task that was impossible under capitalism.[58]

Chonchol's concrete interest in the practical problems of agro-food systems would also lead him to write a set of technical texts throughout the 1960s, in which he explored the complex relation between economic development and agrarian reform. In a 1967 article on the topic, he suggests that the process of land redistribution that would ensue from an agrarian reform was not to be reduced to a mere matter of social justice; it was ultimately one of economic development understood as self-government and national unity. If the land question remained unsolved, Chonchol argued, there would be no political democracy for the popular masses, and Chile would remain a disunited caste society.[59] Moreover, Chonchol questioned the idea that the pattern of industrialisation applied in Western Europe had to be replicated in Latin America. Departing from such a stagist and unilinear understanding of social change, he advocated for an indigenous approach to agricultural intensification that would enable complex combinations between modern technical inputs and also labour-intensive tasks that could create employment for the rural poor.[60] But he was also critical of the autarchic tendencies that were brewing within the narrow nationalism of some political traditions in Latin America. The development of a robust endogenous market for foodstuffs, he argued, would have to be imbricated within an internationalist framework of foreign trade that would increase the political leverage of dependent economies and act as a geopolitical bulwark against the protectionist tendencies of the Western core.

Inspired by liberation theology and by communitarianism, Chonchol also became invested in the design of intermediary bodies and of pluralistic property regimes that could offer an alternative to the utilitarian individualism of liberalism as well as to the rigid collectivism of state socialism. He developed a close personal and intellectual relationship with Paulo Freire during the years he spent in Santiago writing *The Pedagogy of the Oppressed* and working at Chile's National Institute for Agricultural Development (INDAP).[61] In this ground-breaking book, Freire was adamant that modernisation should not be conflated with development. For the author, there cannot be genuine development in a society that suffers from cultural invasion, and development is therefore only possible as a genuine outcome of a process of creativity, creation, and soul-searching that is generated internally by a self-governing polity. For this reason, Freire considered that popular education was a fundamental mechanism for engendering the capacities for self-government that real development entailed.[62] Inspired by these ideas, Chonchol introduced various initiatives for rural popular education and political organisation that included unionisation, the creation of cooperatives, and the publication of booklets that sought to elevate the political consciousness of the peasantry.[63]

In agronomic terms, his aspiration to reconcile the transition to socialism with a more expansive understanding of human individuality would also eventually translate into an attempt to foster productive forms that could counter the intrinsic contradictions and inefficiencies of mass industrial production (as embodied either in the large capitalist farm or in the Soviet *kolkhoz*), as well as those of petty commodity production. He was inspired by the early efforts of the Cuban revolution to chart a different path to that of Soviet collectivisation, one in which forms of individual land tenure would be designed to coexist with cooperatives and with larger productive units of socialised labour.[64] Although the Agrarian Reform Law was passed in 1967 under the Christian Democratic government of Eduardo Frei Montalva, Chonchol would later enlarge its initial design in order to create a novel, integrated amalgam of productive systems that reflected the country's agronomical and socio-cultural heterogeneity. A tier of individually-owned farms became synergistically combined with a network of farming cooperatives, as well as with larger productive units, termed Productive Centres (CEPROS) and Agrarian Reform Centres (CERAS). The former were devised to act as training facilities for medium-scale agricultural production, whilst the latter sought to rationalise the use of geographically remote and unpopulated lands – especially the Magallanes region – for grain and livestock production.[65]

Although the Vuskovic Plan and the Agrarian Reform became the two core pillars of Popular Unity's development strategy, neither Vuskovic nor Chonchol were able to foresee the reactionary forces that they would unleash.

Sabotage of development

In a 1977 postscript to *Development and Dependency in Latin America*, Cardoso and Faletto reflected on the emerging authoritarian regimes that had crept across the region, often as a response to popular and democratic efforts to ascertain economic sovereignty. Far from episodical, Cardoso and Faletto argued that this authoritarian turn was instead symptomatic of a broader 'Bonapartisation' of political power that had rendered the state apparatus more directly subservient to the interests of oligarchies and transnational corporations.[66] In this emerging new formation of Latin American dependent development, Cardoso and Faletto pointed out, authentic popular demands are considered suspicious, subversive, and are therefore met with repression. Insofar as the demands of racial minorities, of feminist groups, and student movements, among others, are increasingly seen as a challenge to the existing state of things, these authors warned that the public interest itself was becoming problematically conflated with the defence of the enterprise system. In a 1978 book titled *Socialismo o fascismo* [Socialism or Fascism],[67] Theotônio Dos Santos expanded on this insight by suggesting that the authoritarian turn that began with the 1964 coup in Brazil was not an instance of reactionary oligarchies resisting the process of bourgeois modernisation. Rather, Dos Santos argued that the combination of fascist ideology and political repression became the hallmark of a new pattern of global capitalist expansion where state violence became more directly harnessed as a lever of free-market reforms.[68]

The 1973 military coup in Chile did not mark, of course, the first moment of reaction to the project of endogenous development in the region; important historical precedents include the US-backed overthrow of the Jacobo Árbenz government in Guatemala in 1954 as well as the 1964 coup against the João Goulart government in Brazil. The case of Chile, however, acquired the status of a canonical example of the trend theorised by Dos Santos, given the relatively high levels of foreign industrial penetration and monopolistic integration that characterised the country by 1973.[69] Also, the stakes were exceptionally high considering that the political program of Allende's presidential campaign was framed in avowedly developmentalist and libertarian terms; the declared objective of the UP government would not only be to curb the oligarchic and imperialist forces that were leading to widespread social suffering, but to overhaul the productive and technological structure of the national economy.[70]

Once in office, UP demonstrated an impressive determination to pursue execution of the Agrarian Reform and the Vuskovic Plan, the core pillars of its development strategy. To begin with, the UP government (with Chonchol as its Minister of Agriculture) greatly accelerated the process of land redistribution that had begun during the previous government. The Frei administration expropriated 3.5 million hectares during the 1965-1970 period, whilst the Allende administration managed to expropriate 8.8 million hectares during the 1970-1972 period.[71] The emergence of the peasantry as a political actor was also clearly demonstrated by the number of people involved in peasant unions, which rose from 2,118 individuals in 1965 to 282,617 in 1972.[72]

Archivo de Láminas y Estampas Biblioteca Nacional de Chile.

In terms of the Vuskovic Plan, the UP government was also able to set up the Social Property Sector (APS), which enabled the nationalisation or requisitioning of 377 firms in strategic sectors such as mining, industry, forestry, construction, retail and fishing. Because the banking system was also an important element of the UP's development strategy, the government was able to exert control over 16 banks whose combined portfolio accounted for 90 percent of all credit allocations in the country.[73] During its first year, the economic results of the UP government were astonishing. GDP growth amounted to 9 percent, while industrial production grew by 13 percent. Unemployment also decreased, going from 8.3 in 1970 to just 3.8 percent in 1971, whilst real income increased by 20 percent – chiefly as a result of aggressive wage increase policies.[74] Although a detailed account of the economic intricacies of the UP project is well beyond the scope of this article, it is important to note that a set of unforeseen circumstances – both domestic and international – soon began to threaten macroeconomic stability and undermined the government's political footing. Food shortages caused by a major earthquake and extreme weather conditions were exacerbated by international volatility in copper prices; this, in turn, led to high trade imbalances and to an escalating fiscal deficit, which went from 15.3 to 30.5 percent during the 1971-1973 period.[75]

Although macroeconomic pressures posed important challenges, it was the variegated mechanisms of reaction which ultimately led to an escalation of political conflict that created the conditions for the overthrow of the government in 1973. Termed 'economic sabotage' by Allende and Vuskovic, the reactionary tactics deployed against the UP's strategy of development involved a diverse set of actors and mechanisms. To begin with, the government faced a parliamentary blockade that thwarted a progressive tax reform that would have provided some leeway for its fiscal spending programs.[76] At the international level, and following Richard Nixon's infamous mandate to make the Chilean economy 'scream', the US administration and its network of closely-aligned international banks and foreign aid institutions (such as the World Bank, the Inter-American Development Bank, and USAID) withdrew access to crucial credit instruments and aid programs. Private credit extended by US banks to Chile plummeted, going from USD 219 million to USD 32 million during the 1970-1972 period, whilst foreign lending from the Inter-American Development Bank went from USD 310 million in the 1960-1970 period, to a meagre USD 2 million during the 1970-1973 period.[77] The financial blockade was also met with a commercial blockade that rendered Chile unable to gain access to technical inputs and spare parts for industrial and agricultural production.

In an essay written from exile and titled 'Indictment of imperialism', Pedro Vuskovic would later argue that the economic boycott suffered by Chile was indicative of the concrete political and instrumental power that the core was able to exert over dependent economies.[78] Moreover, Vuskovic claimed that 'the tragic experience of the Chilean people' acted as an exemplary, world-historical reminder of the unbearably high social and human cost that projects for democratic self-determination would have to endure in the future.[79] The backlash suffered by the UP government, however, involved more than parliamentary *realpolitik* and foreign intervention. In fact, the case of Chile is also reminiscent of the fact that dependency relations are not to be simplistically reduced to those of the interstate system; rather, they quickly metastasise into the domestic class struggle in ways that are often complex and unpredictable. The turn of events in Chile strongly resonated with the idea that dependency relations often lead to the emergence of a 'lumpenbourgeoisie' whose material interests are aligned with those of foreign capital and therefore at odds with the general or national interest.[80] An aggressive media and propaganda campaign was set into motion by some of the major economic groups in the country in order to foster an environment of fear and uncertainty among the population. As Casals points out,[81] the media apparatus conveyed the idea that the UP's undeclared objective was to establish a totalitarian dictatorship that would destroy religion, the family, the nation and private property.

It was during late 1971 that the campaign against the UP – initially led by domestic oligarchic groups and the US – escalated into what Casals refers to as a formidable 'counter-revolutionary bloc' that included petty retailers, landowners, right-wing paramilitary groups, as well as wide sectors of the middle-class and the political centre.[82] It was the Bosses' Strike (alternatively known as *paro camionero* or truck drivers' strike) of October 1972 that further coordinated the various reactionary forces operating against the government, setting the country directly on the trail to the military coup that would come the following year. Due to rumours that the UP government was about to nationalise the private cargo sector, members of the national trucking federation decided to stop the transport of basic consumer goods and also to block some of the country's main roads for a period of nearly one month. Aside from paralysing a large portion of Chile's transport infrastructure, the Bosses' Strike also incited actions by petty retailers who closed their shops, thereby leading to food hoarding, economic panic, and thus widespread outrage against the government.[83]

It was against this background of escalating sociopolitical conflict that both Pedro Vuskovic and Jacques Chonchol were pressed to resign, the former in June of 1972 and the latter in December of that same year; at the same time the dream of a 'popular option' for development began to fade away.

Conclusions

This article has intended to establish a dialogue between two emerging agendas of scholarly research that have so far developed in isolation from each other, but whose assumptions are complementary. One of them is concerned with the effort to reclaim the forgotten legacy of Latin American theories of development, especially against the historical erasure that either oversimplifies their key tenets or that severs the theory from the dreams, aspirations, and mass emancipatory struggles that inspired it. The other has to do with accounts that have rediscovered the eminently republican understanding of freedom that informed the design and implementation of novel anti-oligarchic, anti-racist, and anti-imperialist institutions in crucial periods of Latin American history. It is an understanding of freedom as non-domination from an arbitrary will or from capitalist impersonal power, the article has argued, which lies at the heart of the normative and epistemological sensibility that informs Latin American theories of development and dependency. On this basis, the article has also intended to reclaim the concept of development from liberal and poststructuralist interpretations that reduce it either to the governance of poverty, or to a neocolonial discourse of power, respectively. The experience of Popular Unity in Chile helps to demonstrate a wider point, that Latin American societies were not passive recipients of the Western development project, but often advanced original and revolutionary understandings of what genuine human and social progress should be about.

It was by harnessing a politics of immanent critique that intellectuals from the Latin American School, rather than refrain from using the concept of development, mobilised it to reclaim a seat at the table and to challenge the Western economic orthodoxy in its own terms.[84] As Macarena Marey has recently argued, neoliberal dispossession has by now advanced to such an extent that it has even severed us from our emancipatory vocabulary.[85]

Serigraphy by Agrupación de Plásticos Jóvenes (APJ) for the anti-dictatorship campaign of the 1980 plebiscite. Reproduced from Nicole Cristi and Javiera Manzi, Resistencia gráfica. Dictadura en Chile (Santiago: LOM Ediciones, 2016).

Marey, a major proponent of Latin American plebeian republicanism, insists that we can no longer afford to surrender words to those who are not willing to consider us as equals. As the case of UP shows, the idea of development has embodied longstanding popular aspirations for wellbeing, progress and economic sovereignty, and therefore for *political* freedom. These ideals, it should be noted, continue to be relevant for the labouring classes, and it is for this reason that social theory should take them seriously. Accordingly, it would not only be elitist but also politically dangerous to abandon these social values to the apparatus of multilateral neoliberal governance and to the political right, as the post-development tradition urges us to do. The task at hand, then, is to lay bare their distorted and ideological forms, and to reinterpret them in emancipatory and radically-democratic ways. Debemos disputarle el 2023 marks the fiftieth anniversary of the military coup that was orchestrated against Popular Unity, and it is a year in which the threat of authoritarianism is once again looming over the region. Commemoration of Popular Unity, then, should help us to reclaim some of the explanatory power, the emancipatory content, and the strategic vision of the theories of development that emerged during this convoluted historical period.

Martín Arboleda is Assistant Professor of Sociology at Universidad Diego Portales, Santiago de Chile. He is the author of Planetary Mine: Territories of Extraction under Late Capitalism *(Verso, 2020), as well as* Gobernar la utopía: sobre la planificación y el poder popular *(Caja Negra Editora, 2021).*

Notes

1. Wolfgang Sachs, ed., *The Development Dictionary: A Guide to Knowledge as Power* (London: Zed Books, 2010 [1992]); Arturo Escobar, *Encountering Development: The Making and Unmaking of the Third World* (Princeton: Princeton University Press, 1995).
2. Maristella Svampa, *Debates latinoamericanos: indianismo, desarrollo, dependencia y populismo* (Buenos Aires: Edhasa, 2016); Aram Ziai, 'Post-development', *The Routledge Handbook of Latin American Development*, ed. Julie Cupples et al. (London and New York: Routledge, 2019).
3. Fernando Leiva, 'Toward a Critique of Latin American Neostructuralism', *Latin American Politics and Society* 50:4 (2018), 1–25.
4. Claudio Katz, *La teoría de la dependencia, cincuenta años después* (Buenos Aires: Batalla de Ideas, 2018); Cristóbal Kay, 'Theotônio Dos Santos (1936–2018): The Revolutionary Intellectual Who Pioneered Dependency Theory', *Development and Change* 51:2 (2019), 599–630; Christy Thornton, *Revolution in Development: Mexico and the Governance of the Global Economy* (Oakland: University of California Press, 2020); Aldo Madariaga and Stefano Palestini, eds., *Dependent Capitalisms in Contemporary Latin America and Europe* (Cham: Palgrave MacMillan, 2021); Ronald Chilcote and Joanna Salém Vasconcelos, 'Whither Development Theory?', *Latin American Perspectives* 49:1 (2022), 4–17; Margarita Fajardo, *The World that Latin America Created: The United Nations Economic Commission for Latin America in the Development Era* (Cambridge: Harvard University Press, 2022). For radical development theories beyond Latin America, see Ingrid Harvold Kvangraven, 'Beyond the Stereotype: Restating the Relevance of the Dependency Research Program', *Development and Change* 52:1 (2020), 76–112; Max Ajl, 'Auto-centered Development and Indigenous Technics: Slaheddine el-Amami and Tunisian Delinking', *Journal of Peasant Studies* 46:6 (2019), 1240–1263.
5. Alex Gourevitch and Corey Robin, 'Freedom Now', *Polity* 52:3 (2020), 384–398; William Clare Roberts, 'Marx's Social Republic: Political Not Metaphysical', *Historical Materialism* 27:2 (2019), 41–58; Camila Vergara, *Systemic Corruption: Constitutional Ideas for an Anti-Oligarchic Republic* (Princeton: Princeton University Press, 2020); María Julia Bertomeu, 'Reflexiones republicanas sobre la libertad y la dominación: conceptos y actores', in *Teorías de la república y prácticas republicanas*, ed. Macarena Marey (Barcelona: Herder, 2021); Bruno Leipold, 'Chains and Invisible Threads: Liberty and Domination in Marx's Account of Wage-Slavery', in *Rethinking Liberty Before Liberalism*, ed. Hannah Dawson and Annelien De Dijn (Cambridge: Cambridge University Press, 2022); James Muldoon, 'A Socialist Republican Theory of Freedom and Government', *European Journal of Political Theory* 21:1 (2022), 47–67.
6. Nick Nesbitt, *Universal Emancipation: The Haitian Revolution and the Radical Enlightenment* (Charlottesville: University of Virginia Press, 2008); James Sanders, *The Vanguard of the Atlantic World: Creating Modernity, Nation and Democracy in Nineteenth Century Latin America* (Durham NC: Duke University Press, 2014); Hilda Sábato, *Republics of the New World: The Revolutionary Political Experiment in Nineteenth-Century Latin America* (Princeton: Princeton University Press, 2021); Luciana Cadahia and Valeria Coronel, 'Volver al archivo: de las fantasías decoloniales a la imaginación republicana', in *Teorías de la república y prácticas republicanas*, ed. Macarena Marey; José Antonio Figueroa, *Republicanos negros: guerras por la igualdad, racismo y relativismo cultural* (Quito: Crítica, 2022).
7. José Miguel Ahumada, 'Bringing Freedom Back to Developmentalism: Industrialisation as National Independence', *Cambridge Journal of Economics*, published online

ahead of print, 26 July 2023.

8. Vânia Bambirra, '*Memorial*', Fundação Universidade de Brasília, 1991; Kay, 'Theotonio Dos Santos'; Fajardo, *The World that Latin America Created*.

9. Sergio Bitar, 'Elementos para una nueva estrategia de desarrollo para Chile', *Nueva Sociedad* 23 (1976), 36–46; Joshua Frens-String, 'A Popular Option for Development? Reconsidering the Rise and Fall of Chile's Political Economy of Socialism', *Radical Americas* 6:1 (2021).

10. Thornton 2023, 'Developmentalism as Internationalism: Toward a Global Historical Sociology of the Development Project', *Sociology of Development* 9:1 (2023), 33–55.

11. See for example Thornton, *Revolution in Development*; Fajardo, *The World that Latin America Created*; Felipe Antunes de Oliveira and Ingrid H. Kvangraven, 'Back to Dakar: Decolonising International Political Economy through Dependency Theory', *Review of International Political Economy*, published online 13 March 2023.

12. Cadahia and Coronel, 'Volver al archivo'; see also Sanders, *The Vanguard of the Atlantic World*.

13. The concept of the Latin American School of Development has been proposed by Cristóbal Kay as a means to reflect on the broad epistemological framework that results from an integrated understanding of structuralist and dependency traditions. See Cristóbal Kay, *Latin American Theories of Development and Underdevelopment* [1989] (London and New York: Routledge, 2013), 2.

14. For Prebisch's contributions to theories of the world-system, see Andrés Rivarola, 'Thinking Big from the Periphery: Raúl Prebisch and the World System', in *The Global Political Economy of Raúl Prebisch*, ed. Matias Margulis (London: Routledge, 2017).

15. For the relationship between the Mexican Revolution and development theory, see Thornton, *Revolution in Development*. For anti-oligarchic and anti-imperialist efforts of nation-building, see Guanche, *La libertad como destino*.

16. See Ernesto Che Guevara, *La planificación socialista y su significado* (Santiago: Quimantú, 1972); see also Michael Löwy, *The Marxism of Che Guevara: Philosophy, Economics, Revolutionary Warfare* (Plymouth: Rowman & Littlefield, 1973).

17. Ernesto Che Guevara, '*On Development*', 1964 address to the General Assembly of the United Nations, https://www.marxists.org/archive/guevara/1964/03/25.htm.

18. For the relation between the Cuban Revolution and Latin American theories of dependency, see Ivette Lozoya, *Intelectuales y revolución: Científicos sociales latinoamericanos en el MIR chileno (1963–1973)* (Santiago: Ariadna Ediciones, 2020), Diego Giller, *Espectros dependentistas: Variaciones sobre 'la teoría de la dependencia' y los marxismos latinoamericanos* (Buenos Aires: Universidad Nacional General Sarmiento, 2021).

19. Kvangraven, 'Beyond the Stereotype'; Madariaga and Palestini, *Dependent Capitalisms in Latin America and Europe*.

20. Kay, *Latin American Theories of Development and Underdevelopment*.

21. Ruy Mauro Marini, *The Dialectics of Dependency* [1973] trans. Amanda Latimer (New York: Monthly Review Pres, 2023). For an overview of the internal nuances between structuralist economics and Marxist dependency theory, see Mariano Féliz, 'Notes for a Discussion of Unequal Exchange and the Marxist Theory of Dependency', *Historical Materialism* 29:4 (2021), 114–152.

22. Leiva, 'Toward a Critique of Latin American Neostructuralism'.

23. Svampa, *Debates latinoamericanos*; Kvangraven, 'Beyond the Stereotype'.

24. Fernando Henrique Cardoso and Enzo Faletto, *Dependencia y desarrollo en América Latina: un ensayo de caracterización sociológica* [1969] (México: Siglo XXI, 2003).

25. Vânia Bambirra, *El capitalismo dependiente latinoamericano* [1974] (Mexico DF: Siglo XXI, 2011), 113–114.

26. Madariaga and Palestini. *Dependent Capitalisms in Latin America and Europe*. For the relationship between theories of freedom and socialist economic planning in Latin America, see Martín Arboleda and Francisca Benítez, 'Education for National Liberation: Theories of Freedom and Dependency in the Practical Pedagogy of Marta Harnecker and Gabriela Uribe', *Historical Materialism*, in press.

27. See Philip Pettit, *Republicanism: A Theory of Freedom and Government* (Oxford: Oxford University Press, 1999); Skinner, *Liberty Before Liberalism* [1998] (Cambridge: Cambridge University Press, 2012); Skinner, 'A Third Concept of Liberty', *Procedures of the British Academy* 117 (2017), 237–268.

28. For an overview of this point, see Annelien De Dijn, *Freedom: An Unruly History* (Cambridge: Harvard University Press, 2021); see also Philip Pettit, 'A Republican Law of Peoples', *European Journal of Political Theory* 9:1 (2010), 70–94; Cécile Laborde and Myriam Ronzoni, 'What is a Free State? Internationalism and Globalisation', *Political Studies* 64:2 (2016), 279–296.

29. See Antoni Domènech, *El eclipse de la fraternidad: una revisión republicana de la tradición socialista* (Madrid: Akal, 2019); Roberts, *Marx's Inferno: The Political Theory of Capital* (Princeton: Princeton University Press, 2017).

30. Roberts, 'Marx's Social Republic'; Bruno Leipold, 'Chains and Invisible Threads'.

31. For a programmatic statement on the revival of this tradition in Latin America, see Macarena Marey, ed., *Teorías de la república y prácticas republicanas*.

32. León Rozitchner, *Filosofía y emancipación. Simón Rodríguez: el triunfo de un fracaso ejemplar* [1980] (Buenos Aires: Ediciones Biblioteca Nacional, 2012); Guanche, *La libertad como destino*; Sanders, *The Vanguard of the Atlantic World*; José Antonio Figueroa, *Republicanos negros*; Cadahia and Coronel, 'Volver al archivo'; Sábato, *Republics of the New World*.
33. Vânia Bambirra, *Teoría de la dependencia: una anticrítica* (México DF: Era Ediciones, 1978), 19.
34. Ahumada, 'Bringing Freedom Back to Developmentalism'.
35. Kay, 'Latin American Theories of Development and Underdevelopment', 18.
36. Ahumada, 'Bringing Freedom Back to Developmentalism'.
37. Amartya Sen, *Development as Freedom* (New York: Alfred Knopf, 2000).
38. Wolfgang Sachs, 'El Diccionario del desarrollo reconsiderado', in *Pluriverso: un diccionario del posdesarrollo*, ed. Ashish Kothari et al. (Barcelona: Icaria, 2019).
39. Ha-Joon Chang, '*Hamlet* without the Prince of Denmark: How Development has Disappeared from Today's Development Discourse', in *Towards New Developmentalism: Market as Means Rather than Master*, ed. Sharukh Khan and Jens Christiansen (London: Routledge, 2010).
40. Fajardo, *The World that Latin America Created*, 121.
41. Löwy, *The Marxism of Che Guevara*, 42.
42. Jorge Arrate and Carlos Ruiz, eds., *Génesis y ascenso del socialismo chileno: una antología hasta 1973* (Santiago: LOM Ediciones, 2020).
43. Ibid., 42.
44. Arrate and Ruiz, *Génesis y ascenso del socialismo chileno*; Sergio Grez, *Los anarquistas y el movimiento obrero: la alborada de 'la idea' en Chile, 1893–1915* (Santiago, LOM Ediciones, 2012).
45. Julio Pinto, 'Hacer la revolución en Chile', in *Cuando hicimos historia: la experiencia de la Unidad Popular*, ed. Julio Pinto (Santiago: LOM Ediciones, 2005).
46. Juan Cristóbal Cárdenas, 'Una historia sepultada: el Centro de Estudios Socioeconómicos de la Universidad de Chile, 1965–1973 (a 50 años de su fundación)', *De Raíz Diversa* 2:3 (2015), 121–140; Francisca Benítez, '"Una misma unidad histórica": Vânia Bambirra y el capitalismo dependiente de América Latina', *Cuadernos de Teoría Social* 5:9 (2019), 22–36; Fajardo, *The World that Latin America Created*.
47. Sergio Bitar, 'Elementos para una nueva estrategia de desarrollo para Chile', *Nueva Sociedad* 23 (1976), 36–46.
48. Ibid., 36; see also Frens-String, 'A Popular Option for Development'.
49. Pedro Vuskovic, 'Distribución del ingreso y opciones de desarrollo', in *Pedro Vuskovic Bravo: obras escogidas sobre Chile*, ed. Raúl Maldonado [1970] (Santiago: CEPLA, 1993).
50. Vuskovic, 'Distribución del ingreso y opciones de desarrollo'.
51. Vuskovic, 'Distribución del ingreso y opciones de desarrollo', 194.
52. Frens-String, 'A Popular Option for Development'.
53. Reinaldo Ruiz, 'Los fundamentos económicos del programa de gobierno de la Unidad Popular a 35 años de su declaración', *Universum* 1:20 (2005), 152–167; see also Pedro Vuskovic, 'Política económica y poder político', in *Pedro Vuskovic Bravo*, ed. Maldonado.
54. Franck Gaudichaud, *Chile 1970–1973. Mil días que estremecieron al mundo: Poder popular, cordones industriales y socialismo durante el gobierno de Salvador Allende* (Santiago: LOM Ediciones, 2016); Fajardo, *The World that Latin America Created*.
55. Vuskovic, 'Distribución del ingreso y opciones de desarrollo'; Vuskovic, 'La política de transformación y el corto plazo', in *Pedro Vuskovic Bravo*, ed. Maldonado; Vuskovic, 'Política económica y poder político'.
56. Claudio Robles, *Jacques Chonchol: un cristiano revolucionario en la política chilena del siglo XX* (Santiago: Ediciones Universidad Finis Terrae, 2016).
57. María Angélica Illanes and Flor Recabal, 'Liberación y democracia en la tierra: historia y memoria de la reforma agraria–Unidad Popular, Chile, 1971–1973', in *Fiesta y drama: nuevas historias de la Unidad Popular*, ed. Julio Pinto (Santiago: LOM Ediciones, 2014); Claudio Robles, *Jacques Chonchol*.
58. Jacques Chonchol and Julio Silva Solar, *Desarrollo sin capitalismo: hacia un mundo comunitario* (Caracas: Nuevo Orden, 1964).
59. Jacques Chonchol, 'El desarrollo de América Latina y la reforma agraria', *Revista Mexicana de Sociología* 29:2 (1967), 259.
60. Chonchol, 'El desarrollo de América Latina y la reforma agraria'.
61. Claudio Robles, 'Jacques Chonchol', 206.
62. Paulo Freire, *The Pedagogy of the Oppressed* (New York and London: Continuum, 2000 [1970]).
63. Jacques Chonchol, 'El campesinado y la política agraria de la Unidad Popular (1970–1973)', in *La vía chilena al socialismo 50 años después: Tomo I*, ed. Robert Austin Henry et al. (Buenos Aires: CLACSO, 2020); Eugenia Palieraki, 'Revolución rural y protagonismo campesino (Chile, 1967–1973)', in *La vía chilena al socialismo*, ed. Henry et al.
64. Jacques Chonchol, 'Análisis crítico de la reforma agraria cubana', *El Trimestre Económico* 30:117 (1963), 69–143; see also Cristóbal Kay, 'Agrarian Reform and the Class Struggle in Chile', *Latin American Perspectives* 5:3

(1978), 117–142.

65. Bellisario, 'The Chilean Agrarian Transformation'; Chonchol, 'Ley de Reforma Agraria y de Sindicalización Campesina: Balance a 50 Años', in *Reforma Agraria Chilena 50 Años: Historia y Reflexiones* (Santiago: Biblioteca del Congreso Nacional de Chile, 2017); Arboleda, 'Recetas para la agricultura del futuro: entrevista con Jacques Chonchol', *Jacobin América Latina* 5 (2022), 66–72.

66. Fernando Henrique Cardoso and Enzo Faletto, 'Post-scriptum a 'Dependencia y desarrollo en América Latina'', *Desarrollo Económico* 17:66 (1977), 273–299.

67. Theotônio Dos Santos, *Socialismo o fascismo: el nuevo carácter de la dependencia y el dilema latinoamericano* (Mexico DF: Edicol, 1978).

68. Ibid.

69. Ibid.

70. Mario Garcés, *La Unidad Popular y la revolución en Chile* (Santiago: LOM Ediciones, 2021).

71. Illanes and Recabal, 'Liberación y democracia en la tierra', 32; Bellisario, 'Chilean Agrarian Transformation'.

72. Kay, 'Agrarian Reform and the Class Struggle in Chile', 125.

73. Patricio Meller, *Un siglo de economía política chilena (1890–1990)* (Santiago: Editorial Andrés Bello, 1999), 147–149; Gaudichaud, *Chile 1970–1973. Mil días que estremecieron al mundo*, chapter 4.

74. Garcés, *La Unidad Popular y la revolución en Chile*, 173.

75. Meller, *Un siglo de economía política chilena (1890–1990)*, 124; Frens-String, 'A popular option for development?'

76. Meller, *Un siglo de economía política chilena (1890–1990)*, 131.

77. Joshua Frens-String, *Hungry for Revolution: The Politics of Food and the Making of Modern Chile* (Oakland: University of California Press, 2021), 183.

78. Pedro Vuskovic, 'Acusación al imperialismo', In *Génesis y ascenso del socialismo chileno* [1976], ed. Jorge Arrate and Carlos Ruiz (Santiago: LOM Ediciones, 2021).

79. Ibid.

80. André Gunder Frank, *Lumpenburguesía: lumpendesarrollo, dependencia, clase y política en Latinoamérica* (Buenos Aires: Periferia, 1973); Kay, 'Theotonio Dos Santos (1936–2018)'.

81. Marcelo Casals, 'La contrarrevolución chilena: raíces, dinámicas y legados de la movilización de masas contra la unidad popular', *Radical Americas* 6:1 (2021).

82. Casals, 'La contrarrevolución chilena'.

83. Casals, 'La contrarrevolución chilena'; Frens-String, *Hungry for Revolution*.

84. See Thornton, 'Revolution in Development'.

85. Macarena Marey, 'Debemos disputarle el republicanismo a la derecha', *Jacobin América Latina*, https://jacobinlat.com/2023/05/17/debemos-disputarle-el-republicanismo-a-la-derecha/. See also Macarena Marey, 'Contra el posibilismo, o por qué disputarle el republicanismo a la derecha', *Políticas de la Memoria*, forthcoming.

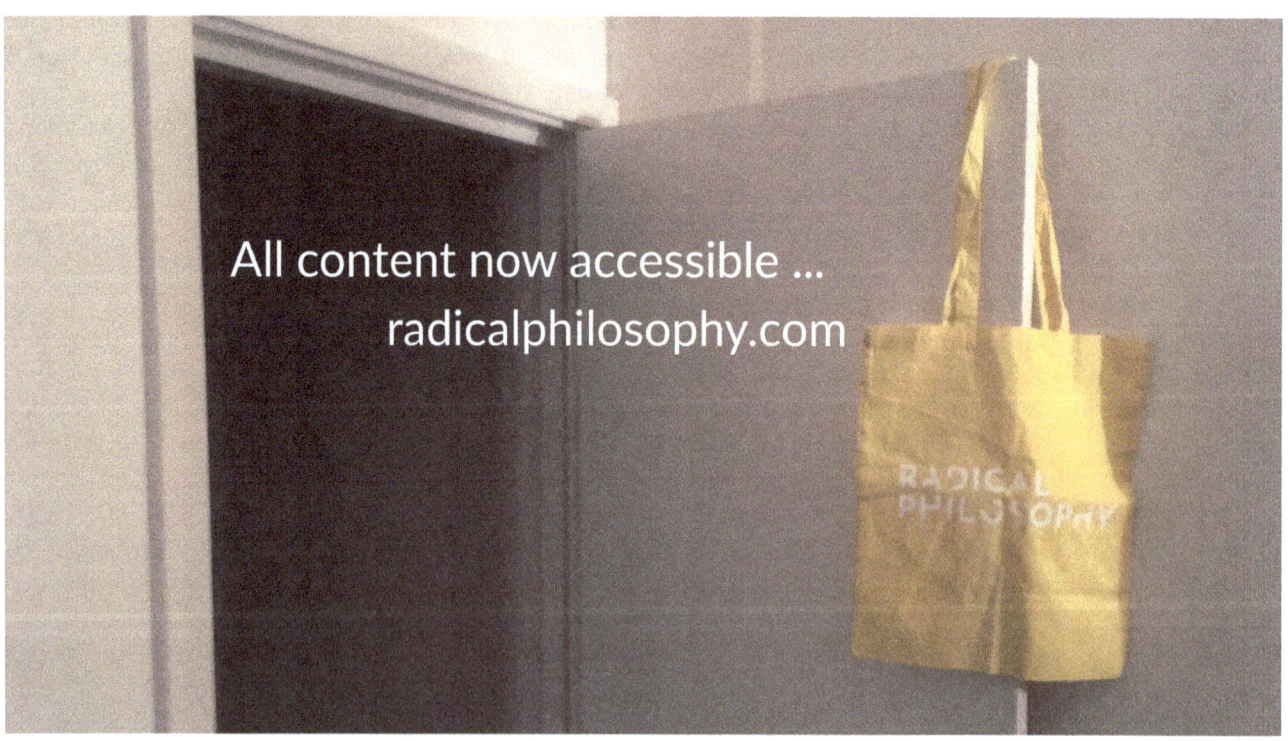

A contest over titles

The canonisation of the Frankfurt School as 'permanent exiles'

Ryan Crawford

Prevailing images of the Frankfurt School have long relied upon an idea of their origins that is far from self-evident. Premised upon the curious allure associated with such notions as 'transcendental homelessness' and 'extraterritoriality', and enhanced more recently by a vogue for all things 'exilic', this canonised image of critical theory has identified members' life and work with an especially melancholic form of messianic philosophy, and their origins with a quintessentially Jewish story of estrangement. In this way, the Frankfurt School's status as exemplary German-Jewish exiles has become a byword for conditions of displacement and isolation celebrated, strangely, as a position of privilege for the critical intellectual as such. Like all such stories, however, the power of this particular tale rests upon its simplicity, an effacement of history pleasing more to its interpreters than to its subjects. It is perhaps no coincidence, then, that the Frankfurt School's canonisation should begin with a contest over titles and identities in which its earliest representatives criticised the very practice of assigning retroactive origins to former members of the Institute for Social Research in a way that has since become hegemonic. To understand how this image of the Frankfurt School was first created, and how it continues to obscure what is most radical about the social and political import of critical theory's past, means returning to the circumstances of the Frankfurt School's inaugural history.

The first comprehensive account of what has come to be called the 'first-generation' of critical theory, *The Dialectical Imagination: A History of the Frankfurt School and the Institute of Social Research, 1923-1950*, began its life in 1967 when a twenty-three-year-old doctoral candidate made the felicitous decision to focus upon a little-researched area of study at an especially auspicious time and place. For Martin Jay, the budding American historian who would soon become the foremost Anglophone authority on the Frankfurt School, it was indeed a 'stroke of good fortune.'[1] His advisor, H. Stuart Hughes, was close personal friends with several former Institute members and associates, and thus able to provide his student with letters of introduction to figures instrumental to the latter's research. Equally significant was the sense of excitement with which the American New Left greeted any sign of the Frankfurt School's potential relevance for their own intellectual and political pursuits.[2] And yet, despite this fascination, there were as yet very few published translations of Institute members' work, and a paucity of research into their origins. To address this situation, Jay set out in the summer of 1968 for Berkeley, California, to meet and examine the voluminous correspondence of Leo Löwenthal, a former Institute member then working at the local state university. That material, as Jay would later recall, came to constitute the 'richest primary source' for his book, and provided the occasion for a lifelong friendship between the two.[3] Not long afterwards, during the winter and early spring of 1969, Jay continued his research by travelling first to West Germany, and then on to Switzerland, for interviews with such early luminaries as one-time Institute directors Friedrich Pollock and Max Horkheimer, then-director Theodor W. Adorno, as well as 'second-generation' figures like Jürgen Habermas, Alfred Schmidt and Albrecht Wellmer. Over the course of his research, Jay would benefit from further interviews with Herbert Marcuse, Erich

Fromm and other former members of the Institute, as well as correspondence, conversations and manuscript notes from a wide range of figures, among whom Jay would later mention Felix J. Weil in particular, the Institute's longtime benefactor and a central force behind its origin and development, with whom Jay 'carried on an extensive and spirited correspondence', even though their 'interpretation of certain issues remain[ed] somewhat at odds.'[4] Composed at a time when many of its central figures were still alive and able to tell their stories, that inaugural history's unique incorporation of first-hand testimony and inclusion of extensive archival research combined to create the standard reference work that *The Dialectical Imagination* remains to this day. This did not mean, however, that Jay's relations with former Institute members were without their share of controversy, or that the resulting work did not elicit criticisms at the time. In the decades since the book's 1973 publication, Jay has answered his critics with characteristic aplomb at the same time as he has facilitated the work of several generations of scholars, writing often and admirably about those forms of identification which first drew him to his subjects, friendships with former Institute members that may have affected his judgment, as well as those conflicts that only reached him, as it were, 'from beyond the grave.'[5]

One such controversy emerged in the years immediately prior to the publication of that first book-length, pathbreaking study, pitting its author against critical theory's earliest representatives in a contest over titles. For while *The Dialectical Imagination* has long since proven so apt a title as to have inspired imitators of its own, that title was not the first choice of its author. Revising for publication the dissertation upon which his book would be based, Jay was then searching for a catchier title than the more strictly academic one he had used before, and initially considered calling his book 'Permanent Exiles'–a phrase he already used some years before in 'The Permanent Exile of Theodor W. Adorno', an essay written upon Adorno's 1969 death and published in the American Zionist magazine, *Midstream*, to which Jay frequently contributed during those early years.[6] In the winter of 1972, however, Jay was still in contact with several surviving Institute members and quickly learned of their absolute abhorrence of his proposed title. 'Fundamentally wrong and damaging' is how Weil described it; 'an outrage' is how Horkheimer was said to have regarded it.[7] 'I just talked to Horkheimer', Weil informed the young historian, 'and discovered that he dislikes your book title "Permanent Exiles" even more than I do, because it is so utterly misleading.'[8] And, indeed, Horkheimer's own letters to Jay had already made clear just how 'problematic' and 'misleading' the former viewed such a characterisation of their work.[9] For even the most generous accounting of the historical record can hardly support the idea that their exile was in any way permanent, as Horkheimer and Weil were at pains to point out. That Jay was aware of that claim's historical inaccuracy can hardly be doubted. For him, however, its appropriateness did not rest solely on its conformity with the facts, but on how it functioned as a metaphor for describing his own view of Frankfurt School members' life, work and identity. Fifty years ago – and still today – that appellation does indeed exude the aura of some unplaceable allure. What to our ears sounds like a compliment, however, is precisely what seemed to Weil, not only inaccurate, but an insult and an outrage. Indeed, so clearly did that intended honorific appear to Weil a smear that, upon hearing it, he made a thinly veiled threat to persuade Jay against it: suggesting that if Jay still used the title, in defiance of Horkheimer and Weil's protests, then the book's opening pages might no longer include the promised foreword from Horkheimer that Weil had himself helped to secure. In its absence, that first history of the Institute would no longer appear as though it had been endorsed by the Institute's longtime director in a way which might lead readers to believe that Jay's book was an authorised, court history.[10] Understandably, the proposed title was then dropped, the published book included Horkheimer's foreword, and continues to bear its now-inimitable title. But even though Jay abandoned that title some fifty years ago, that does not mean he thought it inappropriate. Less than a decade and a half later, in fact, he used that very title again, explaining how the phrase 'permanent exiles' seemed to him an 'accurate and evocative term to describe the Frankfurt School as a whole.'[11] And on this point several former Institute members appear to have agreed. Löwenthal and Marcuse, for instance, were said to have thought the title 'rang true' and encouraged Jay to use it.[12] So what, then, did Weil and Horkheimer find so objectionable in that title and proposed description of their lives and work?

Note first the distance separating what has come to be called critical theory from what Institute members understood by that term in the fact that our own ears no longer bristle at the sound of a phrase – *permanent exiles*–which once sent two of its earliest representatives into such vehement and united opposition. At the time of the Jay-Weil correspondence, Institute members' understanding of their own lives clearly belonged to a historical sensorium which has since been almost entirely lost. For the contemporary reader, however, that difference is still discernible wherever Weil's 1971-1972 correspondence turns its attention to that contest over titles and identities from which *The Dialectical Imagination* eventually emerged. Indeed, it is at precisely those points where Weil contradicts critical theory's received image, insisting that Jay reconsider and remove reference to an aspect of that image against which he constantly protested – but which is today seen as so self-evident as to seem beyond dispute – that the so-called foundations of critical theory become considerably less stable than Jay supposed or as we might ourselves still think today. For what the correspondence between Weil and Jay demonstrates is that Institute members' opposition to that title was but a single point around which a far larger concern came to concentrate itself – namely, Weil's sense that Jay sought to place the Frankfurt School within a distinctly Jewish tradition that Weil questioned and criticised in almost every single letter. Indeed, it is only within the larger context of Weil's critique of what he called Jay's 'treatment of the "Jewish" question' that Institute members' opposition to still-popular designations of the Frankfurt School as 'permanent exiles' becomes at all comprehensible.[13]

Minefields from the history of ideas

From late January 1971 to early April 1972, and over the course of nearly three dozen letters, Weil was at all times concerned about how the Institute would be characterised and, upon reading Jay's manuscript and discussing the content with its author, made clear that he neither understood nor agreed with the paramount importance *The Dialectical Imagination* accorded the Frankfurt School's supposed Jewishness. Though 'fascinated by the amount of research' which went into the manuscript, and complimentary of Jay's 'excellent understanding of that turbulent period', Weil continually opposed the terms, arguments and evidence upon which the author relied when attributing Jewish identity and influence to Institute members' life and work.[14] And while Jay would neither then nor afterwards accept his correspondent's account of the Institute's origins, development and influences, he could have hardly found a better, more knowledgeable source about such matters than Felix Weil. For Weil was not only the founder and chief benefactor of the Institute; he was also the single most important force behind the idea and implementation of that form of social research for which the Frankfurt School later attained such renown: a distinctly Marxist form of intellectual production both pluralistic and undogmatic, as well as a unique framework for collective, multidisciplinary work whose socialist inspiration created an independent structure unprecedented for the time.[15]

To realise such a project, Weil drew upon his experience with various then-contemporary social, political and intellectual currents – including his engagement with socialist and communist movements – and then, with the aid of his father's wealth and his own, went on to establish the conditions for the Institute's success. The result was an institution through which Weil and the organisational bodies he created and coordinated exercised considerable autonomy in selecting the directors of the Institute with whom Weil then collaborated, overseeing the personnel, production and overall direction of the Institute. Given Weil's outsized role in the Institute's origin and development, it is no surprise that he should have considered the Institute his 'life's work', and found himself particularly concerned by Jay's decision to refract the Frankfurt School's social and institutional history through the prism of Jewish identity and influence, rather than the far more diverse, and indeed decidedly more political, range of factors uniting the Institute's life and work.[16] Later empowered by Horkheimer to review, assess and approve Jay's manuscript before its author was granted permission to use Horkheimer's foreword or the materials culled from their respective interviews and correspondence,[17] Weil would consistently take up and criticise Jay's treatment of the '"Jewish" question' in his role as the last living and still-healthy representative of that group of 'three survivors [from] the 1920-1930 period of the Institute', as Weil referred to Pollock, Horkheimer and himself;[18] the original 'triumvirate', as Horkheimer called them.[19] For this reason, and at the time dismayed by the 'necrology' which followed Pollock's recent death, as well as the continuing confusion 'about who did what when', Weil resolved, as he said, to 'do my part in setting the record straight', using various archival materials at his disposal, dedicating his early morning hours to reading Jay's manuscript when he should have been asleep, and planning to allocate time on weekends and holidays to helping as best he could.[20]

'Re[garding] your M[anuscript]', Weil writes Jay on 16 May 1971, 'there is one respect in which I dislike it and would like you to change it.'[21] For what Weil had discovered in the very first chapter of Jay's manuscript was that he was described there, to his surprise and increasing exasperation, as the son of a 'German-born Jewish merchant', while Friedrich Pollock was called the son of a 'Jewish businessman', Horkheimer the son of a 'prominent Jewish manufacturer', and Henryk Grossman was said to come from a 'family of Jewish mine-owners.'[22] And because Weil could not understand the rationale behind such designations, he implored Jay to explain: 'why do you feel the need of stressing wherever you introduce a new character, that he is or was Jewish?'[23] For Weil, Jay's repeated identification of Institute members according to their supposed Jewishness was especially peculiar because, when it came to other Institute members, that same tendency was not applied consistently. Instead, whenever Institute members' 'religion (or race?)' might be characterised as either Christian or Aryan, those markers of identity went unmentioned.[24] 'Now the question is', Weil remarks, 'whether you understand "Jewish" as a religion or as a race or nationality.'[25] And concludes: 'I can't imagine you, like Hitler, consider it a race.'[26] For while Löwenthal and Fromm undoubtedly came from 'Jewish orthodox families', according to Weil, 'all the others were of Jewish-liberal or even baptized Christian origin … and not one ever was a service-attending Jew', while still others were unmistakably 'Christian by origin'.[27] Concerning himself, Weil tells Jay he was born Catholic and, like his parents before him, never attended religious services or considered himself Jewish in the least. 'I, [for instance]', Weil continues, 'was not the son of a German-born Jewish merchant, but the son of a German-born merchant who was an atheist.'[28] For even though Weil's parents had indeed been born into Orthodox and Reform Jewish families, 'both refused to join a Jewish congregation after they immigrated into Argentina around 1890.'[29] Indeed, his parents were either atheists or agnostics, and not only scandalised the local Jewish community of Argentina by not having Weil circumcised, but also made no protest when their son's name was supplemented by the name of the Catholic saint on whose day he was born; in sum, then, as Weil informed Jay, he 'grew up creedless, as I wasn't baptized either.'[30] 'Now', he continues, 'can you honestly say that I came from a Jewish family?' 'Only', he concludes, 'if you accept the Hitler method of the Jewish grandmother.'[31]

Concerning other Institute members, the situation seemed to Weil no less vexed. In the case of Pollock and Horkheimer, both 'ceased to be "Jewish" in the religious sense' as soon as 'they became adults.'[32] For this reason, Institute members could hardly be said to have been united by the fact that they were all 'assimilated Jews', as Weil made clear in his very first letter, since Jay uses that term 'without explaining it' – and despite the fact that it encompasses a vast and by no means homogenous range of people: from baptised Jews to the children of baptised Jews, from avowed atheists to those who considered Judaism no more than a religion and thus regarded themselves as 'good German[s]' instead.[33] Not to mention, of course, those who never considered themselves Jews in the first place and were never 'considered Jews until the Nürnberg Act made them Jews' on the basis of racist determinations of their ancestry.[34] Regardless of whether Institute members might be more 'accurately' described – in Nazi terms, Weil adds – as either Aryan or Jewish, such designations would be in each case inaccurate, since they all 'felt as plain atheists.'[35] For this reason, Weil recommended dropping those religious, ethnic and/or racial references, including a note of clarification instead. Should Jay still wish to address the issue, however, he might defer to Weil, raising the question of 'whether it was true that almost all of the earlier Institut members were of Jewish origin', and then quote Weil as saying:

> The answer depends upon what you consider 'Jewish': before the Nazis branded me and other persons 'with at least one Jewish grandparent' as 'Jews', even if they belonged to a Christian religion, I would not have considered myself nor anyone in our group a Jew, and certainly there was not a single one among us who ever attended Jewish religious services – orthodox or liberal – other than as a guest as a wedding. And there were some among us who even Hitler could not have branded as 'Jews': for instance, [Institute members and associates] Wittfogel, Korsch, or Massing.[36]

If unsatisfied with this addendum, however, Jay might take up the commonplace according to which 'it has sometimes been stated that the Institut group "were all Jews"', and then conclude, on the basis of his own authority, but no longer deferring to Weil, that in Jay's own estimation 'none of them was a Jew.'[37] 'Of course, I like the second suggestion *much better*', Weil tells Jay, since the latter would make the point even 'more authoritative'.[38]

Given their continuing debate about such matters, as well as *The Dialectical Imagination's* inclusion of the very '"Jewish" references' Weil recommended excluding, the book's author appears to have been largely unpersuaded by Weil's arguments.[39] Nonetheless, Weil persisted because he could not understand whether Jay's attribution of Jewish identity was meant to rest upon notions of descent or ancestry, race or religion, ethnicity or nationality. 'It seems that for you', he tells his correspondent, '... "Jewish" simultaneously means the religion, the nationality ... and perhaps also the race', with the result, Weil concludes, that 'if "religion" doesn't apply' for the putative Jewishness of any specific individual, then Jewishness can still be assigned because, in such cases, 'you [mean] the ethnic descent or the race, or vice versa.'[40] This kind of peculiar logic of identity, based as it is on religious or non-elective forms of identity-based inheritance, creates untold confusions, as Weil makes clear by referring to the self-evident absurdities resulting from similar determinations during the time of the Third Reich. Yet, to Weil's dismay, Jay's manuscript consistently employed such categories, as when writing, for instance, about how 'obvious' it is that 'if one seeks a common thread which runs through [Institute members'] individual biographies', then that 'common thread' is quite clearly their shared birth in Jewish families.[41] For Weil, however, it was by no means 'obvious' that their purported Jewishness ever served such a function, which is why he 'most *emphatically* stress[es] that the "Jewish" origins of most members of the Institut group was mere coincidence', and that Jay's repeated reference to 'Jewish families', identities and influences is not only 'misleading' but 'convey[s] a totally wrong impression.'[42] After time and again finding in Jay's manuscript such attributions of ill-fitting identity assigned to colleagues he knew so well, Weil hazards a guess about the criteria used in words designed to provoke: 'I was sort of waiting to see you hold, with Hitler', he writes Jay, in parentheses, 'that "a Jew is a person descended from Jews", while Goering said, repeating the 1880 Mayor of Vienna, Lueger, "I shall tell who is a Jew or not!"'[43]

Aside from Weil's concerns about such retroactive ascriptions of Jewish identity, what he found perhaps even more galling was Jay's portrayal of such identities' influence on the Institute's life and work. 'You seem to hold', Weil observes, 'that we became Socialists and Revolutionaries as a consequence of our Jewishness.'[44] To this, however, Weil can only repeat that 'with us neither religion nor ethnic origin played any role.'[45] 'When our initial group got together to foster revolutionary socialism, nothing was farther from our mind than ideas about Jewish [sic], or any other religion, ancestry, ethnic kinship, skin color, etc., as a common element. We looked for total dedication from scientific conviction.'[46] And so he tells Jay that if his manuscript is to be published in the form in which it was written, then he will write a review challenging its claims. 'I would write this in a review', he tells Jay, and goes on to address an imaginary reader interested in Jay's book:

Although couched in cautious terms ... the author evidently wants to see our group's work, although he admires it and approves of it, as a consequence of our Jewishness, without realizing that nothing was farther from our mind and that he thus revives the old chestnut of the all-encompassing Jewish conspiracy against Germany (and thus justifies whatever is left of this Nazi concept).[47]

'I shudder at the idea [of] how our work will be interpreted after our deaths', Weil continues, 'when we no longer can talk back.'[48] For while Pollock, 'now already gone', Weil adds, himself 'talked back' in a letter to Jay, 'evidently to no avail', Weil will not for that reason remain silent.[49] 'Well, I am still alive for some time', he writes, continuing his mock-review, 'and vehemently disagree with the author's interpretation (not to say prejudice).'[50] For while Jay has every right to his own opinion, interpretations should be based on 'solid evidence', according to Weil, not on the author's own 'preconceived notions', adding to his mock-review the following caricature of '[t]he author's interpretation', which, according to Weil

> reminds me of the German scholar who as editor of an edition of Goethe's Diaries appended a endnote to Goethe's words 'Of all women in my life I loved Christine the most.'

The endnote [from the scholar] read 'Here Goethe erred. On the contrary, his love for Lilly was by far greater ...'[51]

This is an unkind parody of Jay's position, no doubt, but it was also informed by concerns both substantial and not at all uncommon in relations between historical actors and their interpreters. Elsewhere, Weil suggests a compromise of sorts. Since Jay had already made it '*quite clear* that almost all of our group were of Jewish descent', the author is told he might 'justifiably ventilate the question whether our radicalism had anything to do with this' – but on the condition that he then 'print Pollock's and my letters saying this was not the case.'[52] Concerning the purported influence of antisemitism on their early thinking – a claim the whole 'triumvirate' appears to have opposed – Weil underscored Pollock's earlier statements about the absence of any Weimar-era legal barriers for those considered Jewish, adding that whatever discrimination persisted was of a purely social nature – vacation landlords who wouldn't rent to people with Jewish-sounding names ('Abraham Lincoln', he notes, 'would have been rejected out-of-hand'), as well as student fraternities that did not accept Jews – but that these kinds of discrimination did not matter at all.[53]

Closing his letter, Weil ends in resignation: 'All I can do now is to help you at least to be as accurate as possible.'[54]

In time, however, Weil would relent in several respects, telling Jay that 'as long as you don't write that I was the son of a Jewish merchant, I am satisfied',[55] even if he continued to point out how Jay confuses 'the "Jewish" question' by using 'Jewish' for one person when referring to a religion and then, without explanation, using 'Jewish' as a stand-in for ethnic descent for another.[56] Where his own person is concerned, however, Weil is adamant that Jay exclude any reference to his own purported Jewishness. 'For if you say that I came from a Jewish family or joined with our group because of our common Jewishness it would be wrong – and I would resent it. True, I had on my father's side orthodox Jewish grandparents and liberal on my mother's side, but it was only Hitler who declared me a Jew ... So don't you do it, too, please.'[57] Further, Weil explains that, on account of his Argentine birth, even the idea that Hitler declared him a Jew is not quite accurate – 'I don't mean me personally', he writes, 'I was never a German!' – and that Hitler's declaration of who was and was not Jewish did not affect his own sense of identity: 'I deliberately did not say "*made* me a Jew", as I still don't [think?] "Jewish" '.[58] 'In other words', Weil adds, 'despite all my sympathy for Israel, I still don't feel as a Jew, although I know where I come from, and I would never [pretend?] to be a Goy'.[59] A few weeks later, Weil seems to think his arguments and entreaties are having some effect: 'I am glad you are beginning to see the "Jewish" matters my way', he tells Jay, and congratulates him on 'so quickly finding a professorship' at the University of California at Berkeley, where Jay first met Löwenthal, a member of the faculty, three years before.[60] By this time, the controversy surrounding Jay's handling of the so-called '"Jewish" question' had been muted amid discussions about publisher proofs, Weil's request that Jay share his letters with other scholars and suggestions for titles Jay might consider for his forthcoming book – 'gift[s]', Weil called them, like 'The Young Scholars' and 'Rebels With a Cause.'[61]

Not long thereafter, however, Jay appears to have made clear his own preference for the book's title. And Weil, upon learning that Jay wished to call his inaugural history of the Frankfurt School by the title 'Permanent Exiles', went silent for nearly a month, his more conciliatory attitude coming to an abrupt stop. 'I haven't answered your ... letter so far', Weil began his next letter, 'because I didn't want to be negative all the time ... But I mulled and I mulled about "Permanent Exiles", and the longer I mulled the less I liked it.'[62] 'I think I can discern your reasoning behind it', Weil continues, supposing that what Jay likely meant was that 'they were spiritually already exiles while still in Germany'.[63] About this sort of claim, however, Weil and others always made clear that they did not experience discrimination before 1933, while Weil had long insisted that the identity-based foundation of Jay's claim to the Frankfurt School's 'spiritual exile' was no less mistaken. It could hardly be said, then, that the pre-1933 Institute could be in any way characterised as existing in a state of exile, spiritual or historical, identity-based or socially imposed. From 1933 to 1950, they were indeed exiles from Germany but, as Weil points out, 'the Frankfurt School continued and flourished especially after 1950, and from then on they didn't feel exiled any more – they were back home and in a non-nationalist environment.'[64] In this sense, too, it would be mistaken to speak of the life of the Institute in terms of some nebulous notion of exile, spiritual or otherwise. As a result, the claim to 'permanent exile' can hardly be considered accurate.

A month later, Weil informs Jay that he has just gotten off the phone with Horkheimer, recently returned home after two stays in the hospital, and that Horkheimer 'dislikes your book title "Permanent Exiles" even more than I do, because it is so utterly misleading.'[65] As a result, Weil repeats once more his earlier suggestions, and then, a month later, tells Jay that if he means 'Permanent Exiles in the sense of Permanent Outsiders', as Jay appears to have suggested, then 'why not *say* The Permanent Outsiders' instead?[66] At this point, Weil's mention of Horkheimer's opposition could have hardly surprised the author since Jay already received from Horkheimer several letters to that effect. There Horkheimer pointed out that any claim to permanent exile 'seems to me problematic' since Adorno, Pollock and Horkheimer had long since lost any exiled status after returning home to Germany, while others, like Löwenthal and Marcuse, could hardly be considered 'permanent' exiles as they had long since 'made America their home.'[67] In response, Jay sought to explain how his characterisation of their exile as permanent was only meant 'metaphorically', a claim supported, in Jay's mind, by the idea that 'even before their actual emigration, Institute members had been anxious to avoid co-optation and after the war, Critical Theory had maintained its distance from any real "homecoming".'[68] But Horkheimer, as Jay recalls, 'was not placated' by this explanation, and sent Jay an urgent telegram and letter explaining why, as he said, the 'title still seems misleading to me.'[69] There Horkheimer made clear how the interpretation Jay and others would later advance about the Institute's pre-exile (1923-1933) and exile period (1933-1950), according to which they were collectively 'obsessed by "the fear of co-optation and integration" ', as Horkheimer writes, quoting Jay, 'is certainly not precise.'[70] Before Horkheimer himself became director (1923-1931), 'this surely was not the case', he writes, and once he assumed the directorship 'several of us definitely were non-conformists in some ways', Horkheimer admits, 'but no "Exiles" '.[71] Turning to their time in American exile, Horkheimer acknowledges that 'most of us were exiles with regard to fascist Germany, but certainly not with regard to democratic states like the USA and postwar Germany.'[72] Were that to have been the case, Horkheimer points out, they would have never developed close relations with conservative Americans like the President of Columbia University, nor would people like Franz Neumann have returned to postwar Germany to help organise the university in West Berlin, nor would Horkheimer himself have done the same in Frankfurt 'with American and German public funds'.[73]

Two weeks after Horkheimer's letter, Weil would write Jay again to offer 'one more word of caution and argument against the title "Permanent Exiles" ', which Weil considers 'fundamentally wrong and damaging'

> especially because of the reinforcement of the misunderstanding you give by your insistence on saying, or broadly hinting at, the influence the so-called joint ethnical origin of our group is supposed to have had on our way of thinking, the 'Exiles' title will lead retroactively to justify all the attacks our enemies launched against the Institute and the Frankfurt School, to wit, that we as rotten outsiders had no business nor justification in trying to instill 'undeutsche Gedanken' [ungerman thinking] = subversive feelings into German students.[74]

For Horkheimer and Weil, then, when such a title is read alongside the book's related speculations about how the Institute's ideas may have been influenced by 'the so-called joint ethnical origin of our group', as Weil understood Jay to say – and which subsequently has been repeated so often as to have become received wisdom when discussing the Frankfurt School – the proposed title could not help but present an image of the Frankfurt School that was not only fundamentally mistaken and contrary to the lives and works of Institute members, but which also undermined their prior efforts. For this reason, Weil informs Jay that 'Horkheimer considers the Exiles title an outrage', and warns him against its use because, if he were to do so, then Weil tells Jay: 'Don't be surprised if [Horkheimer] now refuses to write a Foreword!'[75] A little more than a week later, this conflict over titles will be brought to a close once a new title, 'The Dialectical Imagination', was proposed as its replacement. In response, Weil tells Jay just how much he and Horkheimer like the new title: it 'sounds intriguing', Weil writes, 'and may help with the sales.'[76]

From pariahdom to prestige

It was undoubtedly right for Weil to have feared how Jay's identification of the Frankfurt School as 'permanent exiles' might lend credence to right-wing fantasies of an alien force peddling ideas designed to undermine the nation, as Jay has himself recently acknowledged. Against the backdrop of the current century's antisemitic and conspiratorial scapegoating of the Frankfurt School as the newest scourge of civilisation, Jay now admits that 'the fears he [Horkheimer] and Weil had about the dangers of foregrounding the Jewish identity of their colleagues were, alas, justified.'[77] At the time, however, as Jay would later say, he did not fully 'understand the source of their anxiety', did not recognise how Weil and Horkheimer 'still felt the sting' of those historical 'slanders', and did not take seriously enough the nationalist right's past and present vilification of those considered 'rootless cosmopolitans'.[78] As we have seen, however, Weil and Horkheimer's objections to Jay's treatment of the 'Jewish question' were in no way reducible to such fears. Nor was it a matter, for them, of coarse political calculation in the sense that their purported Jewishness should be concealed so as not to provoke an antisemitic response. For Weil, the problem was, instead, that it was simply inaccurate to designate Institute members as Jews, either individually or collectively, and that it was especially dubious to do so on the basis of assumptions about

Jewish identity and influence which transform people's origins and ends into the stuff of myths refractory to the facts. In such cases, Jewish identity, ancestry and otherness is accorded an explanatory power that is not only a poor substitute for historical understanding, but which regularly devolves into the very antisemitic stereotypes critical theory meant to surmount. In this sense, it is difficult to ignore how the association of a term like 'permanent exiles' with antisemitic tropes about 'rootless cosmopolitans' and the 'eternally wandering Jew' might have made it difficult for Weil and Horkheimer to regard such a title as a 'badge of honor', as Jay intended.[79] The very homology that has long existed between antisemitic and philosemitic stereotypes like these may thus explain, in part, why Weil and Horkheimer regarded that title as a 'source of reproach' instead, leaving Jay feeling as though he had 'unintentionally entered a minefield' while corresponding with Weil and Horkheimer about such matters.[80]

What Jay then appears to have assumed, 'perhaps naively', as he would later write, was that his search for critical theory's origins in individual Institute members' 'Jewish' ancestry, implicit classification of those people in terms of ethnic, religious or racial descent, and subsequent identification of those 'origins' as a cardinal source for the Institute's life and work would resonate, instead, with a substantially more philosemitic, but not for that reason any less problematic, tradition of ascribing positive characteristics to Jewish identity.[81] Integral to that tradition is a set of practices which frequently reproduce the antisemitic practice of 'unmasking' individuals and groups as Jews, no matter their protests, and which accord outsized influence to non-elective ethnic and/or racial identities in the determination of life and character.[82] Indeed, it was likely considerations such as these which once led Habermas to worry – if only for a moment – that celebrating the German Idealism of such 'Jewish philosophers' as Adorno, Horkheimer, Marcuse and Lukács might thereby 'pin a Jewish star on the exiled and the beaten once again.'[83] More recently, Jay appears to have become more sensitive to certain aspects of these matters since he now notes how the 'exaltation of the eternally marginal Jew' can have its dangers, '[r]omanticizing the unchosen condition of displacement and homelessness' that it is the historian's task to demonstrate as historical through and through.[84]

At the time of *The Dialectical Imagination's* writing, however, Jay's thinking about such matters was still affected by a range of quite different influences. In this sense, *The Dialectical Imagination* is perhaps best seen, like every other act of historical interpretation, as the sum of a complex interplay of interests and identifications, equivocations and antipathies in which projective fantasies and transferential relations combine to create that peculiar form of individual investment necessary for academic labour. Only recently, however, has Jay begun to more fully articulate how the conditions of his own milieu first drew him to his subjects, informing his presentation of the Institute in a way which might make his ideas about the '"Jewish" question', as Weil called it, considerably more comprehensible. In retrospective accounts, Jay has presented his early interest in the Frankfurt School as having been guided by three overriding interests. The first concerns the specific milieu to which Jay and a number of scholars from the late 1960s American reception of critical theory belonged, and which Jay characterises as a 'a generation that was in a sense both part of the New Left and part of the counter culture [sic].'[85] Though by no means 'a full-fledged member of any militant New Left position', Jay considered himself a 'sympathizer' and found in the tradition of Hegelian Marxism, and in Herbert Marcuse in particular, a 'self-justification' of sorts, providing himself and others with the 'permission to be radical.'[86] At the time, however, those interested in such ideas 'had no idea where [Marcuse] came from', and it was precisely this 'unknown dimension' Jay came to regard as a 'mystery to be solved', leaving him 'fascinated by trying to figure out ... Marcuse's own background.'[87] The second source for Jay's early interest was his realisation that so many of those responsible for the so-called intellectual migration from Nazi Germany to the United States were getting older, retiring or passing away, and that those who had 'so enriched American intellectual life' were now 'interested in telling their stories.'[88] These two influences comprise the 'two-part' answer Jay 'normally' gives when asked about his initial interest in critical theory.[89] They do not, however, tell the full story for 'there was [also] a third reason', Jay acknowledges, a 'very personal reason', which involves Jay's own identification with an assimilated, but religiously non-observant, Jewish tradition.[90] And because Jay believed that 'most of the members of the Frankfurt School [also] came from

Jewish backgrounds more or less lacking a strong religious dimension', he came to develop what he called 'a certain identification with these people' in whom he saw represented 'a kind of ideal version of the way in which a truly cultured figure might be.'[91] Elsewhere, and no less candidly, Jay has spoken of having long viewed the representatives of critical theory 'as exemplars of a certain kind of ... normative or aspirational moment of high German-Jewish excellence' with which he early and still continues to identify.[92]

The problem, of course, is that the very people to whom Jay attributed those identities often rejected such ascriptions of Jewishness, and opposed explanations of their life and work based upon those identities. Indeed, as Jay noted in a contemporaneous letter to Leo Löwenthal, throughout his interviews and correspondence he discovered how '[t]he Jewish question is certainly a sensitive one as every time I broach it, I am corrected.'[93] To support his own identity-based interpretation, then, Jay would have to rely upon the writings and ideas of figures more sympathetic to his views. Concerning 'Permanent Exiles', for example, Jay contrasted Weil's and Horkheimer's opposition with the approval of Löwenthal and Marcuse, both of whom remained in the United States, and maintained, in Jay's estimation, a more conflictual relationship with the contemporary world.[94] Still more significant for the resulting book, however, were the resources upon which Jay relied when according Institute members a particular form of Jewish identity despite their opposition. This is perhaps nowhere better evidenced than in the above-mentioned episode in which the title and trope of 'permanent exiles' appeared to Weil, not as the honorific Jay intended, but indissociable from that armband of antisemitic ideology from which a racial, religious and/or ethnic identity was concocted for them, reproducing the very same noxious racial stereotypes in the process. That a pernicious homology between antisemitic and philosemitic stereotypes has long existed, been instrumentalised philosemitically to dubious historical effect,[95] and early criticised by the Frankfurt School itself is today well understood.[96] At the time of *The Dialectical Imagination*'s composition, however, Jay may well have found Institute members' reactions inconceivable, as he would later claim, because he was then 'under the indirect influence' of a work he afterwards credited with '[t]urning the insult of "rootless cosmopolitanism" into a virtue, celebrating the burdensome role of "wandering Jew", [and] valuing restless "homelessness" over stable settlement.'[97] That book, George Steiner's *Language and Silence*, which Jay recalls first encountering in 1968, was one which 'powerfully resonated', as Jay later wrote, 'with the understanding of the Frankfurt School I was beginning to formulate in my dissertation.'[98] And it was, indeed, on the basis of such ideas as these, ideas Jay found suggestive for celebrating 'the virtues of exile and displacement', and 'stress[ing] the benefits of marginalization over its costs', that the historian imagined he had discovered 'a key to make sense of what their [Institute members'] Jewish backgrounds might mean.'[99] The resulting work thus came to crystallise a conflict between Institute members' own sense of the social, political and intellectual spurs to their work and that ascription of Jewish influence to which Jay has remained committed for the last half-century.

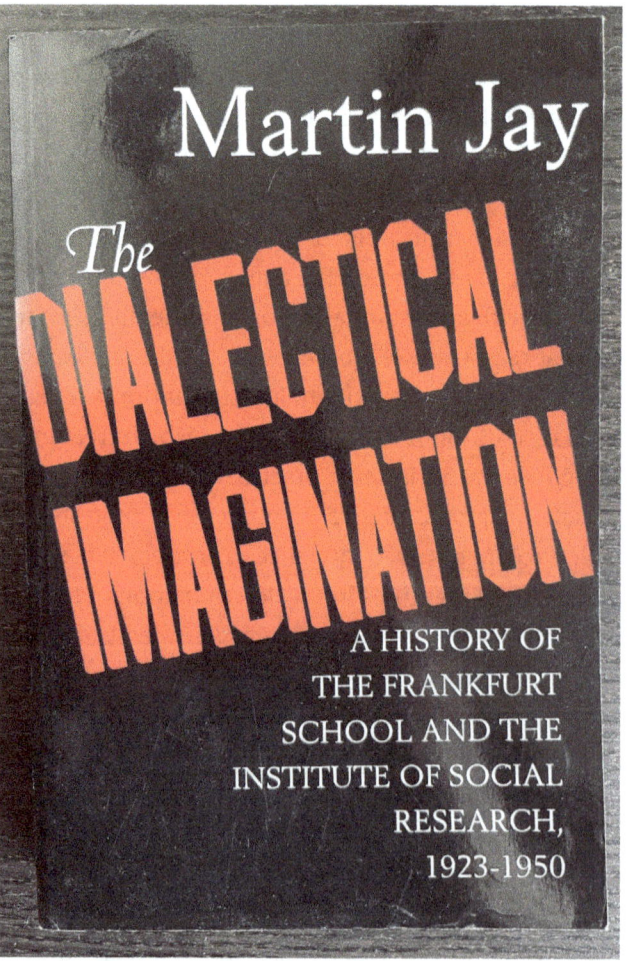

Such a conflict is already evident in the published version of *The Dialectical Imagination* itself. In the latter Jay appears to have followed Weil's advice, making explicit

Institute members' 'vehement rejection of the meaningfulness of Jewishness in their backgrounds',[100] as well as the extent to which they 'den[ied] any significance at all to their ethnic roots.'[101] Indeed, Jay writes, it is clear that 'the overt impact of Judaism as a system of belief seems to have been negligible', that 'the manifest intellectual content of Judaism played no role in the thinking of the Institute's members', and that – aside from Löwenthal, Fromm and Benjamin – '[t]o the others Judaism was a closed book.'[102] Here, as elsewhere, Jay makes clear that his speculations do not intend to suggest that 'the Institut's program can be solely, or even predominantly, attributed to its members' ethnic roots', while also arguing that 'to ignore them entirely is to lose sight of one contributing factor.'[103] As a result, Jay continued searching for 'indirect ways' in which their purported Jewishness 'might have played a role', and thus turned to what he termed 'more broadly sociological or cultural explanations.'[104] For this purpose, Jay adduced a series of speculative links between the Frankfurt School and their purported Jewishness, ranging from the 'elective affinity' said to exist between political radicalism and Judaism to the widespread antisemitism of Wilhelmine and Weimar Germany – Institute members denied both – and from the plainly less compelling idea that Frankfurt School members were prey to 'self-delusions' about the threat of Nazism to the presence of what Jay classified as typically Jewish father-son relations among Institute members, their interest in psychoanalysis, as well as the idea that their writings' 'strong ethical tone' may have derived from the 'values likely to be espoused in a close-knit Jewish home.'[105]

In light of such 'sociological' and 'cultural' explanations, it is perhaps unsurprising that Jay does not simply write of Frankfurt School members having denied significance to their purported ethnic roots, but instead writes that they were '*anxious* to deny *any significance at all* to their ethnic roots'; that Weil did not simply oppose Jay's interpretation but '*heatedly* rejected' the significance of their supposed Jewishness; that Institute members were not assimilated Jews, but '"assimilated" Jews' – the scare quotes Jay's, and presented in such a way as to suggest that their self-professed assimilation was not to be entirely believed.[106] When characterised in this way, it becomes clearer why Jay should have found surprising 'the intensity with which many of the Institut's members denied, and in some cases still deny, any meaning at all to their Jewish identities.'[107] Because *The Dialectical Imagination* neither takes seriously the potential validity of Institute members' refusing such identities, traditions and influences nor inquires into the actual social, intellectual and historical reasons for Frankfurt School members' rejection of Jewish identity, but instead renders such opposition suspicious by speaking of it in terms of just how 'anxious' and 'heated' was the 'intensity' of such denials, compounded in Jay's estimation by the 'general blindness' and 'self-delusions' of Institute members,[108] it is no wonder Jay should come to the conclusion that, as he writes, 'for all their claims to total assimilation and assertions about the lack of discrimination in Weimar, one cannot avoid a sense of their protesting too much.'[109]

For Jay, then, Institute members' accounts of their own lives inevitably appear implausible because the very stridency of their claims is interpreted as evidence of its opposite. Such suspicions as Jay entertains here, however, appear reminiscent of a series of ill-founded assumptions which have long sought to render ridiculous Weimar intellectuals' rejection of ethnic identity and experience of successful assimilation and waning antisemitism by setting it against the backdrop of the Shoah's supposed inevitability. From this perspective, the destruction of European Jewry is made to appear both foreseeable and foreordained, while those who did not earlier accept their 'origins' are belittled, in the words of Samuel Moyn, as being 'wholly self-deluded in their attempted integration … [since] they were fated from the beginning to disappear.'[110] On the basis of this kind of teleological vision of history, however, a 'negative idealisation' of the past, as Moyn calls it,[111] it is perhaps more readily understandable (if not for that reason any less regrettable) that Jay should have gone on to characterise so uncharitably Institute members' protests against his interpretation of the '"Jewish" question', as when he dubbed their reactions a form of 'role-playing' performed by 'the Jew eager to forget his origins.'[112] Yet, as Moyn has noted of similar judgments, such characterisations may owe their success to an 'underlying prejudice', 'a form of "ethnic absolutism" or 'essentialising reduction of identity',[113] as he calls it, most recently suggested by Jay's insistence that 'their Jewish identities, however attenuated, preclude[d] their ever being fully at home in the hegemonic culture of Europe.'[114]

At the time of *The Dialectical Imagination*'s 1973 publication, the objections raised by Weil and Horkheimer did still have some effect: their protests were at least excerpted and recorded in the published book, its title was changed and the attribution of Jewish identity to Weil's father was omitted. But in the decades since, Jay has continued modifying his account of the Frankfurt School's relationship to Judaism and exile, strengthening his earlier interpretation in the process. Following his 1972 decision to give up 'Permanent Exiles' as a title, for example, Jay employed the very same title some thirteen years later for a volume on the Frankfurt School and other former exiles. In his defense, Jay explained that, with reference to the protests of Weil, Pollock and Horkheimer, 'it has always been my conviction that the homecoming of certain Frankfurt School members to Germany did not really end the exile of Critical Theory.'[115] In still later accounts, Jay has returned to the terms of that earlier dispute, claiming of Frankfurt School members that 'they themselves were *content* with being permanent exiles', and insisting that the Frankfurt School's 'history cannot be told, *pace* Felix Weil, without taking into account the Jewish star in the constellation of influences' determining their work.[116] As a result, it should hardly surprise that, in a recent essay on the foundations of critical theory, Jay restores in part what he had initially omitted, describing his former correspondent's father, Hermann Weil, as a 'German-Jewish grain merchant' – just as countless others have done before and since, antisemitically and philosemitically by turns.[117] In this context, it is perhaps instructive to recall the barbed joke Weil once related after questioning Jay's 'treatment of the "Jewish" question.' In that letter, Weil closed with a postscript: 'Do you know the story of the Jew declaiming "I am a Jew and proud of it. If I weren't, I'd be a Jew anyway ... So I might as well be proud of it"?' 'I don't know whether I read this somewhere or made it up myself', Weil observed, 'but I am sure it was your treatment of the matter that inspired me ...'[118]

As the decades passed, this early and important dispute about the Frankfurt School's identity and influences receded from view as the idea took hold that their 'Jewishness' was less a question than a certain origin. Two years after *The Dialectical Imagination* was first published, for instance, the Harvard professor and former doctoral advisor of Martin Jay, H. Stuart Hughes, published a book referencing and repeating without qualification his recent student's assertions, writing of the Frankfurt School that a 'point of common experience' between them was their shared 'Jewish origin', but that, like so many other 'German Jews', 'they preferred most of the time not to speak of the matter or to speak of it with a certain embarrassment.'[119] Less than a decade later, this interpretation received its most significant stamp of approval when George Mosse, the doyen of German Studies, published *German Jews Beyond Judaism* and included the Frankfurt School among its pantheon. Mosse not only drew upon Jay's work to acknowledge Institute members' denial of any link between their work and purported Jewishness, agreeing with them that Judaism ecumenically defined – as either an ancient, intellectual or religious tradition – played no part in their lives, but at the same time insisted upon the central importance of 'their Jewishness' regardless.[120]

In Mosse, as elsewhere, the 'Jewishness' of the Frankfurt School is explained by Institute members' supposed position as 'outsiders' in German society, attention to the notion of alienation, and affinity with left-wing political movements – ensuring that, '[w]hatever their individual concerns were', as Mosse writes, 'the Frankfurt School as a whole' should be considered 'a part of the German-Jewish tradition of *Bildung* and Enlightenment.'[121] By 1990, this interpretation had become canonical enough for Steven S. Schwarzschild to observe that 'The Jewishness of the Frankfurt School ... is long since a truism.'[122] And, indeed, the following thirty years have only witnessed the further strengthening of this truism. In more recent secondary literature, Jack Jacobs' *The Frankfurt School, Jewish Lives, and Antisemitism* is perhaps the most obvious example. For while Jacobs is careful to qualify his assertions about 'Jewish influence' on the Frankfurt School by making clear that the Institute 'was never an explicitly Jewish institution', that he himself does 'not believe that Critical Theory is a Jewish theory', and that the *Dialectic of Enlightenment* is not at all a 'Jewish book in any significant sense', his book-length insistence upon what he calls the Frankfurt School's 'Jewish origin', 'Jewish life paths', 'Jewish roads' and 'Jewish consciousness' cannot help but make his qualifications appear, if not disingenuous, then at least somewhat perfunctory.[123] More recently, this canonised interpretation has reached its apogee in the work of Peter E. Gordon, a former student of Jay who, in a nod to his teacher's momentarily-abandoned title, seeks to now repurpose it by arguing that 'we are all "permanent exiles" ' today.[124]

In line with this interpretation, the past half-century has transformed into a commonplace the idea that the Frankfurt School consisted of German-Jews committed to the reinterpretation of particularly Jewish themes, and that the group's putative distance from prevailing ideologies was not only constitutive of its work, but may also be seen as characteristically Jewish as well – as though Jewish identity, isolation, extraterritoriality and exile should now be seen as the very origin and the end of critical theory's work. When confronted with Weil's objections and arguments, however, that commonplace appears decidedly less compelling, and may inspire in today's reader a palpable sense of discomfort. Indeed, that discomfort is also my own. And yet this earlier contest over origins, titles and identities may also allow us to ask whether more recent notions of identity and intellectual work are sufficient for understanding critical theory's earlier impulses.

At the time of their correspondence, it was precisely this difference between the lives of Institute members and that of their interpreters which led Weil to empathise with Jay, underscoring, with regret, how the impulses of that earlier generation appear to have been lost in the meantime. 'I realize how difficult it must be for a scholar with your background to grasp the political and societal urgency in which we founding members lived and worked', he told Jay: 'We wanted to do our share to have socialism ... if not yesterday then tomorrow.'[125] Such social, political and historical factors, Weil suggests, are at once both more accurate and more illuminating than any identity-based explanatory model. Indeed, the facts of Weil's own history clearly demonstrate the inadequacy of any form of religious, racial, cultural or ethnic Jewishness for understanding his life and work.

Contrary to the well-worn idea that Weil and other Institute members belong to the pantheon of German-Jewish intellectuals driven by *Bildung,* and whose radicalism was motivated by shared Jewish backgrounds, it should be remembered that the most formative influences on the life of the Institute's founder were all of an eminently social and political nature, as Weil's biographer, Hans-Peter Gruber, has recently made clear.[126] These influences include, for instance, Weil's early awareness of South American social injustice, as well as the effects of the First World War, November Revolution, Communist movement and political instability in Weimar Germany. Weil, it should be remembered, was neither Jewish nor German, but an atheist and internationalist born in Argentina whose mother tongue was Spanish. His social consciousness was formed, not by Jewish identity and antisemitism, but by his early apprehension of the divide between his own family's wealth and that of the masses of impoverished workers with whom he grew up. Indeed, it was in solidarity with the indigenous family that was for him a second family that Weil's sense of historical injustice was formed in opposition to the ruling *latifundistas*. Later, upon his relocation to Germany, Weil participated, albeit briefly, in the November Revolution of 1919, became a socialist student agitator, and was imprisoned and expelled from the state of Württemberg for his 'seditious' activities. Moving ever farther to the left, Weil worked for years as a delegate to the Bolshevik-led Communist International in Argentina, and founded the Institute for Social Research as an avowedly Marxist centre for study and research, while also becoming a patron, promoter and publisher of left-wing avant-garde art and literature.

There is little doubt, then, that the spurs to Weil's intellectual and organisational activities were of a manifestly socialist and political nature: in Argentina, the boy who was like an older brother to him was murdered for organising local workers; in Germany, he was imprisoned and expelled for political agitation; in the United States, he was surveilled and suspected for what were believed to be his past and present communist activities. Moreover, as Gruber points out towards the end of his exhaustively researched biography, 'There is not the slightest doubt about Felix Weil's areligious attitude.'[127] For Weil was not only ignorant of and uninterested in his 'origins', but remained an 'avowed atheist' who, his biographer notes, 'understood religion only as a belief system and therefore did not consider himself a Jew.'[128] And, in this, Weil was not at all unusual since 'he came from an areligious family', according to Gruber, in which his sister was also an atheist and both his parents early distanced themselves 'from any religious ideas and practices.'[129] Yet the pull of identity-based explanatory models remains so strong that even Weil's own biographer cannot entirely avoid its effects. For, despite this, Gruber will nevertheless claim that Weil's life represents, in certain respects, a 'personified Jewish history' and that 'his biography ... is exemplary ... of a group of left-wing intellectuals of Jewish origin.'[130]

The First German Institute for the Study of Marxism

As Neil McLaughlin reminds us, the prevalence of certain origin myths in the Frankfurt School's canonisation 'are not about accurate historical reconstruction', but are best conceived as so many integral 'part[s] of a process whereby "contemporary preferences" are legitimated by "providing them with an honorable past".'[131] That the vogue today enjoyed by exile or pariahdom become prestige should accord itself an illustrious pedigree in the life and work of critical theory's past is no guarantee that such identities and equivalences constitute a faithful reconstruction of the Frankfurt School's past. Indeed, it may be more plausibly argued that it is only after abandoning such prejudices that one can then entertain the idea that what critical theory's representatives had to say themselves about their origins and impulses might actually be worth taking seriously. This would mean resisting an otherwise unquestioning reliance upon identity-based models of explanation and exercising greater caution when claiming for contemporary ideas greater validity than those possessed by the people who lived through those times themselves.

Against the perennial practice of explaining away Institute members' rejection of Jewish identity and influence, then, one might follow instead the recent recommendation of Martin Jay to resist the temptation to 'condescendingly "understand" those of past generations by situating them in their historical situation and moment', and no longer chalk up to ignorance or self-delusion ideas which do not appear to have been confirmed by the course of history.[132] Doing so would not only lend greater credence to the many reasons why such identities and models were so strenuously rejected in the first place, but would also preserve that distance between past and present which is otherwise collapsed when making Institute members' life and work conform with our own present. For whenever one now finds the Frankfurt School's image aligned with readymade impulses said to issue from the depths of some individual, collective or social being, one might more plausibly ask after the way such characterisations obscure the extent to which critical theory's most radical contributions are to be found on the very surface of its work.

In this respect, one need look no further than the preface Horkheimer did in fact write when Jay's provisional title was abandoned. For when the Institute's former director discussed what united the various members of the Frankfurt School, he did not identify that 'common thread' of Jewish birth and family backgrounds against which Weil had so protested, but a 'critical approach to existing society' through which, Horkheimer writes, 'a group of men, interested in social theory and from different scholarly backgrounds, came together with the belief that formulating the negative in the epoch of transition was more meaningful than academic careers.'[133] And if this patently more social, political and, indeed, existential determination of critical theory's origins is in fact correct, then a far more compelling explanation for the singularity of critical theory is not only explicit in Horkheimer's words, but plainly evidenced throughout the history of its experiments in social and intellectual production. Upon *The Dialectical Imagination's* 1973 publication, the dubiousness of identity-based explanations was not lost on Jay's own contemporaries. Writing in 1975, for instance, the American critic Douglas Kellner echoed Weil's objections, unwittingly it appears, in his own review of Jay's book, arguing that the author

> seems to place more weight on the Jewish origins of the members of the School than on their commitment to Marxism as the 'common thread running through individual biographies' ... In fact the most important 'common thread running through individual biographies' is a marked anti-capitalist and pro-socialist tendency.[134]

This is not to say, of course, that such attributions of Jewish identity may not serve a salutary purpose when they aim to produce less ethno-nationalism within the ambit of their own identity-based discursive concerns. In this sense, it is perhaps not inappropriate to ask if the prevailing image of the Frankfurt School as quintessentially Jewish is not itself a defense against more restrictive models of Jewish belonging, and might thereby constitute a progressive attempt at developing more expansive notions of diasporic, cosmopolitan Jewish identity as a result. Historically, of course, the ascription of identity is not infrequently developed in response to more orthodox acts of identity exclusion in a way that may prove instructive for understanding the canonisation of critical theory as well. Consider, for instance, Steven S. Schwarzschild's more orthodox portrayal of the Frankfurt School as coming from 'completely acculturated, assimilated, de-Judaised' families whose sons were 'thoroughly ignorant of Jewish culture', and thus possessed only 'suppressed and semi-Jewish instincts.'[135] Such criticisms of the Frankfurt School's insufficient Jewishness led Schwarzschild to characterise Horkheimer's late religious turn as demonstrating 'knowledge the paucity of which would shame a schoolboy',[136] and Hannah Arendt to denounce people like Adorno as 'Aryan stragglers',[137] identifying him, ignominiously, as the 'only half-Jew among Jews'.[138]

Examples like these attest to an intra-Jewish tradition of refusing Jewish identity to those who do not appear to conform to what others consider the necessary attributes of proper Jewishness, a slippery slope, as Evelyn Wilcock has shown.[139] The efforts of Jay and others to advance a more inclusive concept of German-Jewish diasporic identity are, from this perspective, most certainly welcome. Yet, as examples from outside the field of critical theory have shown, even the most laudatory efforts at expanding the scope of Jewish identity to include figures similarly non-nationalistic, non-religious, and non-identifying can often reproduce the very same tendency of subordinating individual lives and works to the exigences of contemporary political expediency, corralling prominent historical figures into one identity, rather than another – and thus creating an illustrious and self-legitimating pedigree for oneself in the process.[140]

For this purpose, there exists today an ever-expanding set of typologies for assigning Jewish identity to those who never identified themselves as such, and who possessed neither a connection to contemporary Jewish communities nor knowledge of Jewish culture – but who, despite this, can still be dubbed Jewish, retroactively, on the basis of such recent redescriptions of refractory figures as 'Non-Jewish Jews',[141] 'German Jews Beyond Judaism', or 'post-traditional Jews',[142] to take a few recent examples. While the sheer variety of these more capacious notions of identity evince a worthy desire to move beyond older notions of blood-based inheritance, such typologies can also seem woefully anachronistic. In this sense, it is perhaps not inappropriate to ask whether prevailing ideas about the Frankfurt School derive less from the life and work of Institute members than from 'our own standpoint', as Jay argues elsewhere, 'a contingent historical context, which generates assumptions that often elude us', and which often acts as an obstacle to recognising, as their contrary, 'the potentially transcendent alternatives presented by earlier thinkers.'[143] By explaining away the social and political realities, and legitimate individual reasons, behind such figures' distance from particular traditions, one also loses sight of how those figures saw themselves as participating within entirely different historical traditions instead.

Photo: Felix Weil Fotografie (1963)

In the case of early critical theory, its actions were determined by the ferment felt by those seeking to understand and transform the contemporary world, uniting Institute members in a series of unprecedented experiments in social and intellectual production irreducible to stories today told by way of identity, influence and other archetypes. Beholden as we now are, however, to the prevailing search for critical theory's roots, bedrock and related orthodoxies, this more radical legacy has been obscured. And yet it is precisely this often-elided history Felix Weil once intimated when suggesting, as the subtitle for Jay's canon-defining book, the idea of calling it – in a manner faithful to the Frankfurt School's past but obscured by its half-century-long canonisation – 'The story of the first German university institution for the study of Marxism.'[144] For it should not be today forgotten that, at the time of the Institute's 1923 inauguration, such an orientation was just as inimical to the social, political and scholarly norms of its time as it is to our own – and so at the moment that avowedly socialist impulse was first announced as the Institute's organising principle, 'we

[all] held our breath', as Weil later recounted, for 'here and now it had happened': 'Marxism was admitted as a teaching principle at a German university.' 'The taboo had been broken.'[145]

Ryan Crawford is Assistant Professor of Political Philosophy at Webster Vienna Private University. He is co-editor of Adorno and the Concept of Genocide *(2016) and* Delimiting Experience: Aesthetics and Philosophy *(2013).*

Notes

1. Peter E. Gordon, 'Conversations with Martin Jay', *Journal of Comparative Literature and Aesthetics* 42:2 (2019), 1.
2. On the personal, professional and political interests driving American scholars' reception of critical theory, see Robert Zwarg, *Die Kritische Theorie in Amerika: Das Nachleben einer Tradition* (Göttingen: Vandernhoeck & Ruprecht, 2017).
3. Gordon, 'Conversations with Martin Jay', 2.
4. Martin Jay, *The Dialectical Imagination: A History of the Frankfurt School and the Institute of Social Research 1923-1950* (Berkeley: University of California Press, 1996), xxxiii.
5. Martin Jay, 'The Ungrateful Dead', *Salmagundi* 123 (Summer 1999), 22–31.
6. Martin Jay, 'The Permanent Exile of Theodor W. Adorno', *Midstream* 15 (December 1969), 62–69. On the magazine's history, see Emily Alice Katz, '"A Questioning of the Jewish Status Quo": *Midstream*, Shlomo Katz, and American Zionist Letters at Midcentury', *Jewish History* 29 (2015), 57-96.
7. Felix J. Weil to Martin Jay, 19 March 1972. Weil's letters are to be found in Martin Jay's personal collection and are here used with his permission. On Jay's correspondence with Weil and Horkheimer, see Martin Jay, *Splinters in Your Eye: Frankfurt School Provocations* (London: Verso, 2020), 19-32.
8. Felix J. Weil to Martin Jay, 13 February 1972.
9. Max Horkheimer to Martin Jay, 31 January 1972; Max Horkheimer to Martin Jay, 5 March 1972, quoted in Jay, *Splinters*, 28.
10. See Jay, *The Dialectical Imagination*, xxxi; and Jay, *Splinters*, 30.
11. Martin Jay, *Permanent Exiles: Essays on the Intellectual Migration from Germany to America* (New York: Columbia University Press, 1986), xii.
12. Ibid.
13. Felix J. Weil to Martin Jay, 29 July 1971
14. Felix J. Weil to Martin Jay, 29 April 1971.
15. For the most complete account of Weil's life and work, see Hans-Peter Gruber, *»Aus der Art geschlagen« Eine politische Biografie von Felix Weil 1898-1975* (Frankfurt: Campus Verlag, 2022).
16. Felix Weil to Gustav Meyer, 16 January 1923; as quoted in Gruber, *»Aus der Art geschlagen«*, 207.
17. On Weil's offer to persuade Horkheimer to write a foreword for Jay's book, subsequent confirmation of Horkheimer's willingness to do so, and later threat that the foreword might no longer be forthcoming, see Weil's letters to Jay from 30 April 1971, 12 June 1971 and 19 March 1972, respectively. On Weil's specifications concerning Jay's permission to quote from interviews and correspondence with Pollock, Horkheimer and himself, see Felix J. Weil to Martin Jay, 30 March 1972.
18. Felix J. Weil to Martin Jay, 28 February 1971.
19. Felix J. Weil to Martin Jay, 29 April 1971.
20. Felix J. Weil to Martin Jay, 28 February 1971; Felix J. Weil to Martin Jay, 28 April and 30 April 1971.
21. Felix J. Weil to Martin Jay, 16 May 1971.
22. Ibid. For corresponding passages, see Jay, *The Dialectical Imagination*, 5–6, 16.
23. Weil to Jay, 16 May 1971.
24. Ibid.
25. Ibid.
26. Ibid.
27. Ibid.
28. Felix J. Weil to Martin Jay, 6 June 1971.
29. Felix J. Weil to Martin Jay, 16 July 1971.
30. Felix J. Weil to Martin Jay, 29 July 1971.
31. Ibid.
32. Felix J. Weil to Martin Jay, 6 June 1971.
33. Felix J. Weil to Martin Jay, 31 January 1971.
34. Ibid.
35. Felix J. Weil to Martin Jay, 6 June 1971.
36. Felix J. Weil to Martin Jay, 16 May 1971.
37. Ibid.
38. Ibid.
39. Felix J. Weil to Martin Jay, 6 June 1971.
40. Felix J. Weil to Martin Jay, 29 July 1971.
41. Felix J. Weil to Martin Jay, 16 July 1971. For the corresponding passage, see Jay, *The Dialectical Imagination*, 31.
42. Felix J. Weil to Martin Jay, 6 June 1971; Felix J. Weil to Martin Jay, 29 July 1971; Felix J. Weil to Martin Jay, 6 June 1971.
43. Felix J. Weil to Martin Jay, 11 June 1971.
44. Ibid.
45. Ibid.
46. Felix J. Weil to Martin Jay, 9 June 1971.
47. Ibid.
48. Ibid.

49. Ibid. For a short excerpt from Pollock's 'protest' letter, see Jay, *The Dialectical Imagination*, 33.
50. Felix J. Weil to Martin Jay, 9 June 1971.
51. Ibid.
52. Felix J. Weil to Martin Jay, 4 September 1971.
53. Felix J. Weil to Martin Jay, 9 June 1971.
54. Ibid.
55. Felix J. Weil to Martin Jay, 9 August 1971.
56. Felix J. Weil to Martin Jay, 24? August 1971.
57. Ibid.
58. Ibid.
59. Ibid.
60. Felix J. Weil to Martin Jay, 4 September 1971.
61. Felix J. Weil to Martin Jay, 24 November 1971; Felix J. Weil to Martin Jay, 5 December 1971.
62. Felix J. Weil to Martin Jay, 5 January 1972.
63. Ibid.
64. Ibid.
65. Felix J. Weil to Martin Jay, 13 February 1972.
66. Felix J. Weil to Martin Jay, 1 March 1972.
67. Max Horkheimer to Martin Jay, 31 January 1972, quoted in Jay, *Splinters*, 28.
68. Jay, *Splinters*, 28.
69. Max Horkheimer to Martin Jay, 5 March 1972, quoted in Jay, *Splinters*, 28.
70. Ibid., quoted in Jay, *Splinters* 29.
71. Ibid.
72. Ibid.
73. Ibid.
74. Felix J. Weil to Martin Jay, 19 March 1972.
75. Ibid.
76. Felix J. Weil to Martin Jay, 30 March 1972.
77. Jay, *Splinters*, 19. For related comments, see also Jay, *Splinters*, 151–172; and Martin Jay, 'Review Forum: Jack Jacobs, The Frankfurt School, Jewish Lives, and Antisemitism', *The German Quarterly* 89.1 (Winter 2016), 86–90.
78. Jay, *Splinters*, 29.
79. Ibid.
80. Ibid.
81. Ibid.
82. On the antisemitic practice of 'unmasking' Jews, see Paul Hanebrink, *A Spectre Haunting Europe: The Myth of Judeo-Bolshevism* (Cambridge, MA: Harvard University Press, 2018).
83. Jürgen Habermas, 'The German Idealism of the German Philosophers', in *Philosophical-Political Profiles*, trans. Frederick G. Lawrence (Cambridge: Polity, 2012), 57.
84. Martin Jay, 'After George Steiner: A Personal Recollection', *Salmagundi* 208-209 (Fall 2020-Winter 2021), 74.
85. Martin Jay, Azucena G. Blanco and Miguel Alirangues, 'Martin Jay: An Intellectual Picture', *Theory Now: Journal of Literature, Critique and Thought* 2:1 (January-June 2019), 239.
86. Ibid., 240.
87. Ibid.
88. Ibid.
89. Ibid., 239.
90. Ibid., 240.
91. Ibid.
92. Martin Jay, *City Lights Live!: Martin Jay in Conversation with Paul Breines*. YouTube, uploaded by CityLightsBooks, 26 August 2020, https://www.youtube.com/watch?v=7pVrOzFjji4.
93. Letter from Martin Jay to Leo Löwenthal, 16 September 1970. As quoted in Zwarg, *Die Kritische Theorie in Amerika*, 111.
94. Jay, *Permanent Exiles*, xii.
95. See Frank Stern, *The Whitewashing of the Yellow Badge: Antisemitism and Philosemitism in Postwar Germany* (Oxford: Pergamon Press, 1992); Jeffrey K. Olick, *The Sins of the Fathers: Germany, Memory, Method* (Chicago: University of Chicago Press, 2016).
96. See Theodor W. Adorno, 'Prejudice in the Interview Material', in *The Authoritarian Personality* (New York: Harper & Brothers, 1950), 603–653, especially 'Observations on Low-Scoring Subjects', 644–652; and Theodor W. Adorno, 'Zur Bekämpfung des Antisemitismus heute.' *Gesammelte Schriften Band 20.1* (Frankfurt am Main: Suhrkamp, 1986), 360–383.
97. Jay, 'After George Steiner', 74, 73.
98. Ibid., 74.
99. Ibid.
100. Jay, *The Dialectical Imagination*, 33.
101. Ibid., 32.
102. Ibid., 33.
103. Ibid., 34.
104. Ibid.
105. Ibid., 32-35.
106. Ibid., 32; italics mine.
107. Ibid.
108. Ibid.
109. Ibid., 34.
110. Samuel Moyn, 'German Jewry and the Question of Identity Historiography and Theory', *The Leo Baeck Institute Year Book* 41:1 (January 1996), 294.
111. Ibid.
112. Jay, *The Dialectical Imagination*, 34.
113. Moyn, 'German Jewry', 295.
114. Jay, 'After George Steiner', 74.
115. Jay, *Permanent Exiles*, xiii.
116. Jay, 'After George Steiner', 74 (my emphasis); Jay, 'Review Forum', 90.
117. Jay, *Splinters*, 6.

118. Weil to Jay, 29 July 1971. For the source of that joke, see Kurt Tucholsky, *Die Weltbühne*, 8 November 1932, p. 688. As quoted in Istvan Deak, *Weimar Germany's Left-Wing Intellectuals: A Political History of the Weltbühne and Its Circle* (Berkeley: University of California Press), 27.
119. H. Stuart Hughes, *The Sea Change: The Migration of Social Thought 1930-1965* (New York: Harper & Row, 1975), 140–141.
120. George Mosse, *German Jews Beyond Judaism* (Cincinnati: Hebrew Union College Press, 1997), 61.
121. Ibid., 61-62.
122. Steven S. Schwarzschild, 'Adorno and Schoenberg as Jews Between Kant and Hegel', *The Leo Baeck Institute Year Book* 35:1 (January 1990), 449.
123. Jack Jacobs, *The Frankfurt School, Jewish Lives, and Antisemitism* (Cambridge: Cambridge University Press, 2015), 2, 6, 151, 2, 3, 4, 9.
124. Peter E. Gordon, *Migrants in the Profane: Critical Theory and the Question of Secularization* (New Haven: Yale University Press, 2020), 148.
125. Felix J. Weil to Martin Jay, 9 June 1971.
126. The following sketch of Weil's life relies, once more, upon the excellent work of Gruber's »*Aus der Art geschlagen*«.
127. Gruber, »*Aus der Art geschlagen*«, 727.
128. Ibid., 12.
129. Ibid.
130. Ibid., 13.
131. Neil McLaughlin, 'Origin Myths in the Social Sciences: Fromm, the Frankfurt School and the Emergence of Critical Theory', *The Canadian Journal of Sociology* 24:1 (Winter 1999), 111. McLaughlin, it should be noted, is here quoting and paraphrasing the work of Jennifer Platt.
132. Martin Jay, *Genesis and Validity: The Theory and Practice of Intellectual History* (Philadelphia: University of Pennsylvania Press, 2022), 16.
133. Max Horkheimer, 'Foreword', in Jay, *The Dialectical Imagination*, xxv. For Jay's own use of Horkheimer's foreword, defending himself against Weil's objections, and tacitly supporting Horkheimer's late religious rewriting of critical theory, see, Jay, *Splinters*, 19–32. For critiques of those who take Institute members' religiously-inflected late statements at face value, see Felix J. Weil to Martin Jay, 27 June 1971; and Jonathon Catlin, 'Review: The Frankfurt School, Jewish Lives, and Antisemitism, by Jack Jacobs', *Antisemitism Studies* 1: 2 (Fall 2017), 415–423.
134. Douglas Kellner, 'The Frankfurt School Revisited: A Critique of Martin Jay's *The Dialectical Imagination*', *New German Critique* 4 (Winter 1975), 133.
135. Schwarzschild, 'Adorno and Schoenberg', 450–451, 454.
136. Ibid., 451.
137. As quoted in Zwarg, *Die Kritische Theorie in Amerika*, 147.
138. Hannah Arendt and Karl Jaspers, *Correspondence 1926-1969*, eds. Lotte Kohler and Hans Saner, trans. Robert and Rita Kimber (San Diego: Harcourt Brace & Company, 1992), 644.
139. Evelyn Wilcock, 'Negative Identity: Mixed German Jewish Descent as Factor in the Reception of Theodor Adorno', *New German Critique* 81 (Autumn 2000), 169–187.
140. See, for instance, Judith Butler, *Parting Ways: Jewishness and the Critique of Zionism* (New York: Columbia University Press; 2013); Sarah Hammerschlag, 'Outside the Canon: Judith Butler and the Trials of Jewish Philosophy', *Political Theology* 16:4 (2015), 367–370; and Julie E. Cooper, 'A Diasporic Critique of Diasporism: The Question of Jewish Political Agency', *Political Theory* 43:1 (February 2015), 80–110.
141. Isaac Deutscher, *The Non-Jewish Jew and Other Essays* (London: Verso, 2017).
142. Paul Mendes-Flohr, *Cultural Disjunctions: Post-Traditional Jewish Identities* (Chicago: University of Chicago Press, 2021).
143. Jay, *Genesis and Validity*, 16.
144. Felix J. Weil to Martin Jay, 5 December 1971.
145. As quoted in Gruber, »*Aus der Art geschlagen*«, 214

Grammars of the figure in the Iranian Uprising

Austin Gross

In modern times, the present becomes a didactic question. The new must be learned and there is no textbook.

The readings that follow were stirred by images from the streets of Iran and by a pseudonymous author's early attempt to conceptualise her present.[1] Her essay, under the byline 'L', took stock of new forms of action as they emerged and of the powers of the image that animated them.

But we will begin with another scene: a dressing room at the *Theater am Schiffbauerdamm* in Weimar-era Berlin.

In the summer of 1934, Walter Benjamin jotted an abrégé of a conversation with Bertolt Brecht on the subject of didactic poetry. Brecht took one of his own *Lehrgedichte* as example, a 'didactic poem on the art of acting for Carola Neher.'[2] Two variants exist,[3] but only one fits their conversation, and it is, as yet, untranslated.

> **Advice to the actress C.N.**
>
> Refresh yourself, friend
> From ice-water in the copper bowl
> – Open your eyes, underwater, wash them –
> Dry yourself with the rough towel and read
> The difficult lines of your part from the sheet on the wall.
> Know: this you do for yourself and do it exemplarily.[4]

Carola Neher was Brecht's star for whom he wrote the part of Polly Peachum in *The Threepenny Opera*. This didactic poem speaks to her backstage. We are invited to eavesdrop.

According to Brecht, Carola Neher learned from him how to wash her face.[5] That is, to give a new purpose to the same actions. She had hitherto washed 'so as not to be dirty';[6] to be presentable, or pleasing. What she learns is to wash without why: 'this you do for yourself, *für dich*.'

Für sich has no one-to-one equivalent in English. In everyday German, it more often means *per se* than *pro se*. Valences of 'this you do by yourself' and '... on your own' are pertinent too. But downhill the verse, past 'and', we are taught something new. Here, the didactic poem speaks of exemplarity.

When C.N. performs, she does not follow a model, but authorises herself from herself. Virtuosity in acting consists in this self-authorisation. Yet C.N. does not refuse to learn, that is, does not claim the authority of raw impulse or nature. She learns her part, and she learns by example: her own. Her art, the art of the actor, which she perfected, sustains itself in learning and teaching 'for herself', without why and without graduation.

Between C.N. and herself, teacher and learner, a third element intervenes: a ferry between two banks. This element is an image (*Vor-bild*). Here, Brecht's poem concedes its limit. What verses give to overhear, C.N. can show.

Twelve days after Jina Amini's murder, when Jina had already metamorphosed into *Jin* and *Jiyan* (Woman and Life), and the Kurdish slogan, *Jin, Jiyan, Azadi* (Woman, Life, Freedom), echoed in every translation,[7] an essay was published on the website of a women's safety organisation, Harass Watch.[8] Both of the English translations available online drop part of the title, so I'll start out by reproducing it in full. What comes first is a subheading. The main title follows.

انقلاب فیگوراتیو زنانه؛ اندرکنش بدن‌ها و تصاویرشان

Feminine Figurative Revolution; Interplay between Bodies and their Images

زنان در آینه تاریخ خود

Women in the Mirror of their Own History[9]

L proposed a history of her present, in the course of an uprising that drew its poetry from the future. She identified what she named 'figure' as the uprising's singularity and 'character.'[10] For L, nothing discursive, no slogan could come close; not even 'Woman, Life, Freedom.'

Gülsün Karamustafa, Prison Paintings [Hapishane Resimleri], 1972. Salt Research, Harika-Kemali Söylemezoğlu Archive.[11]

As L develops the concept of the figure, she cites and interprets a series of examples. Almost all of them are photos or stills which had become so much a part of the daily life of Iranians in those weeks that she had no need to include them in her essay. Others are drawn from deeper 'within the mirror', from 'the figure of all the women before her …'

> The figure of the sitting woman. The figure of the standing woman. The figure of the woman carrying a sign in Tabriz, eye-to-eye with the forces of repression. The figure of the woman who ties her hair. The picture of the dance circle around a bonfire in Bandar Abbas.

She is silent, in action or dancing. She is in action, yet 'fixed' in freeze-frame; she is not here to please, or to impress; she is not the figure of an individual, a face belonging to a name; she is in profile and she is a crowd, from a wide angle; she does not distinguish herself from others, like a soldier from a civilian; her gesture is 'everyday', or, one could also say, 'everyone's'; she is distinctive, yet anyone. These images lay a formal outline of the figure.

But to define the figure by what is in the picture would miss the point, as it would to equate C.N.'s exemplarity with a bowl of water and a rough towel. The figure is not something that can be hung on a wall or saved to disk. It 'drives' us, 'stimulates'. Or, put the other way round, I 'strike' a figure. From either side, a figure is not seen, but 'takes'. There is no such thing as 'pre-figuration'. The image does not precede the act.

> The space between me and the images I had desired had grown very small. I myself *was* those images. I would suddenly see myself in a circle burning headscarves, as though we had always been burning scarves. […]
> You say to yourself that you should light a cigarette, and you see yourself there, [already] smoking a cigarette. You say: I should get going, and you see yourself in the crowd. You've been there the whole time.[12]

L also calls this temporality 'warmth': a Farsi expression, akin to 'the heat of the moment' but different in scope and without the connotation of transgression. When the body is 'warm', writes L, I am not afraid, and my actions go beyond my fear and my intentions.

> The body is 'warm' when it is being beaten, and we don't experience pain in the way we might expect. Then you say to yourself that you should light a cigarette, and you see yourself there, smoking a cigarette. You say: I should get going, and you see yourself in the crowd. You've been there the whole time.

In 'warmth', she outruns herself. She suddenly is, has become, her own figure.

The figure is a tense, writes L: 'present perfect'. But is that all? It's true that the present perfect excludes intention and abrogates distances: 'I have been there the whole time.' But the figure has its own hope, and its own power of promise.

The figure is not a promise given to L, nor hers to the future. L writes of '[t]he desire to be that promissory figure.'[13] To be that promise, 'for herself.'

L does not refer to Brecht's didactic poem, any more than she employs the word 'didactic'. Yet her concept of figure opens a new angle on the didactic *Vor-bild*: C.N.'s self-exemplarity is also performed in a kind of present perfect. Producing her own example, she has outrun herself in a sense. But she has done so within the ethical self-relation denoted by 'for yourself'. L, for her part, has left her own behind.

> Now, the figure has freed itself from the bondage of the face. It is a general, faceless figure, covered with a mask, effaced for reasons of security, an image shot from behind, nameless, anonymous.

Nonetheless, in L's paratext, names, faces and secrets steal onto the stage. She opens with a dedication: '*For Zhina [or Jina], for Niloofar, for Elaheh, for Mahsa, for Elmira, and for those whose names I have yet to call*'.[14] Some are the names of women killed or imprisoned, but L invokes each by first name. The byline carries an endnote glossing the pseudonym, the letter 'L'. The letter, she says, alludes to something private from her relationship to her beloved. In a way, it's something more intimate than her legal name.

> My beloved once chose to title a project 'L' that may or may not have been referring to me. Engrossed in the experience of this revolutionary space, so akin to the experience of love, I want to push aside my constant hesitation about this L's reference, and instead own it along with my beloved's gesture. My signing of this essay as L is a revolutionary appropriation of [their] gesture. This naming not only keeps me secure from the threats of government forces, but frees me in my idea of love, at the very moment that names have become ciphers [*ramz*].[15]

This endnote places the entire essay under love's sign. Her love for her beloved and her love for the people on the street pass into one another, by the intercession of a name that has become a password or symbol (*ramz*), a mediator between her text and her endnotes.

The essay's third and final endnote is the longest of the three. L 'render[s] common' a private letter which she had written to her beloved in 2020. In the present of the uprising, she says, her letter has become common property. And, in fact, the entirety of her essay was its commentary.

A video had been circulating online of the liberation of Qasr Prison in 1979. We see the freed inmates and their loved ones embrace on the square in front of the prison.[16] L was struck by a face.

> I wrote to my beloved after I watched a viral video of the opening [*bâz*] of the gates of Qasr Prison and the freeing of political prisoners months before the 1979 Revolution. I wrote this on August 2, 2020:
>
> 'Tonight I saw the video of the freeing [*āzādī*] of prisoners on the internet. Again and again. Would that I could be the one brushing that woman's hair aside from her forehead? ... You need not say anything. It's enough to brush aside the hair from the forehead in front of you to recognize her and become certain that she is there, and it's you who reveals her face.
>
> Is it you?
>
> Yes, it's me.
>
> A face for everyone. ... How can you recognize someone in the crowd in the moment of revolution? When every organ of the body goes beyond its self-awareness and the ways it has learned to be. By brushing aside the hair and seeking a rare memory. A black mole next to the right ear ...'
>
> I now make this private letter common property in these revolutionary conditions :) This letter no longer belongs only to my beloved, but to all the bodies on the street that I have loved so dearly.[17]

The heart of L's essay beats here, in the mirroring alternation between collective figures and the beloved to whom she writes under the image of a face revealed and recognised in the lightness of a lock of hair stubbornly tumbling over her brow as we take our first giddy steps in the open.

But to state the hard fact: prison was coming. The regime answered Woman, Life, Freedom the only way they knew how: brutal, stupid force, a slap in the face, despite the would-be subtleties of their secret police and intelligence agents. The people on the street were beaten and killed. Thousands of girls were poisoned through school lunches because women had made something so powerful happen. Protestors were convicted on the basis of forced confessions, that is, confessions extracted under psychological and physical torture, as well as the threat of retaliation against family members. They were served prison sentences, others executed.

In solitary confinement, in the interrogation room, what image will help you? Off the street, out of the open, without the moment's warmth, is a figure still yours?

The courage of long-time political prisoners, like Niloufar Bayani, Morad Tahbaz, Sepideh Kashani-Doust, Sepideh Qoliyan ... became very important. A friend of mine, who is an ex-inmate of Evin Prison, worked all autumn to get their statements published. She told me: 'Most young people don't know yet what they will face. They have mostly not done prison time. That's why it's so important to write, now, to warn them about the tactics and psychological torture that will be used to extract forced confessions. So that they can resist it, and not be surprised, and know that others have made it through, and that if they crack they do not need to feel ashamed. It is important for the long-term prisoners to speak, now.'

G. Karamustafa, Prison Paintings, 1972. Salt Research. Harika-Kemali Söylemezoğlu Archive.

In 1937, Brecht learned that Carola Neher, who had also fled in 1933, was now a prisoner in a camp in the Soviet Union. He wrote a second *Lehrgedicht* for her, truer and deeper than the first, which he never published. No longer 'to' her, because no letter could reach her, the poem was placed under her initials.

Washing[18]
C.N.[19]

When I showed you years ago
How you should wash yourself in the early morning
With bits of ice in the water
Of the little copper pot
Plunging face in, eyes open
While you patted dry with the rough towel
I read, from the sheet on the wall, the heavy lines
Of your role, and said:
This you do for yourself and do it
exemplarily [*vorbildlich*].

Now I hear, you must be in captivity.
The letters I wrote for you [*für dich*]
Remain unanswered. The friends I approached for you
Are silent. I can do nothing for you. How
Might your morning be? Will you still do something for yourself [*für dich*]?
Hopefully and responsibly
With good movements, exemplary ones?

Its first stanza recollects Brecht's first poem, but prison casts a shadow on the memory. The time of day has changed. C.N. is no longer washing to 'refresh' herself amidst a day's work, but in the early morning, to begin another day and stay human. 'The heavy lines of your role': we reread their difficulty, where *schwierig* becomes *schwer* ... The same lesson, *verbatim*, closes the stanza, but, in prison, this lesson changes meaning. History has brought out its consequences.

Care and exemplarity – the 'for yourself', forwards and backwards – make it possible to go on learning and teaching in prison. The way C.N. has learned to learn is the only one that can allow her to study after losing the open world. But nothing is guaranteed. We are not with her. Her morning is the night of a question.

At the poem's end, new words appear: 'Hopefully and responsibly.' No promise is given from outside. This hope, this promise, she must become it. If she can, at all.

When she was free, Carola Neher knew how to teach and learn 'for herself', 'on her own'. Can she do so where she is today?

Like the first, this poem too concedes its limit: however her morning may be, it is for everyone else a night. Yet an image of the night, of the question of the morning and the act that answers it, is what we so much wish for, today, what we need to stay brave as the state cracks down. But now the actor's art forsakes us. Eurydice, an image that falls.

I remember another conversation with my friend. She was angry about the mess that new, especially short-term, inmates make. 'There are rules in the ward! Some new prisoners come in and do whatever they want … TV blasting, at all hours, messes in the common space … But they know *nothing*. You just got here, to serve a short sentence, but the ward has been here for decades, and I've been here for four years, and N was a prisoner for twelve years already.'

'They made me so angry. Always drama and a lot of noise; they completely disrespect P, or S. She has been through enough, just listen to her and don't make a constant annoyance. But there are always new ones, and it's always the same headache.'

'You were also new', I replied. 'But you weren't like that. Maybe that's what helped you, I mean, helped you not to crack.'

'Everybody cracks.'

'But when you cracked, you weren't alone, and you had teachers. You could ask N or P for advice, "Please, tell me how you've held yourself together."'

'No, you don't bother her. She has enough.'

'Oh', I said and shut up.

'You don't have to ask her. Just watch her walk.'

Under international pressure, the state tried to save appearances. In mid-March, one of my friend's fellow-prisoners was released from Evin. She had served almost five years for taking part in the worker's struggle at the Haft Tappeh sugarcane mill. BBC Persian and other news outlets reposted a video of her release.[20]

In the short video, Sepideh Qoliyan is skipping down the hill in front of Evin prison. She is red and gold from head to toe, bouquets in both hands and under her arms, overflowing, with rings of flowers on her head.

As she bounces down the street, she spins around, cups a hand to her mouth, and sings from the bottom of her lungs.

Khamenei, you are Zahhāk, we will put you underground.[21]

Someone touches her elbow, trying, it seems, to retain her. She yells again.

Khamenei, you are Zahhāk, we will put you underground.

The whole clip lasts only a few seconds, then loops.

She was dressed for celebration and her song meant, 'Who do you think you'll fool, granting concessions as though it were all a misunderstanding? Do you think I will thank you for my release, after you took five years of my life away? Hypocrites. Do you think we will stop now, as you give ground? You're afraid. You're on your back foot now, and we'll push, and you'll fall.'

I shared her image with everyone I knew because of the hope it gave me, and bounced with her joy, all day, not knowing that she was arrested hours later. Her mother too. They were driving south, towards their home. The intelligence service took her to Block 209 at Evin Prison, the interrogation block where those who are arrested are kept, at first, in solitary confinement for an undefined duration. It is a place where people are tortured and threatened, psychologically and physically, in order to force a confession.

The second image unplugged the first. It was unbearable to see her again in her dress with her flowers because it was impossible to see both images at the same time. Her morning was just a question.

But after the shock, one sees that she knew. She knew exactly what would happen. If you can stand to look at her again, you'll see where she is. It is already there, in her smile, song, bounce. There are not two images, here, a day and a night, but one. Sepideh's sun. Nothing was secret.

Brecht could only ask how C.N.'s mornings might be; whether she did something 'for herself', whether she washed 'hopefully and responsibly'. What he can't say, and she can't show, Sepideh Qoliyan radiates. Just watch her walk.

G. Karamustafa, Prison Paintings, 1972. Salt Research, Harika-Kemali Söylemezoğlu Archive. [Political prisoner Sepideh Qolian shared this painting on her Instagram account on September 9, 2021, with a post reporting on the conditions of those living in Bushehr Central Prison]

These pages are a shadow cast by the figures of the Iranian uprising.

A figure 'takes' in a situation, when someone runs ahead of herself, when she 'strikes' its pose before she expects it. Because this was not my case the figures of the Iranian uprising were never truly figures for me. The shadow they cast was, yes, hope. But my words do not carry any risk. Only, under her initials, the break between my *for* and *you*.

In the first days of the uprising, a grammatical figure crystallised on Persian social media: *baraye*, 'for'. Shervin Hajipour collected around thirty *baraye* from social media and set them to music.[22]

Some are hopes or loyalties; others denounce or refuse. All are promises and each promise is its author's own. Like Sepideh Qoliyan and so many others, Shervin Hajipour was arrested, full of hope and staking everything.

Baraye ('For')[23]

For dancing in the alleys
For the fear when kissing
For my sister, your sister, our sisters
For changing rusted minds
For the shame of poverty
For the regret of living an ordinary life
For the dumpster-diving children and their wishes
For this dictatorial economy
For this polluted air
For Valiasr and its worn-out trees
For Pirooz and the possibility of his extinction
For the innocent banned stray dogs
For the unstoppable tears
For the scene of repeating this moment
For the smiling faces
For students and their future
For this forced heaven
For the imprisoned elite students
For the Afghan kids
For all these fors that are beyond repetition

> For all of these meaningless slogans
> For the collapse of fake buildings
> For the feeling of peace
> For the sun after these long nights
> For anxiety and sleeping pills
> For man, homeland, prosperity
> For the girl who wished to be a boy
> For woman, life, freedom
> For freedom
> For freedom
> For freedom[24]

Notes

1. Published first on Harass Watch in the second week of the uprising (counting from Mahsa Amini's murder on September 16 2022).

2. Walter Benjamin, 'Notizen Svendborg Sommer 1934', in *Gesammelte Schriften. 6: Fragmente, autobiographische Schriften*, 1. Aufl., [Nachdr.], Suhrkamp-Taschenbuch Wissenschaft 936 (Frankfurt: Suhrkamp, 2006), 524. My translation.

3. Benjamin's German editors (*GS6*, 816) refer to an early-1930s title, 'Advice to the actress C. N.' (*'Rat an die Schauspielerin C. N.'*). This is, however, the title of two different poems, of which only one treats the 'art of the actor.' The relevant version is, however, absent from Brecht's Suhrkamp *Gesammelte Werke*. Fortunately, it was included in the *Große kommentierte Berliner und Frankfurter Ausgabe*, or BFA, of Brecht's works. See Joyce Crick, 'Power and Powerlessness: Brecht's Poems to Carola Neher', *German Life and Letters* 53:3 (July 2000): 314–24. This pre-1934 poem is echoed by a third, datable to 1937, to which we will return.

4. From Brecht's *Frankfurter Ausgabe*, cited in Crick, 316:

> *Rat an die Schauspielerin C.N.*
> Erfrische dich, Freundin
> An dem Wasser aus dem Kupferkessel mit den Eisstücken
> – Öffne die Augen unter dem Wasser, wasch sie –
> Trockne dich ab mit dem rauhen Tuch und lies
> Vom Blatt an der Wand die schwierigen Zeilen der Rolle.
> Wisse, das tust du für dich und tue es vorbildlich.

The translation provided here adapts Willet's translation of a variant bearing the same title: Bertolt Brecht, *Poems, 1913-1956*, ed. John Willett (New York: Routledge, 1987), 179–180.

5. Benjamin, 'Conversations with Brecht', in *Understanding Brecht* (London: Verso, 1998), 106.

6. Benjamin, 'Conversations', 106.

7. *Zan, Zendegi, Azadi – Jen, Zand, Ajoi* – Woman, Life, Freedom

8. 'Zenan', https://harasswatch.com/news/2049/

9. 'Zenan'. Translated with assistance from Aras Amiri.

10. Two translations are available. I will cite the former.
   'Figuring a Women's Revolution: Bodies Interacting with Their Images', Jadaliyya, https://www.jadaliyya.com/Details/44479
   'Women Reflected in Their Own History', e-flux, https://www.e-flux.com/notes/497512/women-reflected-in-their-own-history

11. This image and the following ones belong to a single series of paintings, which can be found at: https://archives.saltresearch.org/handle/123456789/190443.

12. Cigarette smoke renders teargas less caustic.

13. For this sentence, I have cited the *e-flux* translation.

14. After those she can invoke, she calls on the 'names I have yet to call'. These are not anonymous, either: they are names. Here, the present perfect opens onto the future: '… have yet to call'.

15. Translation modified; L, 'Zenan'. *e-flux* is right to give gender-neutral 'them', since Persian does not have gendered nouns or pronouns.

16. '1357 – azada jem'ea az zendanaan saasa az zendan qesr – aban', https://www.aparat.com/v/c2Li8?t=90

17. L, 'Figuring'. For Farsi interpolations, 'Zenan'.

18. Bertolt Brecht, *Poems, 1913-1956*, 290. German from Bertolt Brecht, *Gedichte 2*, ed. Elisabeth Hauptmann, vol. 9, *Gesammelte Werke* (Frankfurt am Main: Suhrkamp Verlag), 1967.

19. When my friend, who teaches so much, was imprisoned five years ago, this poem became hers. She has since been released.

20. Reposted by BBC Persian, Sepideh Qoliyan's original post remains on her feed. sepide_qoliyan, Instagram, 15 March 2023, https://www.instagram.com/reel/Cpz7dfKvWZS/

21. Zahhāk is a monster from ancient Persian mythology.)

22. 'Baraye Shervin Hajipour (Full Version with English Lyrics) – Baraye', Youtube, https://www.youtube.com/watch?v=LY_U5QfeQQc

23. 'Shervin Hajipour – Baraye', *Genius.com*, https://wwww.genius.com/Shervin-hajipour-baraye-lyrics – with two modifications ('women' to 'woman' and 'men' to 'man', in the last six lines).

24. Shervin Hajipour was released on bail. Sepideh Qoliyan is back in prison, sentenced to two more years. She is out of block 209 and back in the main ward. Next week will mark the one-year anniversary of Jina Amini's murder and of the beginning and first warmth of the movement. It will no doubt be commemorated. We know what promise the people of Iran have become. What will their morning bring? *September 2023 / Shahrivar 1402*

Aijaz Ahmad (1941–2022) in memoriam

Perseverance in the midst of defeat
On Aijaz Ahmad's political writings
Ammar Ali Jan

Defeat shapes the subjectivity of the global Left in the contemporary era. The twin collapse of actually existing socialism and revolutionary nationalisms in the late twentieth century deprived the international communist movement of material support as well as ideological anchorage. A reactionary thesis stemming out of this defeat proclaimed the triumphant victory of global capitalism against socialist despotism, with the combination of liberal democracy and the free market punctuating the definitive end of the tumultuous sequence of revolutionary upheavals that marked modernity, from the French Revolution to the Bolshevik revolution to anticolonial struggles.

This triumphalism was paralleled by what Domenico Losurdo has called the 'self-flagellation of the vanquished', a subjectivity that feels ashamed of its own past.[1] The latter is evident in the form of erstwhile radical political parties that abandoned the idea of a structural transformation of the world in favour of issue-based movements, inadvertently facilitating their integration into the dominant order. At the ideological level, a wide gamut of left-wing, postmodern and postcolonial theorists converged in their criticism of actually existing socialisms, dismissal of Marxism as 'class reductionism' and displacement of materialist analysis by a cultural critique of imperialism.

These transformations were part of an intellectual atmosphere that made the Communist Movement of the twentieth century, with its gigantic achievements and obvious shortcomings, illegible to a range of political activists in the contemporary era. Aijaz Ahmad, as inheritor of this complex legacy, became one of its most eloquent defenders against reactionary attacks and its obfuscation by what he termed the 'Post-condition'.[2] By discussing his work on the rise of the far-right in South Asia, I argue that Ahmad can be read as a theorist of defeat – a disposition that allowed him to explain the counterrevolutions that he witnessed through the historical transformations of our era without abandoning the principles of class struggle and its theoretical correlate, historical materialism, as key weapons in the fight against reactionary forces.

Experiencing defeat

Some of Ahmad's harshest criticisms were reserved for what he termed the 'ironic, detached critic' based in Western academia – someone whose intellectual production was geared towards the academic publishing industry rather than stemming out of any concrete political struggles.[3] Ahmad embedded his own theoretical work within the unfolding struggles in the Global South in which he was an enthusiastic participant. Born and brought up in India, Ahmad moved to Pakistan in his late teens, before returning to India in the 1980s while also living and working in Canada and the US. He belonged to the last generation of individuals in the subcontinent who could claim both India and Pakistan as their homelands. In his career as a militant, he experienced the defeats of the Left in both countries. Here, I want to discuss his work on the coming to power of a right-wing military dictatorship in Pakistan and the rise of Hindu fundamentalism in India. I suggest that many of Ahmad's later criticisms against postmodernism were rooted in his early political writings, where he confronted the simultaneous decline of the Left and the rise of a parochial and punishing form of cultural nationalism.

During the 1970s, Aijaz Ahmad was a member of the Mazdoor Kisan Party (Workers and Peasants Party) in Pakistan and worked actively to organise the party across the country. One of Ahmad's most underrated and magisterial essays, 'Democracy and Dictatorship in Pakistan', was written while he was active in the Pakistani Left.[4] The essay includes his analysis of the rise of the left-wing populist Zulfiqar Ali Bhutto (1966 to 1970), his stint in power (1971 to 1977) and his government's overthrow by the right-wing dictatorship of General Zia-ul-Haq (1977). Written in 1978, one year after the coup d'etat and one year before Bhutto was hanged by the military junta, the essay excavated the myriad contradictions that underpin postcolonial society, offering a Marxist account of the limits of bourgeois radicalism and the dangers of right-wing reaction.

Ahmad pointed out that Bhutto's populist government was ridden with ideological and social contradictions as it tried to manoeuvre between its working class support base and the interests of the entrenched ruling elites. Bhutto nationalised major industries, initiated land reforms, increased rural credit and moved towards an independent foreign policy. At the same time, he handed over control of industries to bureaucratic elites, failed to implement land reforms, and accepted harsh austerity measures from the IMF. More crucially, Bhutto relied on the Pakistan military, which had gained global notoriety for conducting a brutal military operation in East Pakistan (now Bangladesh) in 1971, to crush his left-wing political opponents. In an ironic twist, the same military overthrew Bhutto's government in a coup d'etat on the 5th of July, 1977.

Ahmad was quick to note that Bhutto had done enough to terrify the ruling elites but without substantially undermining their power. The July coup was their reaction against the mildly pro-labour policies of the Bhutto government, a reaction that deployed the veneer of religion. Instead of signalling an 'authentic' awakening, Islam was used by the reactionary elites to displace the language of socialism and class struggle in their quest to eliminate threats to their property and privilege. As the Zia regime turned the repressive apparatus into the primary vehicle for politics, it used the intertwining discourses of religion and national security to imprison and torture political opponents, introduced public floggings, disbanded trade unions and students unions, and turned Pakistan into a frontline state in a US-sponsored 'Jihad' against the Soviet-backed government in Afghanistan, a situation that led many – including Ahmad – to flee into exile.

In the 1980s, Ahmad arrived in India, where he worked closely with social movements and remained close to the Communist Party of India (Marxist). Following the collapse of the Soviet Union, India witnessed the abrupt liberalisation of the economy as well as the meteoric rise of the Hindu fundamentalist Bharatiya Janata Party (BJP). Writing in the aftermath of the destruction of the Babri mosque by Hindu fanatics in 1992, Ahmad traced the growing strength of reactionary forces in his essay 'Right-wing Politics and the Cultures of Cruelty', which has become a classic for understanding the rise of religious nationalism in India.[5]

Ahmad argued that India's incorporation into the free market system had created immense social tensions, leading to a decline in support for the traditional secular parties, especially the Congress. Sensing a weak centre, a 'counter-revolutionary elite' stunned the country by mobilising the masses in a series of communal riots and 'revivalist terror', strategically using electoral calculus, implicit state support and political violence in a coordinated 'hurricane from below' to propel the BJP to power. The ideological war waged by the Hindu Right included a set of presumptions that would come to dominate the thinking of reactionary movements, including an 'anti-liberal conception of nationalism, anti-rationalist critique of Modernity, anti-humanist assaults on the politics of liberation, in a rhetoric of "blood and belonging", and in the name of a glorious past that never was.'[6]

The End of History, manifested in the form of the Hindu Right, produced an insular and punishing politics that targeted minorities in pursuit of a homogenous identity and celebrated the most retrogressive elements from India's past. Today, with the continued dominance of Narendra Modi's BJP in India and the Pakistani military's tightening grip over the country's politics, Ahmad's words of caution on the rise of regressive, illiberal identitarian politics appear prophetic.

Defending the revolutionary tradition

Ahmad's later criticism of postcolonial theorists who celebrated 'alterity' and cultural nationalism stemmed from his intimate experience with authoritarianism in the Global South. Rather than taking comfort in cultural explanations, Ahmad characterised the rise of religious nationalisms in South Asia as a violent response to labour militancy and democratic aspirations of marginalised communities, linking their emergence to objective conditions such as the dislocations caused by neoliberalism and the geostrategic imperatives of US imperialism in the region.

The 1980s and 1990s experienced far-right offensives on a planetary scale, from the Iranian Revolution to the fall of the Socialist bloc and its replacement by oligarchs. This political defeat was matched by an ideological retreat in academia that discarded Marxism as yet another metanarrative of colonial modernity and sought to replace it with micro struggles around identity and cultural difference. By contrast, experience had taught Ahmad the disastrous consequences of abandoning grand projects of emancipation. His criticism of Lyotard and other postmodern thinkers for their celebration of the end of metanarratives stemmed from the recognition that in the midst of violent communal passions, unbridled neoliberalism, pervasive militarism and grand millenarian fantasies of resurrecting an imagined past, the only universalism that was obliterated from popular (and academic) discourses was the egalitarian promise of emancipation.[7] The end of the universalism of the Left manifested itself in the rise of universal horror.

Walter Benjamin famously stated that '*even the dead will not be safe from the enemy if he wins*'.[8] The defeats of the Left have resulted in a concerted assault on the memory of revolutionary movements, including their stigmatisation by conservative and postcolonial thinkers, albeit for different reasons. Ahmad's theoretical work, including his polemics with the giants of literary theory, is an attempt to come to terms with these failures without abandoning the democratic impulse inherent in them. His belated defence of the Soviet Union, which he considered an essential pillar of support to anti-imperialist struggles in the Global South, was part of his attempt to salvage the genuine solidarities and internationalisms produced by socialist states at a time when the academic world had confined them to the dustbins of history.[9]

Ahmad's insistence on holding onto the memory of revolutionary pasts despite experiencing catastrophic defeats showed that he believed that the human adventure is not finished, that there could still be an alternative trajectory for humanity different from the mediocrity of the contemporary moment. In this regard, Ahmad's legacy is one of hope in dark times and the courage to sustain it in the face of repeated defeat and pervasive ideological disorientation. It is a provocation to the Left to shake off the paralysing subjectivity of shame, resume the difficult task of creatively rethinking Marxism grounded in the accumulated experience of revolutionary movements and link theoretical texts to existing political struggles in order to rebuild global solidarities – a task in which nothing less than the future of humanity is at stake.

Ammar Ali Jan is a historian of communist thought in the Global South and a member of the Haqooq-e-Khalq (People's Rights) Party.

Notes

1. Domenico Losurdo, 'Flight from History? The Communist Movement between Self-Criticism and Self-Contempt', *Nature, Society, and Thought* 13:3 (2000), 457–514.
2. Aijaz Ahmad, 'Post Colonial Theory and the "Post-" Condition', *Socialist Register* 33 (1997), 353–381.
3. Aijaz Ahmad, *In Theory: Nations, Classes, Literatures* (London: Verso: 2008).
4. Aijaz Ahmad, 'Democracy and Dictatorship in Pakistan', *Journal of Contemporary Asia* 1:5 (1978), 477–512.
5. Aijaz Ahmad, 'Right-wing Politics and the Cultures of Cruelty', *Social Scientist* 26:10 (1998), 3–25.
6. Ahmad, 'Right-wing Politics', 4.
7. See Ahmad, 'Post Colonial Theory and the 'Post'-Condition'.
8. Walter Benjamin, *Selected Writings, Volume 4, 1938-1949*, ed. Michael Jennings (Cambridge: Harvard University Press, 2006), 389–400.
9. Aijaz Ahmad, 'Originality of the October Revolution', *Marxist* 33:1-2 (2017), 1–18.

Decoding the 'Bandung Moment'
Aijaz Ahmad on decolonisation
Rafeef Ziadah

Aijaz Ahmad's work traversed several disciplines: literary criticism, history, Marxist theory and philosophy, politics and political economy. His book *In Theory* navigated the intersections of class, nationalism and literature, offering a critique of postcolonial theory at the height of its popularity.[10] His insights in essays like 'Imperialism of our time' were a thought-provoking commentary on the continuities of imperialism written as the US and its allies launched a second war on Iraq following years of deadly sanctions.[11] In this work, Ahmad centred historical analysis, while offering astute observations on the influence of the US knowledge industry in shaping global elites after World War II. Such analysis was critical to the burgeoning anti-war movement and the debates surrounding the concept of the 'new imperialism' at the time. In what follows, I reflect on two aspects of his writing that offer valuable insights for contemporary debates around decolonisation: first, his analysis of the historic Bandung conference in 1955, which brought together leaders from newly independent or soon-to-be independent Asian and African states, marking a significant moment in the history of decolonisation. Second, his critique of the academic operationalisation of the term 'Orientalism' and its implications.

The Bandung Moment

Ahmad's attention to colonialism and imperialism is striking, particularly in contrast to certain Western Marxist perspectives that neglect their role in the development of capitalism. He insisted that 'colonialism was not an incidental, epiphenomenal or episodic feature of the development of capitalism', adding that 'neglect of this fact has marred much Marxist theory of capitalism'.[12] Like other scholars shaped by and through anticolonial struggles, he understood both analytically, but also at a visceral level, the place of colonialism in shaping the world we live in. Unable to reclaim Indian citizenship due to legal provisions that prevented those who became Pakistani citizens after partition from doing so, Ahmad was acutely aware of the contradictions and power struggles within postcolonial states and the array of elite formations that emerged through anti-colonial struggles.

Amidst the renewed interest in uncovering the neglected histories of decolonisation, including the place of the Bandung conference in consolidating Afro-Asian solidarity, Ahmad's work helps us to move beyond a hagiographic retelling of that moment. First, it is relevant to note that the contemporary effort to uncover anticolonial histories emerges in the face of a persistent historical amnesia and 'post-imperial melancholia', particularly prevalent in England, where the loss and legacy of formal Empire remain unaddressed.[13] This act of historical erasure perpetuates the misconception that anticolonial movements ultimately resulted in failed experiments, corrupt states and dictatorial regimes – flattening the terrain of decolonisation and reducing it to a simplistic narrative of Cold War politics. In this sense, I consider Ahmad's analysis essential in helping us to decipher and reconstruct a more nuanced understanding of the past, one that goes beyond mere narration, serving as a valuable resource to inform our present aspirations for decolonisation.

In his chapter 'Three Worlds Theory and Bandung' (*In Theory*, chapter 8), Ahmad methodically endeavours to decode the official language employed in Bandung and situates the conference within the regional dynamics of the time. For example, he notes that China and India, two of the major actors of the conference, 'both needed a forum where they could assert their leadership – part collaborative part competing – in the region.'[14] He writes that, in this context, the term Third World 'does not come to us as a mere descriptive category, to designate a geographical location or a specific relation with imperialism alone. It carries within it contradictory layers of meaning and political purpose', noting that 'in the conception of its chief nationalist exponents – Nehru, Nasser, Sukarno – the term was indissolubly linked to the containment of communism and a "mixed" economy of the private and state capitalist sectors'.[15] In this way, Ahmad captures the ambitions of decolonisation, but also the tragedy of its truncation by nationalist priorities within the context of 'mixed' economies.

Ahmad's examination of the term 'Third World' thus urges us to delve into the internal political dynamics of the main proponents of Bandung, including centrally Egypt and Indonesia under Nasser and Sukarno, respectively. He argues that decoding the language used at the conference is essential, as 'words constantly exceeded their intended meanings, simultaneously slippery and hermeticised.'[16] Through this act of decoding, Ahmad masterfully highlights the inherent contradiction of the 'Bandung moment' – its dual character – acknowledging the genuine aspirations and anti-imperialist objectives, while cautioning against its elevation of Third Wordlist nationalism, especially as its key figures were waging domestic battles, often very deadly, against internal opposition movements composed largely of mass communist parties. This is an important thread in the writings of Frantz Fanon, Walter Rodney and Samir Amin, who were similarly attentive to the utilisation of nationalism and anti-imperialist rhetoric to consolidate national capital and 'mixed economies' that helped newly cohering national bourgeoisies to further projects of accumulation in international capitalist circuits.

Ahmad's approach to the Bandung Conference thus goes beyond simplistic celebration or dismissal. Rather, he invites us to conduct a nuanced examination of the competing regional powers, oppositional movements and ideological currents that were contending for hegemony during that period, emphasising that the outcomes were never predetermined. The scope of this analysis and his attentiveness to both regional and internal political dynamics is valuable beyond the Bandung moment of course. It invites us to always consider multiple scales and to reflect on the disparity between official anti-imperialist rhetoric and the actual actions of states in relation to local opposition. In the contemporary political landscape, attending to this distinction is crucial.

Orientalism and after

Ahmad's rejection of an essentialised Third World aligns with his critique of Edward Said's *Orientalism* (articulated in chapter 5 of *In Theory*). Ahmad was particularly concerned by the imposition of a binary between East and West and especially by the placement of Marxist theory within this binary. More specifically he took issue with Said's dismissal of Marx as being part of the Orientalist canon. This specific chapter of Ahmad's work was met with both acclaim and controversy. Benita Parry saw it as 'a critique mishandled'.[17] In hindsight, the tone and framing of the debate appears to have been a missed opportunity for a more 'reparative reading' that could have fostered a constructive engagement between Said and Ahmad.[18]

However, to fully understand the contentious nature of the debate, it is important to consider the historical context in which Ahmad was writing. This period was characterised by the neoliberal turn that emerged after the collapse of the Soviet Union and the end of the Cold War. There was a prevailing perception of dissolution and a belief that Marxism had become irrelevant, leading to its dismissal as an orientalist relic of the past. Ahmad's critique, therefore, exhibited a noticeable defensiveness that, at times, overshadowed the central arguments put forth. These arguments around postcolonialism, presented differently by various scholars, point to the shortcomings of the West/East binary in Said's writing, which can lead to overlooking the dynamics of class and racial hierarchies within postcolonial states as well as the long history of oppositional Marxist movements in the process of decolonisation.[19]

Despite disagreements over Ahmad's approach to *Orientalism* as a text, there is a crucial lesson in this chapter that I continue to find very useful. Even as it sometimes conflated Said's use of the term 'Orientalism' with its subsequent usage, the essay highlighted its instrumentalisation by elite scholars from the global South to assert their putatively subaltern status in the metropolitan academy while disregarding the internal hierarchies within their societies (and their own place within them). This observation remains relevant today as it pushes us to consider how terminologies that emerge within a certain context can go on to have different lives. For example, this can be gleaned in the widespread embrace of Antonio Gramsci's concept of 'hegemony', which at times overlooks his focus on the role of subaltern classes. Similarly, terms such as 'intersectionality' and 'decolonisation' have been reduced through their popularisation to a superficial understanding focused solely on diversity.

Ahmad's analysis of 'orientalism' prompts us to trace the trajectory of concepts and critically assess how they are later operationalised and assimilated within the context of neoliberal university settings. This is particularly relevant today when considering the various understandings of decolonising the curriculum, for instance. On the one hand, radical student demands advocate for a transformed university system that encompasses free education and anti-racist curricula. On the other, lies a shallow approach that aligns well with market-driven education, treating the process as a mere marketing exercise aimed at appealing to diverse audiences. Ahmad's approach is useful for navigating the inherent tensions within such concepts.

Aijaz Ahmad fearlessly explored a wide range of subjects, capturing the essence of the political moment and movements beyond the classroom. Through his writing, he ignited critical debates that, even amidst disagreement, proved instrumental in enhancing our analytical perspectives. His insights will continue to be invaluable in understanding the nuances and intersections of class, nationalism and literature.

Rafeef Ziadah is Senior Lecturer in Politics and Public Policy in the Department of International Development, KCL.

Notes

10. Aijaz Ahmad, *In Theory: Classes, Nations, Literatures* (London: Verso, 1994).
11. Aijaz Ahmad, 'Imperialism of our time', *Socialist Register* 40 (2004), 43–62.
12. Ahmad, 'Imperialism of our time', 53.
13. Paul Gilroy, *Postcolonial Melancholia* (New York: Columbia University Press, 2005).
14. Ahmad, *In Theory*, 294.
15. Ahmad, *In Theory*, 307.
16. Ahmad, *In Theory*, 297.
17. Benita Parry, 'A Critique Mishandled', *Social Text* 35 (1993), 121–133.
18. Rahul Rao, 'Recovering Reparative Readings of Postcolonialism and Marxism', *Critical Sociology* 43:4-5 (2017), 587–598.
19. Sadik Jalal Al-'Azm, 'Orientalism and Orientalism in Reverse', *Khamsin* 8 (1981), 5–26; James Clifford, Review of *Orientalism* in *History and Theory* 19:2 (1980), 204–23; Benita Parry, *Postcolonial Studies: A Materialist Critique* (Abingdon: Routledge, 2004); Neil Lazarus, 'The Fetish of "the West" in Postcolonial Theory', in *Marxism, Modernity and Postcolonial Studies*, eds. Crystal Bartolovich and Neil Lazarus (Cambridge: Cambridge University Press, 2002), 43–64.

Reading 'the Signs of Our Times'
Aijaz Ahmad on literature and the world
Rashmi Varma

With the publication of *In Theory* in 1992, Aijaz Ahmad threw a spanner into the works of what seemed at the time to be the relentless march of postcolonial theory within departments of English and comparative literary studies in the Anglo-American academy.[20] The increasing power of this purportedly new field of study was made possible, Ahmad would argue, because postcolonial theory had been comprehensively and uncritically hitched to the poststructuralist wagon. In this context, *In Theory*'s appearance became an event because it announced, with a bang, the voice of an India-born Marxist scholar based in India and the US whose powerful polemic set about demolishing the theoretical edifice in which Homi Bhabha, Edward Said and Gayatri Spivak had established themselves as the holy trinity of the field of postcolonial studies. Ahmad, like Arif Dirlik and E. San Juan Jr., among others, was pointing to the fact that these academics had found a foothold within the Western academy precisely at the moment of the defeat of Third World liberation movements and the decline of Marxism as a theoretical and practical resource that was precipitated by the modish tendencies of deconstruction and colonial discourse theory.[21] For Ahmad, the emergence of the field of postcolonial studies and Third World literature was thus based on the elision of what he considered to be 'the fundamental dialectic – between imperialism, decolonization, and the struggles for socialism'.[22]

Ahmad's blistering critique of erstwhile Third World academics as belonging to the 'comprador class' that was divorced from grassroots movements for socialist transformation was, however, seen even by progressive and Left-oriented scholars as unnecessarily personalised and lacking in generosity. Other insights into how exile and migrancy were being valorised as the archetypal postcolonial condition while 'submerging the class question',[23] and how colonial discourse theory was dismissive of questions of political economy and of politics *per se*, were developed with greater engagement with the field of literary studies by postcolonial studies' internal dissidents such as Benita Parry and Neil Lazarus.[24] But while theirs could be seen as 'interventions' in the culturalist critiques of imperialism that had come to define ways of doing postcolonial studies, Ahmad's ambition was to unsettle the very intellectual ground upon which the theory and field had taken root.

Beyond the polemic, of course, Said, Spivak and Bhabha, among others, had critical differences and were substantially different from each other, but that is not immediately relevant to this piece. It is also important to note that Ahmad was hardly reticent in his attack on a Marxist literary critic such as Fredric Jameson (whom he, in a strange move, designated as a comrade who was also 'a civilisational other') for his theorisation of Third World literature, although in subsequent iterations he acknowledged Jameson's contributions to a materialist dialectical reading of literature in the context of late capitalism and seemed to regret, 'as a matter of considerable personal irritation', that his criticisms of Jameson were opportunistically weaponised by poststructuralist critics hostile to Marxism.[25] In her defence of Said against Ahmad's critique, Parry wrote of her 'distaste for the conduct of an argument which, in deploying recrimination as an analytic strategy, misrepresenting the substance of alternative enquiries and adducing these to retrograde ideological interests, cannot but recall that device of polemical assassination contrived long ago by traditional Communist Parties in an attempt to disable other left tendencies'.[26] There were others, besides Parry, who were also uncomfortable with his criticisms of individual academics, particularly of Said who was hailed as an important voice speaking for the Palestinian cause in the American imperium, even as they may have been on board with his criticisms of the transparent careerism and professionalisation of the emergent class of postcolonial theorists that was complicit with the capitalist interests of the academy. So whether or not one reads Ahmad's work as divisive and ungenerous, as Parry contends, it is true that one wouldn't turn to him for citations of Marxist literary theorists who were fighting similar battles against the poststructuralist hegemony on the same ground (some of whom, like Parry, had remained for the longest time outside the folds of formal institutional settings). Nevertheless, what Ahmad posited with such brilliance, erudition and audacity was not just a critique of professionalism but a resolute affirmation of anti-professionalism at a time when the Anglo-American academy had become the site of the making of academic stars, with eyewatering salaries and cult followings.[27] Ultimately, Ahmad, who had taught at various universities in Canada and the US and had spent close to three decades teaching at institutions in India, ended up at the University of California at Irvine when the authoritarian Hindu nationalist Narendra Modi came to power in India in 2014. It was an ironic twist of fate since UC Irvine had hosted key poststructuralists earlier and gave them an important base in the US. It must however be said that to the end, Ahmad refused the frills and seductions of postcolonial theory and its institutional power, even as it had begun to wane by the time Ahmad found refuge in Irvine.

Ahmad's incisive critiques of the institutionalisation of Third World literature as an object of First World interests, 'unthinkable without metropolitan mediations', were crucial in injecting a necessary groundedness and materiality to the study of texts amidst the glib celebrations of the arrival of multiculturalism in the Anglo-American academy. But there always seemed to be a troubling gap in his critical writings, between his magisterial accounts (he frequently referred to the importance and necessity of the sweeping account of history) of the formation of fields of study such as postcolonial theory and Third World, Indian and Urdu literature, and his analyses of particular writers and their texts. Writers as varied as Saadat Hasan Manto, Qurratulain Hyder, Salman Rushdie and others, despite their stunning literary talents, remain for Ahmad unable to transcend the limits of their social location and class formation.

Ahmad's interpretations of Salman Rushdie and Arundhati Roy's texts are particularly illustrative of this gap. In both, his reading of the ideology of form becomes entangled with his analysis of the ideology of the author. Thus, while his masterful analyses of post-war Anglo-American academic institutions and the contradictions therein, as well as his synoptic account of Indian and Urdu literature, are forceful and insightful, his actual readings of texts seem to abjure the dialectical mode in favour of ideology critique. Ahmad was, of course, well aware that Marx saw Balzac as providing 'accurate and enduring analyses of post-Revolutionary France' despite his royalism. In a similar vein, he notes that Lenin had considered *Anna Karenina* a great novel even in the face of its social conservatism. Tolstoy's accurate and detailed rendition of the dominant ideologies of his time, in which he himself was wholly complicit, only confirms for Ahmad, as he puts it, that 'fictions can only be read within the conditions of their own possibility which are historical, ideological and formal'. It is the formulation *can only be read* that takes away from literature in particular, and art in general, the utopian possibilities of exceeding and transcending *the conditions of their own possibility*, a limit that Ahmad imposed on his readings and that seems to have haunted his literary criticism.

Ahmad's criticism of Rushdie's *Shame* entails a reading of the novel that sees it as unrelentingly hopeless in its representation of postcolonial Pakistan, which is portrayed as a claustrophobic world with no scope for resistance.[28] While conceding that the novel is written in the mode of political satire, he can only hear in it 'a laughter that laughs too much', engendered by an author who romanticises his outsider position to mock and parody the East from a distance. Ahmad reads the novel as cynical and as playing to the literary gallery of the postmodernist establishment of the time in its valorisation of exile as a universal condition of modernity and its portrayal of the postcolonial world as intrinsically corrupt and bleak. While satire has long been a crucial literary weapon for emancipatory politics, Ahmad finds that the real-life figures of Bhutto and Zia who are lampooned in the novel were in fact dangerous tyrants, too dangerous to be laughed at. I don't think Rushdie would disagree with the former claim, but the proposition that some tyrants are too dangerous to be mocked seems to deny satire its potency. Rushdie's satire fails because ultimately, for Ahmad, resistance must conform to, and should be mediated via, a particular mode of organised working class politics that he regards as absent from

Rushdie's novel. No doubt Ahmad's unease with Rushdie's work emanated from his own involvement with the Mazdoor Kisan Party (the Workers and Peasants Party, later incarnated as the Communist Mazdoor Kisan Party) in Lahore. There, along with other Left stalwarts such as Feroze Ahmad, Eqbal Ahmad and Hamza Alavi, Ahmad had been part of a 'Professors Group' that organised Marxist study circles for the workers.[29] Even so, one could quibble with his reading of *Shame* and its politics of resistance: while the object of Rushdie's satire is the closed world of Pakistan's elites, it is a world that is fraying because of tensions around class and gender. One is further struck by the underspecification of the working class that Ahmad imagines as the protagonist of all emancipatory literature.

Ahmad's analysis of *Shame* falters especially when he makes the mistake that all teachers of literature tell their students not to make – which is to blur the gap between the narrator of a text and its author. On this account, his reading of Rushdie is also oddly poignant in spite of the many pages that he writes excoriating Rushdie for looking at 'the East' from the perspective of Western theoretical and literary traditions. One can't help but notice their biographical commonalities, even as the differences remain critical. Both were born in India (Ahmad in 1941, Rushdie in 1947 – the year of India's independence) and considered it their original home. Ahmad went to Pakistan to complete his college education, only to leave for the US during the student uprisings of the late 1960s. He returned to Pakistan in the early 1970s after obtaining higher education degrees in the US. He was to leave Pakistan again for the US after the coup by General Zia ul-Haq in 1977, eventually making his way 'back' to India in 1985. The coup was of course the historical event that spurred Rushdie to write *Shame*. The resonances intensify in the fact that Rushdie also tried to return to India to live there (a possibility foreclosed by the banning of *The Satanic Verses* in India in 1988) but eventually made his home in the West even as he returned to India unwaveringly in all his fiction. Ultimately, Ahmad's history of having had a Pakistani passport, which he had relinquished, prevented him from gaining Indian citizenship even after decades of living, writing and teaching there.

The differences with Rushdie seemed to unnerve Ahmad far more than the similarities of shared beginnings. He left Pakistan when political corruption and the decimation of the Left seemed all too final, while the narrator of *Shame* (who for Ahmad is none other than Rushdie) seems to have chosen a self-exile enabled by class privilege and family wealth – a deracinated position from which he narrates the tale of corruption and decay in postcolonial Pakistan. This seems to have rattled Ahmad so much that he felt compelled to point out, even against the backdrop of the 1989 *fatwa* issued by Ayatollah Khomeini against Rushdie for blasphemy in writing *The Satanic Verses*, that 'it took a principally *literary* event – the macabre sentencing of Salman Rushdie for selling certain novelizations of Islam to British and American corporate publishing – for protest campaigns against Khomeini to envelop that very literary intelligentsia which had never bothered when that same clerical state had tortured and actually killed countless communists and other patriots.'[30] It was clear by now that Ahmad's sense of solidarity could not be extended to Rushdie who remained for him someone who had turned exile into a lucrative career. We can interpret this withholding of solidarity to a fellow writer either as signifying a singular lack of generosity or as a dogged commitment to the unknown writers assassinated by authoritarian regimes across the world. But does it have to be one or the other?

On Arundhati Roy's Booker Prize-winning novel *The God of Small Things* (1997), Ahmad wrote one of the most critical reviews in the pages of the left-wing *Frontline* magazine for which he was a regular commentator.[31] Here he generously acknowledges Roy as 'the first Indian writer in English' in whose work 'a marvellous stylistic resource becomes available for provincial, vernacular culture without any effect of exoticism or estrangement, and without the book reading as a translation'. Rushdie's style, on the other hand, is too much of a mishmash of the vernacular and the postmodern and too derivative of the Latin American magical realists to qualify as exemplary. But in spite of the fulsome praise for Roy's style, Ahmad finds her novel to be a 'curious mixture of matchless achievement and quite drastic failings', chief among which was how 'the book panders to the prevailing anti-Communist sentiment, which damages it both ideologically and formally'. For Ahmad, Roy's inclusion of a character such as Comrade Pillai, presumably a fictional figure who symbolises the corruptions of the local branch of the Communist Party of India (Marxist) and is complicit in the murderous assault on the 'untouchable' Velutha, demonstrates how she 'has neither a *feel* for Communist politics nor perhaps rudimentary knowledge of it'. Ahmad takes particular exception to the references to E. M. S. Namboodiripad, 'an actual historical figure and a towering presence in Kerala and beyond', declaring them to be libellous and written in 'spite, pure and simple'.[32]

But if Ahmad's objections can seem petty and partisan to some readers, it was on another ground that his critique of Roy converges with his critique of Rushdie – namely, the representation of the erotic as a transcendent form of politics. Acknowledging that Roy writes with great emotional depth and 'with devastating precision' about caste (although finding her less insightful on matters of class), he nonetheless castigates her for suggesting that it is 'private transgression through which one transcends public injuries'.[33] More sympathetic readers might consider this unfair as the novel can also be read as a powerful evocation of a dying provincial feudal order transformed by satellite television, Gulf money and World Bank aid into a world in which an 'untouchable' Paravan like Velutha can not only dare to love an upper-caste woman but also imagine himself as a worker and organise others around him into a class.

In Ahmad's reading, ultimately, both Rushdie and Roy are of necessity tethered to 'the themes and ideologies that are currently dominant in the social fraction' in which they are located and to which they speak. One sees this same tendency to situate the author in their social location and especially their class position in his brilliant account of Urdu literature in the Indian subcontinent.[34] Qurratulain Hyder, for all her literary talents, remains embedded in the bourgeois social class that embraced liberal nationalism as a panacea for the violence and grief of nationalist wars and partitions. As such, on Ahmad's reading, her fiction is unable to transcend the limitations of her privileged inheritances. But there was another side to this coin in Ahmad's belief that 'the most pressing research agendas for literary critics and theorists can arise only out of the situations which they in fact live'.[35] Thus it was that both the writer and the critic must narrate and theorise the lived situations of their class, nation and social location.

In 2000, Ahmad wrote a brilliant essay on world literature and *The Communist Manifesto*.[36] In a period in which 'world literary studies', or what the Warwick Research Collective defines as 'the literature of the capitalist world-system', has come to eclipse older categories of Third World and postcolonial literature, Ahmad's essay should receive a great deal more attention than it has not only for how it demonstrates a more dialectical turn in his critical writings but also for how it posits the utopian possibilities for a genuine socialist transformation via literature.[37] If Marx and Engels wrote their manifesto at a time when capitalism as 'a global unifying force' was becoming visible and demanded critical attention, Ahmad's response came at a time when late capitalist globalisation was seen as promising to shrink the world through communication technologies and finance capital.

Ahmad's essay engages critically with the hope that Marx and Engels had reposed in the idea that a world literature could become what he describes as 'a progressive force within the socialist project'. For Ahmad, this hope was misguided because Marx seems to have assumed some direct, one-to-one relationship between 'world-market' and 'world-literature'. What was to become evident, and what Marx perhaps missed in earlier writings, was that the 'same globalizing market forces which impose upon the world a historically unprecedented unity' also perpetuate 'economic inequality ... between the core countries of capitalism and the rest', an inequality that is 'still very much on the increase'. In other words, world literature was situated on the constitutively unequal and uneven terrain of the world market, an idea that theorists like Franco Moretti, Fredric Jameson and others were also developing in their theorisations of modernity and world literature.

Ahmad's intervention, however, is unique and consequential for the three main arguments it offers: it underscores the salience of the local, the national and the regional in the formation of global capitalism and in the very idea of world literature; it proffers analyses, with characteristically sharp acumen, of the institutionalisation of world literature through processes of unequal translation and cultural and economic accumulation; and it draws a counter-cartography of the field that could help us to imagine literature as mediating a socialist transformation. The first intervention led him to argue that 'all literatures are above all local and national', and that 'from the numerous national and local literatures, there arises a world literature'.[38] In this he is writing against what Marx and Engels thought of as the narrow-mindedness of national literatures that would be rendered more or less impossible by the global expansion of capital. More importantly, Ahmad contends that 'national and local literatures' are not inevitably expressions of 'narrow-mindedness'. Rather, 'they can just as often be genuine expressions of a democratic demand and just cultural aspirations of a people, in a particular place and time, especially in the context of cultural imperialism'. This is a crucial insight that has predictably not gained much traction as it calls on the critic to draw upon immense linguistic, cultural, critical and historical resources and to take important risks, both aspects that were integral to Ahmad's critical practice.

In terms of the second intervention, Ahmad sketches out for us the processes by which world literature has come to displace Third World literature in the Anglo-American academy. But he points out that 'much of what is today seen as "world literature" is in fact produced, through translation and gloss, by the U.S. universities and publishing industry'.[39] In this, he argues, 'the mediating role of English is decisive'.[40] Here we can see traces of movement in Ahmad's thought from his early reflections in *In Theory* where he saw world literature as at worst an 'abstraction' and at best a 'universalist aspiration' in the world's peripheries.[41] In the later piece, he argues, 'something resembling a "world literature" is now part of the cultural experience of the literate classes across the globe, in a way that was unthinkable in Marx's own time but which Marx deduced from the logic of capitalist universalisation itself'.[42]

It is his final intervention – in which Ahmad allows literature to exceed its ideological prism/prison to help us imagine a more equal and just world – that reads like a manifesto for our times. In this, Ahmad sheds his programmatic lens for a dialectical one. He argues that 'for a "world literature" to arise as a "true interdependence of nations", the logic of the "world market" needs to be transcended'. This is because a '"world literature" can only arise if material relations among the different language-literature complexes can be organised in a structure of exchanges that are non-hierarchical, non-exploitative and non-dominative'.[43] Thus, 'for it to serve as an integral part of the socialist project it must be re-conceived not as an accumulation of certain texts for profit but as a social relation among producers scattered all over the globe, in their specific locales, but connected to each other in relations of radical equality'. It is in this formulation that 'world literature' can function akin to socialism itself, as 'a horizon: the measure of a time yet to come'.[44] We can see here how powerfully the deep formal and theoretical structure of *The Communist Manifesto* manifests itself in Ahmad's own writing.

I want to conclude with a personal anecdote, especially since Ahmad remained a deeply private person even as he was a popular teacher and a brilliant public intellectual. In the early 1990s, my husband who was then a PhD student in the US was conducting fieldwork in India and rented Ahmad's beautiful home in New Delhi while he was on a sabbatical in the US. We spent many lovely months in the house, surrounded by the stunning photographs that Ahmad had taken, and chancing upon floating bits of the manuscript of *In Theory* that he had been working on. The pleasing aesthetic ambience of the house felt especially jarring on the occasions when the landline telephone would ring and a torrent of abuse accusing Ahmad of being a Pakistani agent would assault our ears. One day during our stay, the house was broken into, although not much was stolen. The thieves probably left by the back door when we made an unexpected return. We immediately called Ahmad in the US to inform him about this incident. His first reaction, before he inquired about any loss of his possessions, was to ask us to make sure that the police did not harass the two women workers who cleaned the house. As he had feared, as soon as we filed a police report, the cleaners were hauled into the police station and rudely interrogated until we intervened.

This incident imprinted itself on our minds as evidence of the fact that Ahmad lived his life as he wrote about it. He remained the quintessential outsider and figure of exile from the multiple places and positions he occupied for much of his life, stubbornly committed to working-class politics even as the very terrain of the working classes was shifting and the Left globally was facing unprecedented challenges. As one looks back at his life and work, his words on the nineteenth-century Urdu poet Mirza Ghalib who lived on the cusp of the decline of the Mughal empire and the rise of the British East India Company offer uncanny retrospection on his own life and times. Ahmad had written of the poet that, 'surrounded by constant carnage, Ghalib wrote a poetry primarily of losses and consequent grief' that was 'a poetry also of what could have been possible, but was no longer'. Turning to the question of sensibility in Ghalib's poetry, Ahmad finds in it 'a sensibility whose primary virtue was endurance in a world that was growing for him, as for many others of his time and civilization, increasingly unbearable'.[45] The poignancy of Ahmad's evocative translations of Ghalib's poetic ouevre is made more intense by the fact that to the end, Ahmad himself acted as witness to a newly unbearable world even as he was an important and fearless voice who taught and mentored generations of activists and students and remained hopeful of a socialist transformation.[46]

In his revised essay on Edward Said for *In Theory*, Ahmad conceded that his disagreements with Said were articulated from a position of solidarity. He wrote of Said: 'Those of us who admire his courage and yet disagree with him on substantive issues also have to carry on our own critical pursuits. Suppression of criticism, I have come to believe, is not the best way of expressing solidarity'.[47] It is in this spirit of criticism that I offer this essay as a tribute to Aijaz Ahmad.

Rashmi Varma teaches English and Comparative Literary Studies at the University of Warwick.

Notes

20. Aijaz Ahmad, *In Theory: Classes, Nations, Literatures* (London: Verso, 1992).
21. See Arif Dirlik, 'The Postcolonial Aura: Third World Criticism in the Age of Global Capitalism', *Critical Inquiry* 2:2 (1994), 328–356; E. San Juan Jr., *Beyond Postcolonial Theory* (New York: Palgrave Macmillan, 1998).
22. Ahmad, *In Theory*, 9.
23. Ahmad, *In Theory*, 12.
24. See, for instance, Benita Parry, 'Problems in Current Theories of Colonial Discourse', *Oxford Literary Review* 9:1 (1987), 27–58.
25. Ahmad, *In Theory*, 10; Aijaz Ahmad, 'Jameson's Rhetoric of Otherness and the "National Allegory"', *Social Text* 17 (1987), 3–25. See Neil Lazarus's wonderfully incisive reading of Ahmad's critique of Jameson in *The Postcolonial Unconscious* (Cambridge: Cambridge University Press, 2011).
26. Benita Parry, 'Review. *In Theory: Classes, Nations, Literatures* by Aijaz Ahmad', *History Workshop* 36 (1993), 232.
27. It is worth pointing out that Said himself elevated the amateur over the professional intellectual in *Representations of the Intellectual* (London: Vintage, 1996).
28. Ahmad, *In Theory*, 130–165.
29. For a view from Pakistan, see Raza Naeem, 'The Antinomies of Aijaz Ahmad (1941-2022): From Ghalib to Gramsci', *The Friday Times*, 1 April 2022, https://thefridaytimes.com/01-Apr-2022/the-antinomies-of-aijaz-ahmad-1941-2022-from-ghalib-to-gramsci
30. Ahmad, *In Theory*, 34.
31. Aijaz Ahmad, 'Reading Arundhati Roy Politically', *Frontline*, 8 August 1997, reprinted 21 March 2022, https://frontline.thehindu.com/cover-story/reading-arundhati-roy-politically-by-aijaz-ahmad/article38458826.ece
32. E. M. S. Namboodiripad (1909–1908) was a stalwart Communist politician who served as the first Chief Minister of Kerala, in the first instance of a democratically elected Communist government anywhere in the world.
33. Ahmad offers a similar reading of the representation of Sufiya Zenobia as the embodiment of collective shame that bursts out in acts of private revenge in Rushdie's *Shame*.
34. Aijaz Ahmad, *Lineages of the Present: Ideology and Politics in Contemporary South Asia* (London: Verso, 2000).
35. Ahmad, *In Theory*, 15.
36. Aijaz Ahmad, 'The Communist Manifesto and "World Literature"', *Social Scientist* 28:7/8 (2000), 3–30.
37. Warwick Research Collective, *Combined and Uneven Development: Towards a New Theory of World-Literature* (Liverpool: Liverpool University Press, 2015).
38. Ahmad, 'The Communist Manifesto and "World Literature"', 19, 9.
39. Ahmad, 'The Communist Manifesto and "World Literature"', 23.
40. Ahmad, 'The Communist Manifesto and "World Literature"', 27.
41. Ahmad, *In Theory*, 15.
42. Ahmad, 'The Communist Manifesto and "World Literature"', 15.
43. Ahmad, 'The Communist Manifesto and "World Literature"', 28.
44. Ahmad, 'The Communist Manifesto and "World Literature"', 29.
45. Aijaz Ahmad, 'Introduction', in *Ghazals of Ghalib*, ed. Aijaz Ahmad (New Delhi: Oxford University Press, 2012).
46. For the most recent reflections by Ahmad on his life and work, see *Nothing Human is Alien to Me: Aijaz Ahmad in Conversation with Vijay Prashad* (New Delhi: Leftword Books, 2020).
47. Ahmad, *In Theory*, 160.

Centre for Research in Modern European Philosophy

CRMEP BOOKS

Available as free ebooks direct from CRMEP or as paperbacks from Central Books

5 Institution
critical histories of law

4 Afterlives
transcendentals, universals, others

1 Capitalism: concept, idea, image
Aspects of Marx's *Capital* today

2 Thinking art
materialisms, labours, forms

3 Vocations of the political
Mario Tronti & Max Weber

Kingston University London

www.kingston.ac.uk/faculties/kingston-school-of-art/research-and-innovation/crmep/crmep-books

Reviews

Accumulating extinctions

Mark Bould, *The Anthropocene Unconscious: Climate Catastrophe Culture* (London and New York: Verso, 2021). 176pp., £12.99 pb., 978 1 83976 047 1

The Salvage Collective, *The Tragedy of the Worker: Towards the Proletarocene* (London and New York: Verso, 2021). 104pp., £8.99 pb., 978 1 83976 294 9

Catastrophe is inevitably attracting much discussion in relation to film, books, and other entertainment these days, though it is far from a new theme in philosophy. Even in tourism the theme of catastrophe has been taken up in immersive attractions like Quake – Lisbon Earthquake Centre, where one can experience the earthquake of 1755 through all those screens and museum-cum-fairground type immersions that have been doing the rounds for some years. Such immersive representations of catastrophe need to be far enough in the past for attractions to work; an immersive encounter with Hurricane Katrina and New Orleans might not play so well for good reason.

There have been concerns from some that the general culture of climate catastrophe and collapse stories is part of a strange fixation that may let governments and industry off the hook, rendering people fatalistic and passive, and fixing their futures as inevitable, encouraging an 'it's too late' approach. This seems to be overstating the case. It does not appear to be the representations of catastrophism that are so much the problem (though they, too, often tend to ignore the catastrophe suffered by indigenous peoples through colonialism) as the abject failure of governments and corporations to be effectively held to account – wriggling out of things, lying, acting blatantly to nullify any good things, and generally working to make things worse.

These two related books tackle aspects of the not-so slow catastrophe that we are living in. Mark Bould's *The Anthropocene Unconscious* tackles the importance not just of stories that are told of our worlds and where we are going, but also the way criticism could work for the better. The Salvage Collective in the *Tragedy of the Worker* seek to revise the story of the proletarian inheritance of the means of production not as potential glorious revolution but as tragedy in terms of what these productive forces have brought: climate changes, myriad constant pollutions of seas, earth, skies and bodies, extinctions, massive habitat loss, grinding inequalities, pandemics, wars, and more.

In *The Anthropocene Unconscious: Climate Catastrophe Culture*, Bould takes us through literature and film that does not overtly depict climate change but presents a more symbolic, oblique process, seeking to 'discover what happens if we stop assuming a text is not about climate change.' This is not a book that deals with cli-fi literature as such. In his conclusion Bould asks: 'If we start from the position that all cultural texts are about climate change – even if only in the most fleeting, evanescent way, and never denying whatever else they are about – then they are wide open.' He then argues for a rather beautiful way of acting to make meaning meaningful – that this openness is not just a space for dialogues, debates, discussion, but function 'as adventure playgrounds, workshops, studios … invitations to creative play, to thinking through, to action – as close to unalienated labour as we might get.' It suggests a utopian non-elitist and seductive handle on what critique could be, 'making criticism activism'.

Unsurprisingly, it is Amitav Ghosh's argument in *The Great Derangement*, that mainstream art and literature have failed to engage with climate change in any meaningful way due to an inability to properly imagine the urgency and scale of the threat, that is the pivot Bould argues around. Bould both agrees and disagrees with Ghosh's argument that the modern bourgeois novel became focused on individualised psychologies in the narrow setting of predictable regularities of space and time, banishing other than human agencies, and that its focus on the prosaic meant it has failed not only to engage with climate change but also the voluminous forms of extraction, pollution, exploitation that go together with it. Where Ghosh finds a lack however, Bould often finds: 'not silence but expressive aphasia, teeming with tongue-tied questions.' It's a nice image, implying that the form restricts the ability to respond to the provocations of climate changes. But whilst critical of the form of the bourgeois novel (and its focus on main characters that renders it incapable of tackling the complexity of large processes, systems of exploitation), there is also a generosity to some authors that have made efforts with this form, such as Roy's *The God of Small Things* and Kingsnorth's *The Wake* – both read as being intensely about changing climates and past, present and futures; themes Ghosh claims not to find. For Bould there is a sense that what Ghosh means is that the bourgeois novel needs to operate entirely in the subjunctive and become more like Science Fiction; though Ghosh believes the latter does not have the representational stature to help confront reality. Despite these disputes with Ghosh, it might be argued that Bould plays down just how interesting some of Ghosh's arguments were in *The Great Derangement*.

In these discussions of novels, climate change comes, as in much contemporary culture and politics, to stand for the anthropocene, where this encompasses many more disturbingly blatant actions that have degraded people's and more-than-human lives, lands, waters, airs. The anthropocene has rightly been subjected to very broad critiques, both in regard to its colonial aspects and claims that humanity (as a whole) has become a geologic, hydrologic and atmospheric agent of massively transformative capabilities, while at the same time the capitalist system that has supposedly produced this era is utterly unable and unwilling to act effectively to change from its death drive of sustaining unsustainability. Indeed the whole discourse of the anthropocene, as Eileen Crist noted some years ago, veers away from notions of destruction, devastation, deterioration, depradation, to the relatively tame vocabulary of 'humans' changing, transforming, shaping, altering the biosphere. The seductive universalising of the human that has plagued middle-class reformist environmentalism and that resurfaces in anthropocene (and some cruder posthumanist) discourses plays into the hands of corporations and states who have often successfully focused blame on consumers for many environmental problems like waste or plastic pollution. Whilst Bould embraces the many contrary views of the anthropocene, The Salvage Collective go for their own neologising, with their coinage *the proletarocene*, meaning a world where the majority are proletarianised. Like most neologisms around the anthropocene, it is more of an oppositional heuristic, somewhat reductionistic, yet potentially full if it is to include all the socio-ecological dispossessions, exploitations, killings, and other processes that have led to proletarianisation.

Bould's short, odd, playful book could be read backwards from points in the conclusion where we are asked to stop assuming a text is not about climate change. That way of reading may have clarified why the book's examples of cultural texts begin with the *Sharknado* films, a start that snookered me at first, until I got the 'weird weather' link. But Bould is making a point, starting with monsters, and monsters of fatuous films that are decidedly 'low-brow', as a way to begin to get at this 'anthropocene unconscious' that he posits. For etymologically, we have been told by others, the monster both reveals and warns and perhaps gesticulates, with a nod to Jameson, towards hidden violence, exploitation and repressed realities that underlie cultural texts, and the need to rewrite 'the text in terms of a particular master code'. Bould's engagement with monsters then is not of the 'new weird' forms; he seems interested in something else, wanting to argue that the anthropocene (especially those contrary definitions that seek to put something other than 'the human' at the centre of this Age) is the unconscious of the art and literature of our time. As such, criticism is not about finding the true meaning of the text, but can demonstrate that a work is other than it is, confronting 'the silences, the denials, the resistance of which it is formed.'

But there is also, for me, a little niggle in here about how this unconscious anthropocene is noticed. It is a clever touch to argue that even when the mundane novel of contemporary fiction seemingly ignores the growing ecological devastations, carbon burnings, colonialisms, of financial and extractive capitalism, these things are still to be found in unconscious plots and settings. But in the case of the anthropocene unconscious we also get an echo of the debates over when such an age might have started and the fear of capitalism as second nature. Do all transformations of and engagements with the world, all mention of fickle waters, weird weather, count as accumulations of this era, this second nature? Is the world not also dynamic, is there not still an inhuman nature, are we to put everything down to capitalist or human agencies taking systems from a stationary norm? Such niggles aside, Bould's book is rousing, a call to make criticism more useable, to make meaning more meaningful. Though sometimes it gets a little bogged down in long descriptions of texts or films, it is a book that Bould says he is compelled to reprise.

The story of the anthropocene for the Salvage Collective is rather different. They ask: 'What if the world is already lost'? The principal loss and tragedy invoked is the loss of potential inheritance of capitalist productive forces. For the capitalist state, economy and its social relations has been a death drive, a 'death cult', even as it has brought all kinds of seductions for the few and exploitation and suffering for the many. As they argue, the proletarian gravediggers created by capitalism dig not only its grave 'but also that of much organic life on earth'. The tragedy of the worker is then that even should the proletariat become a class for itself, 'it would – will – inherit productive forces inextricable from mass, trans-species death'. As such, whilst this short book does lay out aspects of the state of the world, with the longest chapter making it clear why green capitalism will not help avert climate catastrophe, it is not a catalogue of ecological degradation, rather it is a cataloguing of tragedy from the perspective of those who had been promised that they would inherit a world they had co-produced collectively in alienated form. The 'salvage communism' invoked here by the Salvage Collective recognises catastrophe is here and that 'the decisive struggle is over what to do with the remains'; but, of course, this implies being able to get access to these remains.

The book, which had a previous iteration in the journal *Salvage* in 2019, works in its early part as a reckoning with how socialism has failed to really address the ecological destruction wrought by the productive forces of capitalism. The authors also counter the old orthodox left arguments that environmentalism has simply been a bourgeois movement, reiterating how early struggles over environment were often instigated by workers, communities. As environmental movements emerged, too often figures from what some call a management class sought to develop environmentalisms that ignored workers and became fixated on the reform of consumerism and as such played into the divisive ways capital sought to make the interests of workers seem diametrically opposed to environmental care, and to create a 'job blackmail' in divisions between labour and environmental movements. Too many critical theories can struggle to integrate a deep sense of the ecological dimensions of living, so this short book by the Salvage Collective gives what feels like a reckoning with coming to things late and what this means in terms of struggles to come amid a 'political adaptation to contexts of catastrophe'.

Just as environmentalism is not solely a bourgeois movement, so too has communism not been bereft of ecological thinking. Brief chapters on the early conservationism of the Soviet Union that ran between 1918-1929, and was swept aside by Stalinist bureaucratic rule, bolster the book's arguments – as do chapters on green fascism and Polar politics. It is an important read, one full of both misery and yet optimism to continue to struggle as all politics has been forced to become 'disaster politics'. Like a lot of discussion of climate change or green capitalism, there tends to be too much discussion of U.S. politics, and not enough of other important regions, other important trajectories, like Latin American peasant movements or how to protect patches of more-than-human liveability, as Anna Tsing has put it, or of the processes of repurposing things of the present in order for there to be places, possibilities of future entanglements to co-make new worlds from. Extractive capitalism is working for less and less people, with billions of others 'sacrificed'. The abandonment of the majority whilst the wealthy continue their gilded lives is also a narrative that is emerging strongly in cli-fi – fiction that features a catastrophically changed climate, reflecting how the very rich are themselves responsible for most climate gas pollution globally. A breakout from such narrow narratives is needed, but while the Salvage Collective offer some visions of possibility, they are ultimately few.

Chris Wilbert

Vital institutions

Roberto Esposito, *Institution* (Cambridge: Polity Press, 2022). 160pp., £40.00 hb., £14.99 pb., 978 1 50955 155 2 hb., 978 1 50955 156 9 pb.

The Covid-19 pandemic had the curious result of simultaneously legitimising and de-legitimising discourses of the biopolitical. The longstanding claim of biopolitical theorists that politics and biological life have become inextricable within medicalised forms of governance has become increasingly undeniable. However, the negative construal of that entanglement within dominant accounts of the concept has been subject to increased scrutiny due to the dynamics of pandemic politics. Giorgio Agamben's widely criticised intervention into public debates around lockdown measures during the early stages of the pandemic – a blog post published in February 2020 entitled 'The Invention of an Epidemic' – has opened broader questions concerning the adequacy of the concept to the present. Who are the main proponents today of the idea that there is something inherently dangerous about governments implementing measures to protect the biological well-being of their populations if not the right? The unimaginably large death toll of the pandemic took place against a backdrop of far-right rallies against government interventions such as lockdowns and mask-mandates, of the alt-right spreading conspiracy theories regarding mobile phone infrastructure and vaccinations, and populist leaders of the right advocating letting the virus rip to keep society open for business. In this context, it became increasingly hard to justify the notion that theoretical accounts that foster mistrust in the normative regulation of public health or use of emergency measures to protect the lives of those vulnerable to death are inherently progressive. Such a crisis in the notion of the biopolitical has led some commentators such as the architectural theorist Benjamin Bratton to call for an affirmative form of biopolitics in which the governance of biological life is seen as a necessity rather than a danger.

Roberto Esposito has been calling for a notion of affirmative biopolitics for what is now approaching twenty years and his work is ripe for reassessment. No thinker has emphasised the centrality of concepts of immunity and immunisation to contemporary politics more than Esposito, whose own understanding of biopolitics is better suited to a post-pandemic world than his better-known compatriot. Esposito's reinterpretation of biopolitics through the category of immunisation was always marked by a critical relation to what it saw as an unresolved antinomy at the heart of the Foucauldian notion in which a politics of life (an affirmative biopolitics in which life is the subject of politics) vied with a politics over life (a negative politics in which life was the object of politics). For Esposito, the affirmative model was taken up by Antonio Negri and the negative by Agamben while his own concept of immunisation represented a point of articulation between the two which made sense of their unity.

This positioning within a third space between Agamben and Negri is something that continues to mark Esposito's work to the present. This is evident in his recent work on instituent thought which was first set out in his 2020 book *Pensiero Istituente* and, following the pandemic, re-connected to his thinking on the biopolitical in the work under review here, 2022's *Institution*. Zakiya Hanafi's welcome translation of the term *istituente* as 'instituent' draws our attention to how the work is being positioned between Negri's concept of constituent power and Agamben's work on inoperativity as a destituent power. For Esposito, the instituent represents the alternative to these two 'exhausted' political-ontological paradigms which can be traced to Deleuze and Heidegger, respectively. As such, it marks a shift away from Esposito's earlier Heideggerian-deconstructionist commitments which he would now assign to an exhausted 'destituent' paradigm primarily concerned with undoing modern political categories and their associated institutions. Instead, he mines a range of sources primarily from French sociology and philosophy, German philosophical anthropology and Italian legal institutionalism to develop an affirmative reconceptualisation of institutions. The spine of this thinking is formed by a line of thought that stretches from Merleau-Ponty and Marcel Mauss to Cornelius Castoriadis and Claude Lefort which centres upon thinking institution not only as a noun but also as a verb; as instituent praxis. Lefort's neo-Machiavellian notion of institution is central to this 'instituent paradigm' which is here developed in biopolitical terms.

Institution centres upon the relationship between biological life and institutions via a discussion of the ancient Roman notion of the *vitam instituere*. This serves as a biopolitical image of the 'instituent' in which the dominant notion of the institution with its associations of formal establishment, duration and law are viewed as inherently connected to biological notions of vitality, movement and force. For Esposito, life and institutions are both misunderstood when viewed as divergent entities which have only recently become entangled with one another. Instead, they should be viewed as two moments of a 'single figure' in which institutions are always already vital and life is always already instituted. The book offers an account of how this ambivalent notion of the institution – as both noun and verb, duration and dynamic, form and force – has been historically 'eclipsed' by the dominant state-like model of the institution. It traces the recent historical and political consequences of this eclipse across the political struggles of the 1960s and 1970s to the institutional responses to the Covid-19 pandemic via developments in post-1989 global civil society. Esposito argues that the tendency to theoretically confine institutions within a state-like form – here understood in a dual sense of the state and static – has led to a rigid opposition between conservative institutions and anti-institutional movements. This opposition is evident in political theory on the left (Foucault, Marcuse, Sartre) and right (Schmitt, Gehlen) and reaches its apex in the political struggles of 1960s and 70s (with an emphasis on the Italian 'Years of Lead').

Esposito traces this opposition to the rise of Christian theology, as exemplified by the anti-Roman tendencies of Augustine's *City of God*, which re-imagined the process of social institution to lie totally within the personality of God and thereby replaced the dynamic and functional concept of instituent human practice that, for Esposito, characterised Roman Law with a fixed model of the institution primarily based around authority. Hobbes's Leviathan state, although complicating this picture due to the explicitly socially instituted character of the sovereign person, ultimately comes to cement the notion that all institituive practice should be incorporated within a monolithic authority. As such the state-form comes to eclipse the diverse and dynamic instituent practices of the ambivalent *vitam instituere* and occupy the conceptual space of the term 'institution' leading to its severing from notions of movement. The result are institutions that are unable to change, and movements that are unable to endure.

This eclipse is challenged by the neo-Machievellian 'instituent paradigm' of thought which Esposito is seeking to recover and elaborate. These thinkers reconnect the concept of institution to its obscured 'instituent' (dynamic-creative) moment alongside its more established (state-like) 'instituted' moment. This yields a dynamic and conflictual conception of institution which embraces the productive potential of the negative. Institution contains a paradox however: the instituent refers to a moment of creation of something new, but this newly instituted moment *qua* institution is a 'state' characterised by temporal duration. Thereby the dynamic instituent moment dialectically passes over into its opposite of immobility. Esposito does not simply side with the instituent moment against the instituted moment of institution but rather embraces the tension between innovation and preservation inherent to the concept. Therefore, unlike the constituent paradigm which continually reduces the constituted moment to the constituent, instituent praxis aims seeks to keep the dynamic and static moments in balance. This process hinges on the relations between institution, life and negativity in two senses: institutions perform a limiting function which is needed to channel the flow of life and secure it in time, however their own vitality – their ability to change – requires their continued connection to social conflicts.

Undergirding Esposito's argument is the historical judgement that non-State institutions are growing in political influence at the same time as the Westphalian model of mutually independent sovereign states is in a period of decline. Therefore, the state-like image of institutions is one that has not kept up with historical reality. In practice, institutions have already acquired increasing autonomy from the state, a process which was accelerated in the post-1989 context in which non-state actors became increasingly influential in shaping political projects (NGOs, the EU, the IMF, etc.). This process of politics being displaced to non-state institutions in a 'global civil society' is seen by Esposito as something to be embraced. While neoliberalism is addressed as further evidence of the declining role of the state, its connection to the emergence of 'global civil society' remains largely unexplored beyond the notion that states increasingly lack the power to regulate global flows of capital without extra-state coordination. Instead, we find glowing passages on NGOs which are described as the 'one of the most interesting experiments in innovative instituent praxis'. Although his conflictualist perspective calls for 'taking a stance for some institutions against others', the overall picture is one which feels in danger of unconsciously endorsing a depoliticised and post-democratic notion of global civil society.

The book concludes by returning to the figure of the *vitam instituere* and arguing that the pandemic has proven the interconnection of life and politics and shown the necessity for institutional intervention at their intersection. Esposito claims that such a connection is what has been missing from theoretical accounts of the biopolitical and traces this lack to the genesis of Foucault's concept in opposition to notions of mediation and law which are, in turn, associated with institutions. He argues that contemporary thinking on biopolitics is ironically shaped by a separation of 'life' and 'politics' inherited from Foucault and Arendt's work. Whereas Foucault sees institutions as separate from and repressive of life, Arendt sees life as something inherently non-political which undermines institutions with violent results. Here, Esposito is challenging two of the sources for the negative model of biopolitics represented by Agamben's thinking on 'bare life' whose immediacy Esposito is seeking to overcome with his notion of 'instituted life' (the *vitam instituere*). For him, biological life 'is always instituted, that is, inscribed in a historical and symbolic fabric from which it cannot be separated.' In fact, the negative biopolitical legacies of racist, colonial and totalitarian violence are here ascribed to the breakdown of the institutional mediation of life. Therefore, he concludes that the concept of biopolitics must be integrated with the instituent paradigm to avoid its negative drift towards a thanatopolitcs.

The institutionally-mediated affirmative concept of biopolitics put forward in Esposito's short book represents a generative way forward for the concept in the post-pandemic world. However, serious questions remain over the project and not merely for its highly Eurocentric or even Romanocentric worldview. The politics within the biopolitics put forward here are less clear than their relationship to life. If constituent power can be ascribed to a revolutionary communist politics and destituent power to an insurrectionary anarchism, where might one ideologically place the instituent paradigm? It is possible to imagine its role within a renewed libertarian socialist politics – there are gestures towards this: for example, he argues for the need to reconfigure the logic of welfare beyond the state – however the overriding feeling is of a slow drift towards liberalism. This is evident in the configuration of the post-1968 and post-1989 moments within the book. The movements of the sixties and seventies are reduced to an anti-institutional straw man figure and ultimately come to stand for part of what must be overcome. Meanwhile, the post-1989 decline of the state in the era of 'global civil society' is presented as something that must be embraced as our only horizon of sense. This symptomatically avoids any exploration of the tendencies within the New Left which, for better or worse, argued for working within, across and against institutions including the state. One can think here of the idea of 'Long March Through the Institutions' or the recently re-discovered idea of working 'In and Against the State'. The instituent paradigm relies heavily on the thinkers of *Socialisme ou Barberie* – Lefort and Castoriadis – but its development would benefit from consideration of their early work.

Matt Phull

Law's violence

Oishik Sircar, *Violent Modernities: Cultural Lives of Law in the New India* (New Delhi: Oxford University Press, 2021). 370pp., £40.99 hb., 978 0 19012 792 3

This is a book that resists easy categorisation and, as a result, also resists the typical review process.* I could, for example, note that the book consists of seven essays written as standalone pieces, which address a wide range of topics. Sircar deals with questions as diverse as the authorial style of the famed critical legal theorist Upendra Baxi (Chapter 6), representations of law in cinematic retellings of the Gujarat anti-Muslim pogrom of 2002 (Chapter 3), the inability of rights-claims under the Indian Constitution to deliver justice and emancipation for subaltern actors (Chapter 1), and the complications of being a male feminist (Chapter 7). I could also flag that Chapter 2, dealing with the children of sex workers and the politics of pity and suffering, is co-authored with Debolina Dutta, a choice that puts pressure on the very form of the sole-authored monograph and invites us to think creatively about how to interact with our comrades and co-conspirators through our scholarly work.

The uniqueness of this volume leads Sircar to warn his readers early on that the book can be read both in a fragmented way (depending on one's interest in different topics covered by the essays) or in a traditional cover-to-cover way. If one does the latter (as I did), then this book becomes a – still fragmented – meditation on the relationship between liberal legality, on the one hand, and the joint rise of neoliberalism and Hindutva, on the other. Where both liberals and the far-right understand the relationship between the two ideologies and political systems as fundamentally antagonistic, Sircar suggests that there are important continuities between the two. More specifically, he documents meticulously that law was a central terrain where the promises of liberalism either remained unrealised or were, in fact, realised only to reveal that they entailed more violence and exclusion than its exponents assumed. Even though the book shies away from a strong, unified claim, the implication is that the failures and successes of liberal legalism alike paved the way for the rise of the Hindu far-right. This happened due to the law's tendency to equate secularism with Hinduism, authorise or tolerate violence in the name of 'national security', make the poor and other subaltern actors the object of private pity and public management, and by elevating the nation-state into the ultimate arbitrator and referent of human diversity. In this telling, the three pillars of the postcolonial state, namely the rule of law, secularism and developmentalism, contained the seeds of the ascendance of the Hindu far-right. Sircar shows in detail how events and actors nominally antag-

---

* I want to thank Adil Hasan Khan for his insightful comments and criticisms. All errors remain my own.

onistic to Hindutva, such as India's LGBT+ movement or cinematic representations of the Gujarat pogroms, continuously centre the (Hindu) nation-state and demand deference to the state and its imperatives in exchange for recognition and minimal protection by the law.

Written from a left-critical perspective, then, the book is of interest both to those working on India and its law and to those thinking about the relationship between law and the global resurgence of the far right. In the intersection of the two, Sircar offers glimpses of the rise and fall of post-colonial constitutionalism and how its shortcomings transformed India from an epoch-making experiment in community co-existence and state-led socialist transformation domestically as well as a leader of Non-Alignment internationally into a far-right, neoliberal state with open and celebrated ties with the settler state of Israel over their shared and increasingly militant Islamophobia. For Sircar, acts like the occupation of Kashmir, the proclamation of the infamous state of emergency under Indira Gandhi, and the embrace of state-led authoritarian developmentalism had poisoned the well of post-colonial statehood and its laws long before Modi's BJP came to power in 2014. Hindutva, then, emerges not as the negation of the liberal rule of law but as its monstrous outgrowth. Perhaps more precisely, Sincar emphasises the profound entanglement between the Hindu far-right and neoliberalism, an entanglement encapsulated in Modi's emphasis on the 'Ease of Doing Business' and other indexes as *the* yardsticks of governmental legitimacy and success. In this respect, the date that haunts this book is not the 15th of August 1947, when India became independent, but rather 1991, when the process of neoliberal reforms began in earnest in India, decisively leaving behind the post-independence political aspiration for and post-1976 constitutional commitment to a mixed economy.

This dance between 1947 and 1991 constitutes a tension that runs through Sircar's thinking: on the one hand, the neoliberal turn of the 1990s is repeatedly identified as a pivotal moment in Indian history. Hindutva is rarely

mentioned without its political economic twin, neoliberalism. On the other hand, Sircar casts a much broader net both thematically and temporally. His analysis shows profound distrust towards developmentalism in general, even when it was directed by the state. In his view, the authoritarianism that he sees as inherent in Indian developmentalism was one of the core state ideologies and practices that paved the way for the rise of the Hindu far-right. In this respect, Sircar's account can be situated in long-standing left-wing critiques of Indian developmentalism that emphasised the role of the state as enabler of private capital accumulation and India's version of socialism as an experiment in top-down management, rather than dispersion of control over the economy to direct producers, workers and farmers.

At the same time, his scepticism about rights claims and adjudication goes back to the promulgation of India's Constitution and the early years of the Supreme Court, long before the latter adopted a pro-market, pro-upper middle class and anti-poor interpretation of constitutionally-protected rights. After all, as the very title of the book implies, Sircar's main focus is not successive ideologies or political economic models (liberalism/neoliberalism, state-led developmentalism/neoliberalism) but modernity writ large. Early in the book, Sircar outlines his own understanding of modernity as both a justification for colonialism and a tool in the hands of the colonised as they craft and legitimise their own versions of it. Indeed, very few places represent the latter move more starkly than India, where the colonised – or at least their elite, self-proclaimed representatives – successfully mobilised the imperatives of modernity against Britain. It is then no surprise that the demise of India's experiment in democracy, pluralism and economic transformation would trigger profound scepticism towards the project as a whole. This scepticism is also present in the book's main theoretical anchors: despite Sircar's recurring engagements with Marx and Marxism, his main interlocutors within legal theory (Goodrich, Kapur, McVeigh) have – despite their palpable differences – focused their energies on modernity, and in particular on its transmutations in colonial contexts.

The problem with this emphasis on modernity as the thread that binds together Indian (legal) history is that the modernist credentials of neoliberalism as an ideology, as system of governance and a model of capitalist accumulation are less than stellar. Hayek's and other neoliberals' attacks against state planning – both in the Global North and the Global South – relied on the fundamentally anti-modernist premise of the unknowability of the economy and its participants. This is more than an abstract theoretical point: from the argument that financial markets are too complex and volatile to be regulated effectively by states to fatalistic approaches to the management of infectious diseases, such as COVID-19, from the elevation of 'risk' and 'uncertainty' into central pillars of modern law and governance to the modalities of algorithmic decision-making that cannot be predicted or even reconstructed after the fact, invocations of ignorance and lack of control are not antagonistic to neoliberal states and markets, but rather the very mode through which they operate.

This is, undeniably, not the only modality of law and power today. Legal fields such as constitutional law, international law or human rights remain at least partially committed to their liberal-modernist assumptions. However, to over-emphasise the role of these fields in the rise of neoliberalism or the far-right in India and beyond is to show faith in the omnipotence of liberal legalism commonly exhibited exclusively by liberal legalists. Even though the continuities between liberalism and authoritarianism are very real, overstating their relationship runs the risk of both missing the uniqueness of authoritarian capitalism and of entertaining liberal delusions about its ability to tame the most destructive aspects of the capitalist mode of production.

The above does not translate automatically into a programme of tactical alliance with liberalism in law and beyond. It does, however, translate into a programme for both critical inquiry and radical action that is not determined by the divisions of the past. Analytically, it is important to acknowledge that the postcolonial developmental state (of the liberal, non-liberal and anti-liberal varieties) contained the seeds for the contemporary emergence of far-right forces, but it also contained the seeds for many other futures, both better and worse. (Third World scholars, including Baxi himself, have questioned singular histories of development and emphasised the existence of radical variations.) I am very sympathetic to Sircar's commitment to thinking through and about underlying currents and broader structures that go beyond the contingencies of each separate historical moment (a testament to our shared sympathy toward Marxism). That said, his suspicion that legal practices, arguments and institutions common to liberal democracies carry the potential for immense violence and destruction needs to be constantly balanced against the reminder that fierce battles were fought within, beyond and against the law and that our current predicament is the result of concrete defeats as much as it is the culmination of immanent tendencies.

Ntina Tzouvala

Existential crisis

Terry Pinkard, *Practice, Power, and Forms of Life: Sartre's Appropriation of Hegel and Marx* (Chicago: University of Chicago Press, 2022). 200pp., £28.00 hb., 978 0 22681 324 0

In the space of just three chapters and a 'dénouement,' Terry Pinkard's *Practice, Power, and Forms of Life: Sartre's Appropriation of Hegel and Marx* explicates Jean-Paul Sartre's late work, *Critique of Dialectical Reason* (1960), and along the way enters into the most controversial of the debates surrounding the *Critique*'s reception. The novel argument that Pinkard unfolds tracks the continuity and change in the development in Sartre's thought in the fifteen years leading up to the *Critique*. Key to this development was Sartre's newly found appreciation in the postwar years for the Hegelian side of Marxism, coloured as it was by Kojève and Hyppolite. This forced Sartre to rethink the theoretical assumptions that he relied upon earlier in his career, while still holding fast to many of them, incorporating elements of Hegel 'while maintaining his distance from what he understood the Hegelian position to be'. The figure keeping Sartre from leaning fully into Hegel is Heidegger: in the *Critique*, one finds 'reappropriation of some facets of Hegelianism', Pinkard says, but 'all the while firmly committing himself to what he understood to be an anti-Hegelian view' because of his appropriation of Heidegger's thought.

There are two common treatments of the *Critique of Dialectical Reason*: either it is read as Sartre's attempt to render his early existentialism and some form of Marxism compatible, or Marxism is conspicuously absent, and the work is treated as a theoretical exploration of neo-anarchism. This is not, however, how Sartre himself described the project of the *Critique*. Sartre at the time considered himself a participant in leftist politics, and this was the context that motivated him to pen the work. Pinkard avoids reducing the *Critique* to pure propaganda – in other words, reading in the *Critique* a clean identity between a shabby practical program and its equally poor theoretical buttressing – while also not disregarding Sartre's politics altogether and treating the *Critique* as detached entirely from Sartre's place in history. This is nowhere more true than in the original and perceptive discussion of Sartre and violence at the midpoint of the book.

At the outset of the *Critique*, Sartre is seeking a dialectical theory of subjectivity that can account for group formation and a sense of first-person plurality. Sartre had argued in *Being and Nothingness* (1943) against the coherence of a collective subject. Groups, metaphysically speaking, are illusions that we have because we fail to appreciate our radical individuality. This precludes any meaningful social or political action. Through his engagement with Hegel, Sartre reconsiders the relation between the first person singular and the first-person plural, or, borrowing from his Hegelian reading, 'the "I" that is a "We," and the "We" that is an "I".' In earlier works, Sartre had rejected the Hegelian subject-object dialectic as one that relies on the presupposition that only individuals are real: groups are merely additive agglomerations of individuals. But, according to Pinkard, Sartre came to see a deep problem in this undialectical conception. *Practice, Power, and Forms of Life* traces Sartre's efforts to dialectically relate the 'I' to the 'We' without subsuming one under the other.

To achieve a robust self-consciousness, Pinkard reminds us that the subject 'confronts his own facticity in acting – including his physical makeup and the institutions and norms of where he finds himself.' This facticity determines what actions are possible. In this confrontation, the subject has the choice between activity ('spontaneity') and passivity ('inertia'), between appropriating the conditions for oneself by taking responsibility for one's freedom and being buffeted by 'inert' exterior forces without resistance. So far, this maps onto the Being-in-Itself versus Being-for-Itself distinction found in *Being and Nothingness*. What Pinkard brings out with considerable brilliance is the historical dimension of the new term of art, the 'practico-inert', or the inertia *that we create for ourselves* over and above the natural, given facticity of our lives, but that we *do not recognize as self-created*. 'This', Pinkard recounts, 'is the foundation of alienation.'

Agents too often think of themselves not as engaged subjects but as detached objects, machine-like and prey to external forces, and certainly not in a mutual project shared with other subjects. This otherness ('alterity') is our reaction to the fact of scarcity in our world, where we enter into antagonistic relations with others and risk becoming superfluous. In this world, 'each may be the "extra" one who can be dispensed with.' This scarcity, however artificial and liable to transcendence, 'marks each member of the group both as a possible survivor and as a dispensable surplus member.' Given Pinkard's reminder of our imminent replaceability in capitalism, the resonance of Sartre's concerns with Marx's is clear, but Pinkard does not explore the dissonances. Whereas Marx saw this crisis in our social relations as a contradiction that points beyond itself, Sartre considers the chance that 'the possibility of antagonism' is permanent in any 'structure of plural human activity'. Arguably this scarcity is contingent and is liable to be overcome in a classless society (Pinkard points out that there is no contradiction in thinking of a world without scarcity), but even if the classless society were realised, Pinkard suggests that Sartre would assume that 'the inertia generated by the practico-inert ... would clash with spontaneity to generate yet another breakdown, and yet again it too would be "overtaken" by another.' For Marx, the contradiction is not in human activity *per se* in some transhistorical sense, but only human activity under specific conditions that constantly demonstrate their historical mutability. For Sartre, the contradiction threatens to take on permanent metaphysical significance: it 'never goes away'.

Sartre's intervention into this antagonism is to emphasise our 'monstrous spontaneity', or the terrifying capacity we have to strike a new beginning through resistance to such inertia. However, a difficulty arises when we exercise our spontaneity, making it 'monstrous' to Sartre. It involves a curious dialectical twist whereby one process or activity transforms into its opposite which then undermines it. Actions – individually or collectively – often result in ends that are at odds with the original plans of action ('counter-finality'). Pinkard notes that while for Marx this would have been experienced with more enthusiasm, for Sartre this is a 'tragic conception of dialectic' because it comes with the discovery of a fate that subjects 'have brought on themselves by their own free actions' for which 'they are driven to assume responsibility' despite not 'being in harmony with their world.' Pinkard summarises the point thus:

> The contingent material conditions of one's time and one's place, of where and to whom one is born, are contingent but generate in most circumstances a destiny that can also become a fatality ... Thus, for Sartre, history ultimately has tragedy written into it. Sartrean tragedy was based on human freedom and the traps that pure contingency and counter-finality can lead such freedom to lay

down for itself. By the time of the *Critique* and afterward, it was based on the way in which freedom is exercised to create a destiny and even to create an unwanted fatality. One stakes everything on some view of the 'totality', and there is no way to see whether in fact the 'totality' measures up to anything at all. This is not a matter of our being subject to natural forces beyond our control (which is certainly true of us) but of our freely producing a kind of inertia that leads us into consequences we find horrible and for which we have to take responsibility, since it is we who did it.

The open-ended possibilities to create more and other than we set out to create are experienced by Sartre as terrifying, especially given the mounting disasters of the twentieth century through which he was living. After all, the world socialist revolution had degenerated into its opposite. But Sartre's terror does contrast with the earlier optimism of the nineteenth century. From the classical Marxist view, such disasters are, at bottom, the negative manifestations of our own freedom alienated from us, and this runaway freedom needs to be harnessed through revolution – a view Sartre increasingly rejected.

The critique Sartre offers of the 'Marxist approach of his own time' is a well-rehearsed one: Marxism saw subjects as 'merely swept along by historical forces' in a deterministic logic. Pinkard recounts that 'the problems of Stalinism' were to treat history as 'just an inexorable process of vast social forces working its way to a satisfactory end on its own', when for Sartre, history 'always involved spontaneity' and was a process where individuals made 'their own way through it in conditions that they have never chosen for themselves.' Pinkard writes, 'historical agents cannot eschew responsibility and leave everything up to capital *H* History.' But what is not found in his discussion is a consideration of the extent to which Sartre's reaction to historical fatalism is an equally one-sided voluntarism, a dialectical reminder one finds stressed in Adorno or early Lukács. Sartre thinks that in the face of a reified world, one naturally wants to break out, and one does that as an act of one's will. Sartre hoped for decades to develop an ethics of action, of 'pure spontaneity', and he got nearly five hundred pages into that project before dropping it in frustration. A target of Sartre's *Critique*, Pinkard says, is anyone who would downplay agency in history by smothering spontaneity, and 'he was always unrelenting in his criticism of dogmatic Marxism for having no real place for such agency.' Pinkard, however, does not speculate on how anti-totalitarianism itself contains elements of totalitarianism. A generation earlier, the Marxism of the Second International had degenerated into a naive progressive view that assumed history was on its side and would inevitably march towards emancipation. With such staid Marxism entering into crisis during World War I, it prompted then-socialists like Mussolini to develop fascism as what they conceived to be a more radical way of dealing with the crisis. Sartre's actionist ethics are a result of the same historical pressures to act in the face of the practico-inert.

According to Pinkard, Sartre never broke with what he took 'the promise of Marxism' to be: 'a conception of history as mapping a course to ... a classless society', but, with the inevitability subtracted. What Sartre 'did not have and what he gave up on' was much of a sense of how to fashion such a revolutionary movement, especially after he had given up the mature Marx's idea of the 'dictatorship of the proletariat' (dismissed as 'absurd') and after 'he abandoned any idea that a Marxist "party" ... could play that role.' Pinkard records a striking late confession from Sartre on the party question: 'While I recognize the need of an organization, I must confess that I don't see how the problems which confront any stabilized structure could be resolved.' Brief flirtations with anarchism and libertarian socialism did not satisfy him. Towards the end of his life as an ageing observer of the New Left, he looked to the new 'social movements and practice-oriented underpinnings' as hopeful signs of breaking through the practico-inert. Pinkard's own New Leftism shines forth in the descriptions of Sartre's late preoccupations. Having come of age in the sixties, Pinkard claims that 'what Marxism itself had trouble doing' was adapting to a world where 'class struggle ... cannot be the whole story'; it failed to incorporate 'race, gender, sexual orientation, and generalized ideals of subordination', not to mention 'the "super-exploitation" of the indigenous peoples practiced by European colonialism' and other 'systems of oppression'. On Pinkard's reading, Marxism was unable 'to produce a satisfactory account of the whole of history as culminating in the classless society' according to Sartre, and so alternative paths must be sought. But is it the theoretical account that was unsatisfactory, or the practical attempt to realise it?

Pinkard ends the book by reconstructing what these alternative paths to Marxism must be for Sartre. These future directions for a social and political *ethos* echo traditional ones. The 'man to come', for Sartre, is designated by 'liberty, equality and fraternity'. Pinkard argues that Sartre would have seen his own project as 'the realization of the (originally bourgeois) goals of the 1789 revolution' that could only be actualised in a post-capitalist order. Like Hegel and Marx, Sartre did not wish merely to 'cancel' but to 'cancel and preserve'. Trust the words of a renowned Hegel scholar like Pinkard when he says that 'Sartre ended up with an unfinished version of a kind of somewhat naturalized left-Hegelianism ... shorn of many of Hegel's own commitments' (and Marx's too, I might add). Pinkard ends *Practice, Power, and Forms of Life* with the following note: 'Foucault's quip about Sartre's "pathetic" use of the nineteenth century to probe the problems of the twentieth might have a lot more truth to it after all – even for the twenty-first century.' Pinkard makes us consider symptomatic self-contradictory misrecognitions of the crisis of capitalism that falsifies such attempts to avoid the problem through fidelity to prior liberal-democratic bourgeois thought. Given Sartre's return to a left-Hegelian liberalism out of his rejection of Marxism, readers familiar with Sartre should wonder to what extent Sartre is implicated by his own critique that he articulated in the orphaned introduction to the *Critique* called *Search for a Method*. There, Sartre writes, 'I have often remarked on the fact that an "anti-Marxist" argument is only the apparent rejuvenation of a pre-Marxist idea. A so-called "going beyond" Marxism will be at worst only a return to pre-Marxism; at best, only the rediscovery of a thought already contained in the philosophy which one believes he has gone beyond.'

Ethan Linehan

Symptoms of the image

Emmanuel Alloa, *Looking Through Images. A Phenomenology of Visual Media*, trans. Nils F. Schott (New York: Columbia University Press, 2021). 391pp., £121.00 hb., £30.00 pb., 978 0 23118 792 3 hb., 978 0 23118 793 0 pb.

Emmanuel Alloa's *Looking Through Images* is an exceptionally ambitious book that attempts nothing less than rethinking the fundamental questions of image theory. Originally published in German more than a decade ago, the book weaves together two very different strands of thought. It is primarily a 'phenomenology of visual media', as the subtitle itself declares. Secondly, the phenomenological strand is linked to a historical approach, which Alloa calls an 'archaeology of the Western engagement with images'. The interplay between these two approaches – phenomenology and archaeology – is motivated by Alloa's intention to forestall a traditional criticism of phenomenological analyses: 'bracketing questions of causality and provenance must not mean the absence of reflection on the provenance of one's own categories'.

The book is structured around five long chapters. Each chapter is divided into ten sections and accompanied by so-called 'Illuminations': short, dazzling descriptions of artworks that shed light on the theoretical discussion from a lateral viewpoint. While the first three chapters are entirely devoted to an archaeological reconstruction of the philosophical discourse about images, in the fourth chapter the discussion shifts to key phenomenological authors, before reaching the most original conclusions in Chapter Five. Nils F. Schott deserves much credit for translating Alloa's prose into eloquent English that allows the nuances of the German original to shine through without impairing readability.

The sheer number of topics dealt with in this book may leave the reader – let alone the reviewer – with a sense of inadequacy. But overall Alloa manages to spin the many threads of the book into a cohesive and compelling narrative. The author's primary objective is to articulate a definition of images that encapsulates their unique way of serving as a *medium*. Alloa defines the medium as a being that 'takes on the form of some other being, without being this being'. The image is a medium because it is something *through* which we are able to see something else, although not in the sense of pure transparency, as when we look at a landscape through a window. The book delves into the specific 'logic of this 'through'", demonstrating why images are irreducible to other forms of signification. So, on the one hand, images are a distinctive and irreducible type of media. But, on the other hand, they are particularly indicative of the nature of media at large.

The historical part of the book features a detailed discussion of ancient Greek philosophy, which is followed by an exceptionally learned, though necessarily quick-paced, survey of the long historical period extending from Late Antiquity to Early Modernity. Alloa's main objective here is to identify the historical roots of the traditional 'skepticism concerning images in philosophy'. This skepticism, he contends, has been fuelled by two prevailing theoretical paradigms that, despite appearing to be diametrically opposed, have actually supported each other in obscuring the true nature of images. Using terminology derived from Arthur Danto, Alloa calls these two paradigms the *transparency* and *opacity* theories. In essence, the transparency theory is based on the premise 'that *images are defined by what lies behind them*', thus emphasising their referential or semiotic status, whereas the opacity theory maintains 'that *images are fully determined by their material objecthood*'. These two paradigms are less incompatible than they first appear, in that they share a reductionist perspective. They present a false dichotomy between images as *signs* and images as *things* – a dichotomy that ultimately overlooks precisely the status of the image as a medium.

A third and more productive paradigm can be traced back to Aristotle. In *On the Soul*, Aristotle uses the concept of the *diaphanous* to refer to the medium of vision, i.e., 'that through which and in which that which appears does appear'. Initially used as an adjective – water or air are diaphanous in the sense that they are transparent and allow light through – the diaphanous gradually becomes a noun, thereby referring to the space of visibility itself, an 'as yet nameless shared essential nature of appearing'. This use of the concept is tantamount to the concept of *medium*. On that basis, Alloa spells out as follows the main 'principle' of Aristotle's media theory: '*something appears to a perceiver because the perceiver is affected*. This affecting, however, does not take place immediately; the object of perception [...] does not act directly but mediately and at a distance. What operates the affection here is that which lies "between" the organ and the object of perception: the medium'.

According to Alloa, Aristotle's media theory of vision is partially anticipated by Plato. However, the latter plays a deeply ambivalent role in the book. On the one hand, Plato inaugurated the ontological distinction that supports the dichotomy of opacity and transparency. This is the distinction between something as taken by itself (*kath'autó*) and something in relation to other things (*pros alla*). On the other hand, in his quarrel with both the Sophists and the Eleatics, he recognised that we can only do justice to images if we conceive of them in terms of a coexistence between these two categories. However, overall, Plato treated this peculiar ontology of images not as something to be cherished but rather as the hallmark of a deficient status. Only with Aristotle do we begin to recognise that 'images are interesting in themselves' and irreducible to anything else. Moreover, Alloa points out that Plato treated the image and the act of seeing as two different things. Aristotle reversed this assumption, proposing that 'an image always *appears in* a medium, yet this medium, to make anything visible, must rely on a seeing eye.' This entails an 'originary unity of phenomenality and iconicity': for an image to appear, 'it takes more than just light; it takes an active, living seeing eye to whom the image appears'. It should be apparent from these quotations that Alloa interprets Aristotle as a forerunner of phenomenology.

Chapter Three offers a 'reception history of the diaphanous'. In what reads almost as an etymological pun, however, this exercise in *Geistesgeschichte* turns into a 'ghost story', that is, the story of a haunting absence rather than of an idea. The history of the Western engagement with images is the history of the multifarious ways in which the Aristotelian paradigm was forgotten and the reductionist alternative between transparency and opacity was favoured. Alloa has a gift for revealing how philosophical discussions are often continuous with philological debates about the interpretation of classical texts. Thus, he shows that the transparency paradigm unfolded in parallel with an interpretation of Aristotle that 'spiritualizes the diaphanous', making it entirely immaterial. The opacity paradigm, on the contrary, rests on a materialistic transformation of the medium. This materialistic turn originated with the Stoics and carried over into modern philosophy. (Think here of Descartes's well-known analogy between seeing and operating a stick.)

Taking a bold leap forward, Alloa further suggests that this history comes to a head in twentieth-century image theory. The transparency theory had by this time come to be associated with a 'negation of the image support' that underpins iconological and semiotic approaches. These approaches view the image as an open window, 'a *document* yielding insight.' Opacity theory, on the contrary, looks at the image as an opaque and 'self-contained *monument*'. Both theories have in common a neglect of the medium and a disregard for the phenomenological perspective, which 'describes images in their appearing'. Here, I found myself wishing that the book could help the reader to better understand how it was possible that precisely in the twentieth century, the century in which phenomenology emerged, image theory took so little notice of it. The question becomes all the more relevant as the subsequent chapter is devoted to phenomenological theories of the image.

With regard to Husserl, in particular, Alloa in Chapter Four defends a double interpretive thesis. If one considers the first segment of his career, Husserl seems unable to grasp the irreducibly mediating character of the image, and this limit is related to his attempt to operate a 'liberation from all the symbols, images, and other mediations with which post-Hegelian and, later, neo-Kantian currents had interspersed philosophy in the late nineteenth century'. Starting with the Göttingen lectures of 1904-1905, however, 'another Husserl' comes to the fore: one who no longer sticks to 'the primacy of the immediate', but rather undermines it by means of a newly minted, *triadic* conception of the image. This conception breaks with the dichotomy between the image as a material vehicle and the object it depicts by introducing a third element, namely, the appearance or 'image object', which lies between the two. Elsewhere, this fundamental triad is described in slightly different terms. In the *Crisis*, for instance, Husserl distinguishes between the appearing object (the *what*), the mode of appearing (the *how*), and the addressee of the appearances, the 'datival *to whom*'.

Readers familiar with the philosophy of Charles S. Peirce will find it puzzling that Alloa opposes this triadic conception of the image to what he calls a semiotic conception. For Peirce's semiotics is based on a comparable triadic model in which the distinction between sign-vehicle and sign-object is made possible by the mediation of an 'interpretant', which Peirce describes as that *to which* the sign conveys its meaning. The two models are, of course, not perfectly overlapping. But there are sufficient similarities to indicate that Alloa's tacit assimilation of semiotics with the transparency paradigm and a binary conception of the image would require greater scrutiny than is provided in this book.

Alloa's phenomenological arguments come to a head in the book's final chapter. Drawing inspiration from Nelson Goodman's philosophy of art, he argues that the original question of 'What is an image' must be replaced with the question of '*When* is an image.' That is, rather than drawing a set of necessary and sufficient conditions for something to be an image, we should look for 'symptoms' of pictoriality. This anti-essentialist move derives from the two approaches that give this book its peculiar flavour. The first is historical awareness of the contingent nature of our philosophical categories, including the very category of 'image'. The second is a phenomenological inclination to begin the process of inquiry not with the image as a ready-made object, but rather with the 'much vaster field of the iconic' in which the image is embedded. Drawing from Maurice Merleau-Ponty and William James, Alloa repeatedly insists on the phenomenologically constitutive nature of this surrounding field, these 'fringes of the act of seeing' from which the image springs into the beholder's eye.

Given that they are best interpreted as something radically different from a set of necessary and sufficient conditions of the iconic, it should come as no surprise that Alloa's ten 'symptoms' display porous boundaries. They continuously blend with one another and, in so doing, let at least four overarching themes emerge. Let me take each of these four themes in turn.

1. The most significant and encompassing theme is the image's ability to present its content in an immediate or immediately perspicuous manner. Images, according to Alloa, are synoptic, meaning that their components are presented all at once. This, in turn, entails ellipsis and framing, or the fact that, while presenting their content perspicuously, images will necessarily leave out something else. (Both synopticity and ellipsis, in turn, entail 'flatness' or 'two-dimensionality'. A three-dimensional sculpture is less elliptic and less synoptic than a picture: it leaves out less and cannot present everything all at once.) The image's specific way of conveying content also explains its specific evidential force, which Alloa calls *figurality*. A diagram is particularly effective at convincing and informing because it does so perspicuously and without any need for discursive elaboration. Finally, with the symptom of *presentativity* Alloa captures the image's ability to 'let something other than what is currently visible be seen'. But presentativity is also – following Susanne Langer – the opposite of 'discursivity', i.e., a linear and temporally extended mode of signification.

2. One of the most fascinating aspects of this final chapter is that, just as Alloa sketches the topics of presentativity or synopticity in images, he also suggests that this is 'clearly insufficient to define images [...] What needs explanation, rather, is how it is that images do not keep anything from the eye and yet in them not everything is given visibly from the outset'. In other words, images do not merely present their content perspicuously – they also contain an element of potentiality or indeterminacy. This indeterminacy may be reduced through the interplay with discursive modes of presentation (consider a situation in which a verbal description expresses, describes, or clarifies the content of an image). Images display a fringe or halo of vagueness. They also contain areas in which indeterminacy rather than representational focality becomes predominant – as in the faux marbles of Fra Angelico, which, on closer inspection, are not faux marbles at all but rather abstract 'matrices of meaning in which a figurative force rests in a state of latency'.

3. A further theme is the specific ability of images to indicate and exemplify by dint of their medial nature. While semioticians traditionally take iconicity and indexicality to be two different forms of signification, Alloa argues that images embody a specific kind of *deixis*. That is, images always refer to themselves as much as they refer to something else. They thus possess ostensitivy, that is, a dimension of pure appearance – or 'phenomenal excess' – that shows itself without signifying anything else. If I understand Alloa correctly, this 'phenomenal excess' is nothing other than the medium or *Bildobjekt*. It is the intermediate and diaphanous layer of appearance through which something becomes visible (see also the symptom of *seeing with*). Finally, the 'phenomenal excess' is also the place where a chiasm of gazes occurs. While I look at an image, something springs out and 'demands attention for itself'. In other words, the more you stare at images, the more they stare back at you.

4. A final theme is exemplified by the symptom of variation sensitivity. Goodman would have referred to it as 'density', indicating that images are unlike discrete systems of signification. Even minimal changes in appearance can have consequences for the image's meaning. Therefore, 'no detail, no nuance can per se be declared irrelevant'. This motivates Alloa's provocative claim that 'there are no digital images. Data masses become images only when they are brought into an internally consistent pictorial appearance for receptors capable of perception'. Today we are increasingly discussing a new generation of digital images, specifically those created by generative forms of AI from textual prompts and vast pre-processed datasets. Much of this technology relies on the system's capacity to progressively reduce noise in the collection of pixels comprising a digital image, leveraging linguistic encodings in the process. It would be a timely endeavour to enquire about the specific challenges this novel development poses to a phenomenology of visual media, as well as the consequences that this further linguisticisation of the image may have for the dynamics of the creation, fruition and transmission of pictorial contents.

While it offers a thorough examination of the phenomenological tradition, Alloa's book also engages in close dialogue with an exceptionally broad array of theories, ranging from the classics of Western philosophy to prominent figures in twentieth- and twenty-first-century image theory. In part due to this wide range of references, the book also provides a vital link between philosophical reflection and historical-artistic studies. *Looking Through Images* is a must-read for anyone with a stake in the theory of image, media and imagination.

Tullio Viola

Black anarchism's history and future

Lorenzo Kom'boa Ervin, *Anarchism and the Black Revolution: The Definitive Edition* (London: Pluto Press, 2021). 224pp., £85.00 hb., £19.99 pb., 978 0 74534 580 2 hb., 978 0 74534 581 9 pb.

Should the state be the source of freedom? Should it be a wellspring for the affirmation of humanism? The modern anarchist tradition has repeatedly answered these questions in the negative, thereby distinguishing it from proponents of liberal democracy as well as Marxism-Leninism. Anarchism at its core is anti-statist, arguing that social stability and progress are best gained through more immediate forms of direct democracy and mutual aid. A fostering of and dependence on local community is positioned against bureaucratic state assistance and intervention. Unsurprisingly, anarchism has consequently appealed to activist-intellectuals and communities that have been marginalised by states and, often as a matter of routine, have been policed by states through violence.

These elements provide an explanation as to why anarchist politics would appeal to Black activists. Yet the Black anarchist tradition remains under-examined as a critical position within the history of Black struggle, in addition to being underappreciated as an approach for present and future politics. Lorenzo Kom'boa Ervin's *Anarchism and the Black Revolution* is a vital intervention designed to rectify this situation. It addresses what makes Black anarchism distinctive. 'What sets Black anarchism apart from classical or European anarchism is that it was born out of a rejection of the hierarchical, messianic, and authoritarian embraces that limited so many Black movements prior', William C. Anderson summarises in his foreword to Ervin's book. 'This makes Black anarchism special because it was already doing the terribly undervalued work of internal critique'.

This internal critique emerged from Ervin's own life. His path to anarchism was eventful, mirroring a number of the most important events and organisations during the second half of the last century. Born in Chattanooga, Tennessee, in 1947, he came of political age during the era of the Vietnam War and civil rights movement. His childhood was shaped by Black and working-class life in the Jim Crow South – his father was a chauffeur and his mother a domestic worker. He joined the military during the 1960s only to become an anti-war activist shortly thereafter, leading to a court martial and discharge. Ervin went on to become involved with the Student Nonviolent Coordinating Committee (SNCC) and the Black Panthers. The crackdown on Black radicalism at the time prompted him to hijack a plane to Cuba, where he was imprisoned by the government, including a stint in solitary confinement. He then fled to Czechoslovakia, followed by East Germany, after which he was deported back to the US. These fraught international experiences with socialist states, combined with the suppression he was subjected to by the US government, contributed to his growing disillusionment and skepticism toward governments generally as providing solutions to social problems, whether racism or class inequality.

Time in federal prison further reinforced this critical perspective. Yet it also fortuitously presented him with a new set of ideas. Upon his return to the US, Ervin encountered the attorney and famed prison abolitionist Martin Sostre (1923-2015), who introduced him to the concept of anarchist socialism. The life of Sostre requires its own biography. Black Puerto Rican in background, Sostre began his activism as a member of the Nation of Islam during the early 1960s. He went on to become politically involved on several fronts, including advocating for prisoner rights and education during the 1960s and 1970s as well as opening the Afro-Asian Bookstore in Buffalo, New York, in 1966. He himself was imprisoned before and after this latter moment, including his arrest in July 1967 and sentence to forty-one years on a range of falsified charges including assault and drug possession. Sostre subsequently gained a reputation as a political prisoner with Amnesty International adopting his case in 1973, which led to his sentence being commuted in December 1975 and his release in 1976. In the introduction to *Anarchism and the Black Revolution*, Ervin not only attributes his embrace of anarchism to Sostre but credits him, along with figures like George Jackson (1941-71), for establishing the prison movement that led to the 1971 Attica Prison Rebellion and the continued struggle for prisoners' rights and against mass incarceration today.

Ervin wrote the first edition of *Anarchism and the Black Revolution* while serving a sentence of life imprisonment in a federal penitentiary following his return to the US. Despite these conditions of confinement, the book was published in 1979 as an 84-page pamphlet. Released after fifteen years of his sentence, Ervin published a second edition in 1988 and eventually a third edition in 2012 through presses connected to the Industrial Workers of the World. This new edition from Pluto Press therefore marks the fourth iteration of the book and the first with a publisher with wide international distribution. As a consequence, this latest republication is intended to introduce Black anarchism to a more global audience. It does so by providing a mix of personal history, a summation of key concepts, discussion of issues facing the Black community today, and, above all, an insistent argument as to why anarchism delivers the best approach for addressing such matters.

Consisting of five chapters (including the introduction) plus two forewords and a concluding interview with Ervin, this definitive edition of *Anarchism and the Black Revolution* goes substantially beyond its first appearance as a pamphlet. The introduction offers a brief autobiography by Ervin before going through a list of ten reasons why Black anarchism remains important for revolutionary struggle in the present. These reasons include its role in the prison movement, but also its enduring critical stance against states and state violence, whether the past authoritarianism of Marxist-Leninist governments like that in the Soviet Union or in present-day liberal democracies like the United States, which regularly police their citizens through the threat and practice of violence. Ervin criticises the left liberal wing of the US Democratic Party for this latter reason, but he also directs ire toward Black leaders like Jesse Jackson and Al Sharpton for hijacking the ideals of the 1960s Civil Rights Movement as defined by SNCC and the Black Panthers. He argues that such politicians have diminished their radicalism in favour of alliances with bourgeois interests. Ervin similarly lambasts the founders of #BlackLivesMatter for accruing private homes and monetary wealth for themselves, thus selling out the principles of anti-violence and Black humanism which established the movement. In short, Ervin delivers a sustained critique of the past several decades of Black politics in the US for its reliance on government intervention and legislation as a means of salvation for safeguarding Black rights and livelihood.

Anarchism and the Black Revolution is not purely a work of criticism, however. Supplementing these strident positions are methodical discussions of how and why anarchism provides a meaningful alternative, particularly through its concepts of autonomy, mutual aid and direct democracy. In Chapter One, titled 'Anarchism Defined', Ervin begins by initially describing anarchism as libertarian socialism, though he follows up this characterisation by carefully going through the various types of anarchism, distinguishing, for example, between anarcho-syndicalists, who focus on labour politics, and anarchist-communists, who focus on revolutionary politics. These distinctions can overlap, of course, but Ervin's main point is to undermine the pejorative, essentialist stereotype of the bomb-throwing, nihilistic anarchist. Ervin goes to great lengths to explain the intellectual richness of the anarchist tradition. He also argues for the affinities between anarchism and Black political organisations like SNCC and the Black Panthers, given the aspects of direct democracy and mutual aid that each cultivated. In the case of the latter party, it was only when the leadership style of Huey P. Newton and Bobby Seale became more authoritarian, in Ervin's view, that the movement started to falter internally. Rather than parties, Ervin promotes the anarchist concept of 'affinity groups' which number between three and fifteen people and are organised around collective practices of mutual aid, education, political action and unity. Ervin refers to them as 'groups for living revolution' – the idea being utopian conditions do not come *after* struggle but are created *during* and *through* struggle.

The remaining chapters further explore the challenges and opportunities for Black anarchism.

Chapter Two, 'Capitalism and Racism', promotes 'Black Autonomy' as an alternative strategy apart from conventional trade unionism, which overlooks racism, and Black nationalism, which indulges a misguided sense of political separatism. Ervin writes that the term 'Black' in his usage refers to 'all existing peoples of colour' with Black Autonomy consequently comprising a new type of 'revolutionary organisation' within the anarchist movement that reflects 'a new radical consciousness of race and class'. Structurally, Black Autonomy resists vanguard parties, personality cults and 'any type of Black nation-state', which can result in the reinforcement of hierarchies. Chapter Three, 'Anarchism and the Black Revolution', outlines what the aims of Black anarchism are if establishing a new state is not the primary outcome sought. Central among these, in principle, are collectives and communes that constitute 'liberated zones' beyond the control of capital and the state. Tax boycotts, rent strikes, urban squatting, abolishing militarism, rejecting sexism, community food systems, community councils and labour caucuses, among many other measures, provide complementary techniques for avoiding dependence on existing state and economic structures. Echoing the legendary query of George Padmore regarding Pan-Africanism versus communism as a strategy for Black internationalism, Chapter Four is entitled 'Pan-Africanism or Intercommunalism?', in which Ervin addresses the challenges of building a Black anarchist internationalism. Drawing from the experiences of projects like the Black Autonomy International, he acknowledges the logistical difficulties of building a decentralised, transnational anarchist network. Still, he remains unwavering in his commitment to the possibility and importance of such an endeavour.

The main argument of Ervin's book is clear – namely, the anti-statist political alternative anarchism provides for Black and other activists of colour. Since the Occupy Movement over a decade ago, anarchism has received more mainstream attention through the writings of activists and intellectuals like James Scott and the late David Graeber. In contrast to these thinkers, Ervin's book provides an important intervention by stressing how anarchism provides a strategy not just against global capitalism and the forms of inequality it has created, but also against systemic racism, which has been an accomplice in such disparities. Indeed, there have been numerous publications of late regarding the fact and history of racial capitalism as a concept and condition, but there have arguably been fewer treatises on possible solutions, especially those that offer new ideas and tactics. Though written in a spirit of militancy, *Anarchism and the Black Revolution* is oriented around formulating practical responses to this issue through the essential tenets of anarchism. In the concluding interview with Anderson, Ervin proposes the need to be 'ungovernable' – not in the sense of political chaos and disorganisation, but as a situation and means for reconstituting politics and society through direct democracy and forms of reciprocity, rather than top-down statist measures approximating a revolution from above.

Taken together, *Anarchism and the Black Revolution* is at times repetitive, reflecting its multiple editions over time. As a manifesto, it can also be more speculative, rather than experientially grounded. Some readers will want to learn more about the practicalities of organising through firsthand examples. Nonetheless, Ervin is committed to praxis, not simply theory. He envisions and promotes the idea of a present-day 'practopian' society, generated through everyday practices, rather than an elusive, future-oriented utopian society. As Joy James writes in her introductory essay 'Catalyst', the anarchism that Ervin espouses is revolutionary through its grassroots orientation. Rejecting notions of the vanguard party and the dictatorship of the proletariat, Ervin favours the 'catalyst group' comprised of an 'organic collective', consisting of 'ancestor and survivor; elders/youths; activists; intellectuals; rebels; [and] revolutionary lovers' – their common denominator being 'painfully accumulated experiential knowledge'. In this way, Ervin's approach to anarchism ultimately stresses the power, humanism and revolutionary agency of the masses over political elites. For these and other reasons, *Anarchism and the Black Revolution* speaks to our political moment.

Christopher J. Lee

Containing Russia

Alexander Kluge, *Russia Container*, trans. Alexander Booth (Chicago: Seagull Books, 2022). 392pp., £27.50 hb., 978 1 80309 065 8

Russia Container is not a book about Russia. It's about the images and stories that East Germans had of Soviet Russia before the fall of the Berlin Wall in 1989 and after. Alexander Kluge wrote it 'on commission' by his sister Alexandra Kluge, who, unlike her brother, lived in the German Democratic Republic after the separation of their parents. There Alexandra learnt Russian at school and read Pushkin as well as Russian fairy tales. After her death in 2017 Kluge collected some of her stories about Russia together with other (former East) German stories. The book shows the romantic feeling that East Germans had, and still have, for Russia. It also demonstrates how these passions spilt over to the 'western' part of Germany, or at least to Kluge himself. But the romanticism of the book is not one of exalted ideas of a nation or state, but rather of the individual human experience, which is in a fundamental conflict with abstract ideas and which tries to resist them.

Kluge received the final version of the English translation of *Russia Container* on the day before the Russian tanks invaded Ukrainian territory. He decided to include an introduction which is meant to serve as a 'reading aid'. After 24 February the reader might indeed need help reading *Russia Container* – a book that neither anticipates this event nor deals with other Russian interventions, operations and annexations before 2022. However, if the reader expects Kluge to make sense of the recent events, then the makeshift introduction fails. There Kluge chooses the form of diary entries, which begin with fantasising about the possibility of turning back time. The motive of turning back time suggests that something unamendable has happened, which history cannot rectify. Then he proceeds with a story of James Baker, who as the US Secretary of State travelled to Russia in 1991 with the abstract idea that Russia should not repeat the history of the German Empire after 1918 – humiliation and then total war. It is implicit in Kluge's story that not much was done to prevent this. This could be read as a suggestion that if time could be turned back, it should go to 1991 – although another story in the introduction suggests that 'what is happening in Ukraine' has been developing for over 100 years and that this is why we cannot readily understand what is now happening or why it hurts so much: 'The older [the crystal] is, the harder, the more unreal and more abstract'. The 'reading aid' also includes the opinion of a desperate civilian who suffered the war and who just 'wants peace', no matter who started it. If this was intended as an overview of stories on the war, then it is not representative of their variety. Indeed, there are no stories told by Ukrainians in Kluge's book. Their absence confirms that *Russia Container* is about German stories. In other words, the introduction doubles and reinforces the content of the book rather than offering aid in this traumatic and disorientating situation. It confirms that (East) Germans have not known how the Russian 'crystal' formed itself in relation to Ukraine.

Perhaps there could not have been a worse moment to publish such a book about Russia. But the anachronism of its publication reflects the artistic and literary form of the 'container'. A container for Kluge transports that which has been collected before it would be lost. The *Children's and Household Tales* (*Kinder- und Hausmärchen*) from 1812 is the most vivid example of a container. The Grimm brothers collected fairy tales at a point when the interest in telling stories had already faded. Fairy tales used to evolve, consolidate and renew their narratives and motifs through the process of oral tradition. The Grimm brothers tried to capture them before they vanished once and for all, thereby producing a written, literary culture of these tales. *Children's and Household Tales* is therefore merely a snapshot of the fairy-tale tradition and should not be considered as a finished work. Rather, it is precisely a container of stories, which came into existence in contexts that we do not remember anymore, and which had meaning that we now struggle to understand. Fairy tales are after-images of lost collective memories – a theory which is implicit in Kluge's and Oskar Negt's *History and Obstinacy* (2014, originally published in German in 1981). They are anachronistic in many ways. This is exactly how we could understand the content of Kluge's *Russia Container*: an experience of Russia which is about to vanish.

The book consists of five chapters with many different sections which are not related to each other through narrative. Instead, a socio-historical theme is developed through a variety of different, unrelated stories by Kluge and by other, sometimes fictional storytellers. Thus, the theme appears as a simultaneity of stories. One example are the stories about the pinnacle of the Cold War in 1983, which tell how the US-Navy carried out a manoeuvre at the Soviet borders in the North Sea and how the Soviets learned about the US plans for 'decapitation' (*Enthauptungsschlag*), namely a nuclear bombing of Moscow. These stories are then followed by one from a former East German, who experienced the fall of the Berlin Wall – in his words, the 'annexation' of GDR by FRG – as a 'decapitation', and, as a consequence, began to vote for the nationalist party Alternative für Deutschland, and then moved to Russia. It continues with more stories about NATO manoeuvres near Russian borders and one report by a translator who was 'in Minsk'. What is meant are the meetings around the Minsk Agreements from 2015. The translator describes how the now former German Chancellor Angela Merkel was trying to read the Russian President Vladimir Putin's facial expression and his body language. The historical context of their encounter, namely the war in East Ukraine, is never mentioned.

The simultaneous, and thus non-causal relation of the stories to one another is emphasised by Kluge's own personal story that evolves as part of the Cold War theme: 'The most dangerous moment of the Cold War'. Kluge's contemplation of the sky and his worries about his newborn daughter are obviously unrelated to the events of the grand political stage and yet they appear at once. In 1983 Kluge received an award in Venice for his film *The Power of Feeling* (*Die Macht der Gefühle*). In *Russia Container* he is telling us about how he felt in that moment, namely, anxious that his daughter could catch a cold. This anxiety 'relates' to the anxiety around the Cold War. Putting the personal-individual anxiety together with the socio-political enables a retrospective interpretation of unrelated experiences as interrelated: to think that he sensed the danger of the *Cold* War through his worries about his daughter catching a *cold*. The book produces a side-by-side of experiences, asking the reader to suspend the complexities of the political context.

Kluge's work is thus a plea for the recovery of the significance of individual experience. This plea is directed against rationality and rationalisation that is a key feature of capitalist, including socialist, societies, which tend to suppress the individual as Kluge conceptualises it, namely, as a reservoir of specific capacities. These human capacities are constantly being challenged and undermined by progress which is necessary for socioeconomic development. As a result, humans have developed a resistance to withstand the constant threat of progress, which keeps divesting them from their learned capacities. Obstinacy is the flipside of history (see his and Oskar Negt's *History and Obstinacy*). The (re)collecting of individual experience and its juxtaposition with other individual experiences is important because it captures the way in which people deal with the social and its history.

The conflict between the social and the individual is dramatised in *Russia Container* in passages on the theme of the Stalinist Terror. Pavel Florensky – a theologian *and* mathematician was employed by Leon Trotsky to work on the project of electrification. Florensky was arrested in 1933 for his book on relativity theory and executed in 1937. As a mathematician he believed in numbers, and as a theologian he believed in the divine. The number as a cipher for the ultimate alienation is considered a result of abstraction and rationalisation. Presumably, Florensky believed that he could work on a project that tries to reconcile the holy light with the electric light, thus reconciling spirituality and rationalisation. This identification with what he thought the socialist project meant tragically brought him his death.

Florensky's story demonstrates how radical utopian thinking – namely, the idea that the individual can see him- or herself fully reflected in the social – came into conflict with the state. This and the stories of many other citizens during the Stalinist Terror presumably stand for the impossibility of wiping out the resistance or obstinacy of individuals. Kluge's book begins with stories about the resistance of the Orthodox Christians to the reforms of Nikon in the seventeenth century, which tried to adjust the liturgy to the Greek tradition. The so-called Old Believers resisted and paid with their lives. Obstinacy is a key human characteristic for Kluge, and he understands history as such in relation to this obstinacy.

Individual experience conflicts with the social because the social tends to rationalise and abstract from the individual and his or her experiences. When the individual recognises his or her personal experience in social events or in the social as such, these moments are 'magical', because they are impossible, even though they happen sometimes. Kluge tries to stage or recreate precisely these magical moments in this book.

Russia Container does not describe Russia as a country that could potentially invade Ukraine, but it describes Russia as a country or empire that was itself invaded twice: by Napoleon's and then Hitler's troops. Kluge's chapter on imperialism ('The Plunderer's Eye Turned Towards the Map/The Principle of Abstraction') does not deal with Russia's imperialism but with British and German imperialism. The theme of imperialism is developed by Kluge as a juxtaposition of 'imperialism as love' and 'imperialism as abstraction'. It begins with the story of his sister Alexandra, living in the GDR on a territory conquered by the Soviet army, where she falls in love with Russian culture, with her conqueror. This is followed by a story of Kluge playing soldiers in his school yard. ('All of us students were moved by the prospect of receiving a knight's estate in the Crimea or – alternatively – a latifundium in German East Africa'.) It moves further to the British geo-politician Halford Mackinder, who considered the majority of the territory of the Russian Empire as the so-called 'heartland', which in his theory was globally the most important geopolitical territory and which is an expression of British desires to colonise Eastern Europe and Russia. It proceeds to a story about the writer Rudyard Kipling, who was not a lover of 'his own green, sea-swept island', but a passionate lover of the British colonies, which even had bodily expressions, as if they were 'his own skin'. This passionate, albeit orientalist and in all ways problematic, 'love' is juxtaposed by Kluge to the abstract, cold and 'loveless' imperial conquest of Russia by Hitler's troops. The stories go that Hitler never visited Russia, implicating that he never had an orientalist vision. Furthermore, we are told that the Wehrmacht soldiers never knew exactly why they were invading Russia and never had a desire to live or work there. The image that is mediating the juxtaposition of 'hot' and 'cold' imperialism is the cousin of Yevgeny Onegin, who like Don Juan, was keeping books of his 'conquests'. 'Nothing more horrible, insistent, pitiless than a conqueror who does not want the conquered'. These stories about imperialism are obnoxious in the light of Russia's attempts to conquer Ukraine, but they also reveal something about the German and West-European colonial gaze towards Russia and Eastern Europe.

With Kluge's *Russia Container* we are dealing with a particular method of thinking with motifs, images and stories. The point that is made in the chapter on imperialism is not that we need to distinguish between hot and cold imperialism, but that such stories *did* circulate and some of them still do circulate even if in a different disguise. The motifs or images and certain compositions of those motifs and images retain their relevance and resonance when they are placed in a different context or story. Thinking in narrative structures and motifs is potentially perilous because it can easily be instrumentalised to manipulate readers. But unlike many stories that currently circulate in the press, academic and artistic talks, including Instagram 'stories', which juxtapose the current events with motifs of World War I, World War II, fascism, Hitler, Stalin, etc., Kluge's stories do not claim to be true. In contrast to politics, journalism and other spheres that operate with myths, motifs and narrative, Kluge's book uses images and literature critically, by containing them and by enabling the reader to perceive them as such.

Marina Gerber

Ordoliberal orthodoxy?

Raphaël Fèvre, *A Political Economy of Power: Ordoliberalism in Context, 1932-1950* (Oxford: Oxford University Press, 2021). 280pp., £64.00 hb., 978 0 19760 780 0

George Monbiot's statement in a 2016 *Guardian* article that neoliberalism is the 'ideology at the root of all our problems' still resonates today. A huge body of literature has been dedicated to exploring how neoliberalism has influenced our economic, political and social lives – ranging from Michel Foucault's biopolitical analysis, taken up by scholars such as Wendy Brown, to David Harvey's Marxist critique to Melinda Cooper's feminist analysis. More recently, Quinn Slobodian focused on the influence of Central European strands of neoliberalism and how these shaped the 'globalist' political order. Thus, Raphaël Fèvre's *A Political Economy of Power: Ordoliberalism in Context, 1932-1950* comes at a time when popular and academic interest in neoliberalism and its variants is growing. The specific focus on German neoliberalism, known as ordoliberalism, has also been gaining interest, especially since the 2009 European sovereign debt crisis. Throughout the crisis Germany and the EU were repeatedly accused of sabotaging the world's economic recovery through their excessive austerity measures. Notably, Timothy Geithner, the US Secretary of the Treasury at the time, attacked the continent's 'ordoliberal' austerity measures. In 2016 Angela Merkel, explicitly affirmed her 'firm conviction' in Germany's historical 'ordoliberal principles', which would neither lose 'their importance nor their relevance'.

A scholar of the history of economic thought and philosophy, Fèvre's interest in the epistemological and philosophical foundations of ordoliberalism makes for an insightful understanding of ordoliberalism grounded in firm economic expertise. Fèvre has contributed many valuable articles uncovering ordoliberalism's intellectual history. Rather than positing ordoliberalism as a variant of neoliberalism however, Fèvre understands the ordoliberal project as an 'autonomous form of economic knowledge driven by power issues.' In placing the original ordoliberal project within the German interwar context, he also presents it as reactionary and 'the fruit of interwar doctrines, analyses, and debates' across contemporary social sciences. If ordoliberalism was a reaction to the unique interwar and post-Second World War context, how can we explain its seemingly continuous centrality in German political economy and the EU more generally?

Fèvre considers the present-day ordoliberal orthodoxy as being somewhat removed from, what he calls the 'seminal' or original ordoliberal project. The former is centered around three interrelated axioms. First, the independence of a Central Bank committed to price stability and separate from national sovereignties. Second, an aversion to fiscal policy and increasing (public) debts, identifiable with the recent European policy of monetary and fiscal austerity. Finally, 'a defence of competition based on a structural supply policy as the primary tool to fight unemployment' which pushes for the privatisation of public enterprises and services. On the other hand, he sees the seminal ordoliberal project as attempting to free the market economy from the 'deleterious exercise of illegitimate powers'. In providing a historical look at ordoliberalism, he aims to provide new insights into the true principles at the heart of contemporary ordoliberal orthodoxy.

Fèvre deepens our understanding of the original ordoliberal doctrine by exploring the theoretical foundations of ordoliberal economy (chapter 1), the substantial and contextual elements of one of the most prominent intellectuals proliferating the ordoliberal project, Walter Eucken's analysis of economic orders and market structures (chapter 2), the centrality of power in ordoliberal economic theory (chapter 3), their formulation of a new social question (chapter 4) and the proliferation of the ordoliberal doctrine after the Second World War (chapter 5). The originality of Fèvre's analysis lies in the identification of power as the central subject of ordoliberal political economy, which is a running theme throughout the chapters. Fèvre defines power from the ordoliberal perspective as 'the capacity of an actor to determine the structure of a specific economic order.'

The ordoliberal project has its roots in the Freiburg School of Economics, spearheaded by economists including Walter Eucken (1891-1950) and lawyers such as

Franz Böhm (1895-1977). Wilhelm Röpke (1899-1966) and Alexander Rüstow (1885-1963) formulated ordoliberalism's cultural project. The Minister of Economy and consequent Federal Chancellor Ludwig Erhard and the academic Alfred Müller-Armack (1901-1978) were not strictly speaking ordoliberals, yet 'bore a political project based in part on ordoliberal ideas, which they renamed the "Social Market Economy".' The ordoliberal intellectuals formulated a 'historical diagnosis' built around the human instinct to acquire power as the driving force of history, finding a causal link between historical liberalism in the nineteenth century and the economic planning of the first half of the twentieth century. They found that nineteenth-century laissez-faire liberalism had paved the way for increased concentrations of private economic power, manifesting in cartelised and monopoly market structures, which proved detrimental to 'economic freedom'. This also proved detrimental to political freedom as 'some companies (or sectors) could acquire significant bargaining power over the ruling political/administrative class.' Coupled with the political instability of the Weimar Republic and the Great Depression, 'the state had to increase and intensify the scope of its interventions in the economic process' causing a profound change in the economic order in favour of a centrally planned system. This culminated in the highly cartelised planning economy of the Nazis from 1933 onwards. The ordoliberals therefore saw power relations as the driving force behind both centrally planned and laissez-faire orders and sought to formulate a political economy that decentralised power in favour of a 'third way' between laissez-faire liberalism and central planning.

Fèvre then goes on to show how ordoliberals viewed power as the 'source of an epistemological problem.' Eucken tried to acquire a 'scientific understanding of the driving forces underlying the economic order' and apply theoretical analysis to the economic uses and abuses of power. However, Eucken was aware of the necessity to 'detach scientific production from any ideological hold' and thus drew inspiration from 'Kant, Schopenhauer, and particularly from Husserl and Weber to underpin his thesis of the contamination of scientific knowledge by vested interests.' He thus updated the old German methodological quarrel (*Methodenstreit*) between the Austrian and German Historical Schools regarding the place of theory in economics and the social sciences more generally, as well as the use of history in explaining human action.

The ordoliberals, Eucken in particular, therefore contributed to two of the most significant international economic discussions of the interwar years: the feasibility of socialist calculation in a centrally planned economy and the 'debate over imperfect/monopolistic market structures.' To Eucken, these two debates embodied aspects of the same problem of 'power manifestations in the economy, but on different scales.' In the former debate Eucken agreed with Austrian-orientated economists such as Ludwig von Mises and Friedrich Hayek on the impossibility of proper economic calculation in a socialist-like economy. Eucken's contribution to the latter debate on market structures ties in with this, since he saw monopolistic market structures as assimilating economic power in a similar way to centrally planned economies, just on a smaller scale, and therefore distorting the price mechanism and freedom on the market.

Alongside this, the ordoliberals 'formulated a new social question based on the collapse of human freedom and autonomy under rising private and public economic powers' in which they saw the dispersion of economic power to be the key to overcoming this social question. Rather than looking to Marx and Gustav von Schmoller's '*Sozialpolitik* in the light of the new modes of economic management' such as state planning, state interventionism and the welfare state, the ordoliberals considered market competition as the best tool for disempowering private economic power and therefore also regulating the social body. This belief was crystallised in politics when the law against restrictions on competition came into effect in the Federal Republic of Germany in January 1958, whilst Ludwig Erhard was economics minister.

The epilogue details the ordoliberal project and discourse after the Second World War (1946-50) and how it gained traction in West Germany. This is rooted in the ordoliberal diagnosis of the Allies' management of the postwar West German economy as a continuation of the Nazi planning and price-fixing model. However, this changed with the monetary reform implemented in 1948, described by Fèvre as a 'cunning maneuver of the Anglo-American Bizone in keeping with Western liberal principles and in opposition to the rise of the communist bloc.' However, he stresses that the price liberalisation implemented alongside the currency reform was pushed by the ordoliberals, with Erhard at their helm, who implemented the price liberalisation without consultation with the Allies. Fèvre concludes the epilogue with the powerful statement that 'the ordoliberal crusade for market liberalism was also intended as a crusade against communism.' He continues that 'the real impact of ordoliberal ideas should be sought in their capacity to shape the agenda of the West German state' and 'to exert considerable influence on the postwar ideological context' with the 'West-East leap into the Cold War'.

Ordoliberalism 'contributed to the development of a form of economic rationale for the West German state, presenting itself as architect of an overall vision of society from the perspective of its economic performance.' In other words, West Germany's identity and legitimacy after the Second World War was rooted in its economic freedom and success. Though the original ordoliberal project became diluted with Erhard's 'Social Market Economy' framework and overshadowed by neoclassical economics in the 1960s and the so-called counter-revolution of the late 1970s, the 2009 eurozone crisis brought ordoliberal debates to the fore once more. Fèvre finds it surprising to see the post-crisis political discourses

> echoing programs born in the interwar period and developed for the postwar era some fifty years ago. There is perhaps some irony in the vision of ordoliberalism resurfacing as an ossified model resting on austerity measures, in a form that is a far cry from the first ordoliberals' 'third way', the purpose of which was to free market economy from the deleterious exercise of illegitimate powers.

Fèvre therefore makes it clear that he does not conflate the contemporary declarations of ordoliberal orthodoxy with the ordoliberal project of the interwar era. Though this is largely true, he does not address the continuity regarding the grounding of society in the economy – in turning to competition and the market mechanism to solve social questions. However, this market-centricity could also be attributed to the neoliberal hegemony that prevails today. The ordoliberals were themselves deeply involved in the global neoliberal networks of the mid-twentieth century, such as the Mont Pelerin Society (Röpke was its president in 1961), that bred an international think tank network and the 'neoliberalisation' of global institutions, such as the IMF and the World Bank. Though it is true that the ordoliberals railed against unfettered laissez-faire liberalism and adhered to a 'softer' form of neoliberalism, it nevertheless remained a form of neoliberalism that promoted economic liberalism and rejected government spending and intervention. Rather than positing ordoliberalism as a 'third way' between central planning and laissez-faire, it should, and already has, been reformulated as an attempt to reinvent liberalism. With the Great Depression and general economic instability of the inter- and postwar years, liberalism's appeal was rapidly declining and in need of revitalisation. Fèvre hints at this when discussing the relationship of the ordoliberals to Marx, who they vehemently opposed, recognising that ultimately the ordoliberals aimed to resist fellow scholars' 'anti-capitalist attitude', which 'found a particularly fruitful relay in the public opinion of the "masses".' The ordoliberal engagement with the concept of 'the masses' or 'mass society' is a further point of contention, as it sheds light on especially Röpke's conservative and elitist views on social policy. Despite being insufficiently critical of the ordoliberal doctrine and its effects on German and European society, *A Political Economy of Power* meticulously dissects the seminal ordoliberal project, delving into its epistemology, morphology and methodology in great detail and offering a novel analysis of ordoliberalism through the nexus of power relations.

Isabel Oakes

Drucilla Cornell, 1950-2022

Philosopher-activist of the imaginary domain

Chiara Bottici

I met Drucilla Cornell at the New School for Social Research, shortly after my arrival in the US at a time of political turmoil. I joined the Philosophy Department in 2010, and one of the first things I was invited to do was help organise an international conference called 'The Anarchist Turn'. The conference took place in May 2011 and it gathered an uncharacteristically large audience by academic standards, leaving many of us quite surprised. Little did I know that some of the people who had gathered there would decide not to leave and ended up staying the whole summer, until, in September 2011, the movement called Occupy Wall Street erupted in the streets. People started to flow into the city, Zuccotti Park was occupied, and everywhere a revolutionary ferment was palpable. During OWS, as in the Arab uprisings, the movement's strength was its spontaneous, horizontal character, but, as some of us feared, this may also have been one of its weaknesses: how to make sure that such a movement would not vanish as quickly as it came about?

It is within this framework that a student told me about a visiting professor who was teaching a class on how to create a revolutionary government. Who on the planet had come up with that class, right at that moment, which seemed so much needed? In December, the Arab revolts started and in January, Drucilla Cornell's 'Constituting a Revolutionary Government' class began. In the middle of that revolutionary ferment, sparked by the first protests in Tunis, Drucilla was there, expressing her solidarity with demonstrators, while immersing students in the classical debates of the European left, such as Marx vs. Bakunin, or Lenin vs. Luxemburg, but also putting them in dialogue with authors like Frantz Fanon and Edouard Glissant among others. Drucilla did not simply indulge in rhetoric about 'decolonisation': she questioned the colonial imaginary and its epistemological boundaries in the same way in which she questioned the sexist imaginary in her feminist work. She was suspicious of the word 'decolonisation' because in her view, it often amounted to a rhetorical move that paradoxically reproduced the centrality of the colonial imaginary:[1] if we are simply decolonising 'Kant and Hegel', are we not thereby reproducing the centrality of the white, European male in the philosophical canon? Drucilla Cornell did not just do that: she 'went to the ground' and worked with authors outside of the boundaries imposed by white epistemologies, and thereby not only did she *de facto* question such boundaries, she also helped to build a different imaginary. That was certainly the case for the students who attended that class in 2011 at the New School, who may have joined the class attracted by the names of Marx, Lenin and Mao, and then found themselves reading Fanon, Glissant and the Ubuntu philosophy she had studied in South Africa.

Drucilla Cornell was not just a theorist of the imaginary: she was also a practitioner of it, and the author of many successful plays. She theorised about the 'struggle for redemptive imagination' but she also actively pursed it with passion and generosity. Even though some aspects of her *The Imaginary Domain*, as she herself admitted, may be outdated, the central intuitions of that work remain, in my view, as valid as ever. Once again, that is the result of the fact that, on feminist issues, as well as all others, she 'went to the ground'. At the time when she was working on *The Imaginary Domain*, feminists were brutally divided between those who wanted to abolish sex work and those who embraced it, between the supporters of pornography and those who saw it as a tool for the perpetuation of rape culture or even as a form of rape itself. Drucilla had been an activist and union organiser for many years, so whenever in doubt about academic debates, she went back to the workers themselves, and looked at the material conditions of their labour.[2] When you do that, the very moral question about abolishing or tolerating sex work turns into a much more urgent political question: how can sex workers unionise if you criminalise them? How can we ensure their working conditions are safe and not exploitative? That is why she not only argued against the criminalisation of sex work, but further went on to build a feminist brothel. Instead of adopting a moralist attitude in favour or against pornography, from the comfort of a university office, Drucilla Cornell decided to meet and work with the women in the business. In doing so, one may discover that, although mainstream heterosexual pornography can be extremely violent and detrimental to women's interests, some feminist pornography may actually work in their favour. Hence her central claim that, since we are all sexed beings, we need to be able to have access to a material and psychic space that enables us to individuate as sexed beings. As she wrote: 'There are three conditions that ensure a minimum degree of individuation which I defend as necessary for the equivalent chance to transform ourselves into individuated beings who can participate in public and political life as equal citizens. They are as follows: 1) bodily integrity, 2) access to symbolic forms sufficient to achieve linguistics skills permitting the differentiation of oneself from others, and 3) the protection of the imaginary domain itself'.[3] Consider how such a move enables us to sweep away endless academic discussions on who is the subject of feminism, whether we need 'women' or not for a feminist cause, and whether we can, or should ever attempt, to define what it means to be a woman. No need to indulge in academic definitions of womanhood: just make sure actual people have the symbolic means to define themselves! The very same concept of the imaginary domain, which enabled her to address pressing feminist issues by connecting vital strands in critical theory with psychoanalysis and legal theory, also enabled her to make an original contribution to critical philosophy of race.

Despite a life in the academy, Drucilla Cornell never forgot the lessons she learned as an activist: as a union organiser, as a militant feminist, and as a Black Panther ally.

In a panel at the Goethe Institute in New York City, devoted to celebrating the 200th anniversary of Karl Marx's birth, Drucilla explained why she always shied away from reductive academic readings of Marx. Despite her encounter with Marxism at a time when everything in the study of Marx was about science and economics, Drucilla was instead attracted to his critique of alienation, and how capitalism leads not only to exploitation but also to imperialism and inhuman conditions of labour and life. Hence her critique of the 'scientization of Marx': 'it is part of turning a revolutionary thinker into someone who can get you tenured at Harvard'.[4] But if you read him as a thinker who demanded the immediate abolishing of an inhuman reality and follow in his footsteps, then you are going to be in trouble. On that same occasion, Drucilla Cornell explained how she, indeed, got into trouble, how she was kicked out of Stanford and Columbia, but she also emphatically repeated: 'It was worth it'.

Drucilla Cornell is just gone, but we already miss the lucidity of her thinking, and the courage of her actions. As I think about her struggles for a 'redemptive imagination', I cannot but recall her Facebook profile picture: Drucilla holding a copy of *The Imaginary Domain* and, next to it a sign: 'Let's talk about abortion rights!'

Notes

1. On multiple occasions, we debated this point. I am less skeptical of the word, once we spell out that it is not just a metaphor. She seemed to prefer the word 'creolisation'. See, for instance, the edited volume, *Creolizing Rosa Luxemburg*, she edited with Jane Ann Gordon (Lanham: Rowman & Littlefield, 2021).

2. Luckily enough, one of the lectures she gave in my class has been recorded and saved in OOPS, the free Online Open Public Seminar I directed in 2016. Particularly appreciated was the story of how she helped in unionising sex workers and building a feminist brothel: https://publicseminar.org/2016/05/oops-lecture-gender-and-domination-class-by-drucilla-cornell/.

3. Drucilla Cornell, *The Imaginary Domain: Abortion, Pornography and Sexual Harassment* (New York, Routledge 1995), 4.

4. See the video of her intervention at the following website. To the question 'is Marx still relevant today', she replied by reading a passage from the *Grundrisse* on the alienation of labour conditions: https://thebrooklyninstitute.com/blog/faculty-video-marx-now-a-symposium/.

Bruno Latour, 1947–2022
An untimely death, a work for the future
Patrice Maniglier

Modernity is characterised by its extraordinary capacity to give a mystified image of itself, and the most enduring aim of Bruno Latour's work might be summarised by evoking the subtitle of his last great theoretical work: an anthropology of modernity.[1] Those of us who mourn his death will miss him above all because we have lost one of the most precious allies we had in confronting the great civilisational challenge of our times, the challenge that Latour named as landing Modernity [*faire atterrir la Modernité*].*

One of the great lessons of what intellectual historians one day will no doubt call the 'late Latour' was the event that constitutes our present. Climate change is one of the most spectacular manifestations of it, though not the only one. The destruction of biodiversity, the reduction of the undeveloped surface of the earth, microplastic pollution, and so on, might all be included. As always, the problem is to properly understand the problem itself. The urgency of the present lies in understanding exactly what specific problem it poses. Latour arrived at a clear statement on this point: it is a question of knowing how to bring back within planetary limits a certain mode of terrestrial habitation which has been called modernity.

In the end, his whole project has consisted in the idea of *relativising the moderns*. The relevance of the term 'modernity' may appear doubtful. Indeed, many great minds, one will recall, have tried to say something clear on this point, from Baudelaire to Foucault, passing through Weber, Durkheim, Heidegger, Arendt, Blumenberg, Habermas, Lyotard, Koselleck, Beck, and so on. Yet these are only the ones who have been most explicit on the subject, and the results have been far from convincing.

It would be tempting, therefore, to drop the term and talk about something else, for example, capitalism, the industrial world, colonisation, or whichever well-known historical process or event. Latour stands out from such attempts through the paradoxical firmness with which he always held on to the enigma of the modern.

We have never been modern means two things at the same time. First, as 'moderns' we are not exceptional or radically different from all that has taken place, but are nonetheless different. Second, 'modernity' is a word that prevents an accurate description of this difference, this specificity, and its actual features. It is an event that occurred first in some societies, and which then extended, through colonisation and then decolonisation, to all the Earth's inhabited lands, before finally swallowing the entire planet away in its racing fury.

We may doubt the existence of a great event dividing history in two, with the 'moderns' on one side and all other forms of human existence on the other – *the West and the rest*, as it is said ironically in English. However, we must recognise that a great event of a planetary nature has indeed taken place. It is enough to examine the details of the so-called Great Acceleration, or to concern oneself with the discussions among geologists about the exact dating of the Anthropocene, to realise that something did in fact happened between the end of the eighteenth century and the middle of the twentieth century, which brought about a radical break in the lives not only of some human societies, but of all terrestrial beings, human and non-human.

Once again, climate change stands as the clearest symbol of this event to the collective conscience. How-

---

* A longer version of this text was originally published as 'Bruno Latour: une mort à contre-temps, une œuvre pour l'avenir', AOC, 11 October 2022, https://aoc.media/opinion/2022/10/10/bruno-latour-une-mort-a-contre-temps-une-oeuvre-pour-lavenir/.

ever, the very expression 'sixth extinction' used to characterise what is happening to the world's biodiversity says something about the space of comparability of this event of which we are the contemporaries. This is because our present differs from others in a way that is comparable to only five events that have taken place in the 5 billion years of the Earth's history. Of course, some discuss the relevance of the word 'sixth extinction', but the very fact that it is being discussed itself gives an idea of the horizon in which this discussion is taking place. It is measured in billions of years.

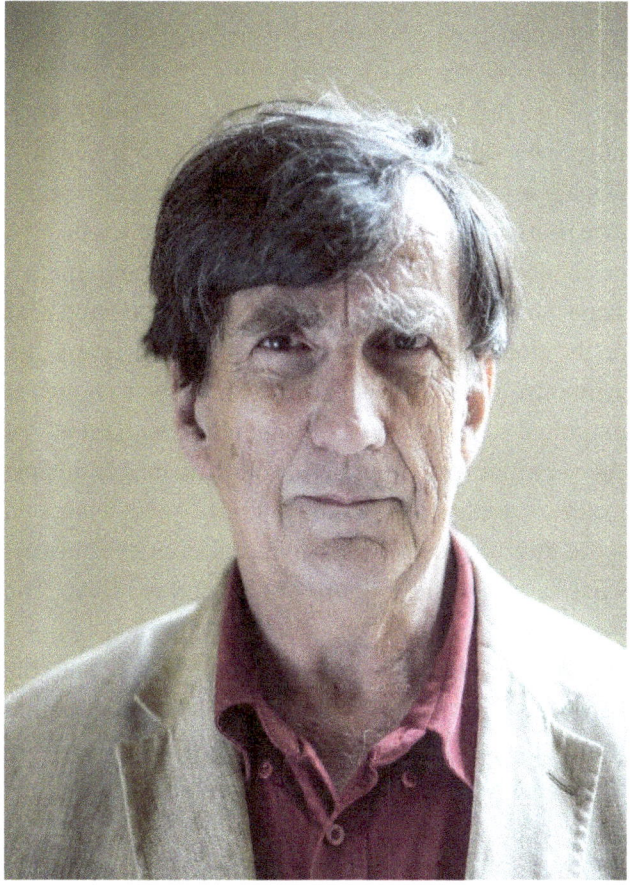

Latour's originality in the contemporary intellectual field lies in the fact that he never gave up the profound conviction that something had indeed happened but we are unable to describe it. The word 'modernity' is for him essentially the name of a question rather than an answer. If it is preferable to other terms (capitalism, anthropocene, industrialism, technoscience, etc.), it is precisely because it is more obscure, more debatable, more controversial. Because of this, it forces us not to rush into believing that we have understood the question. It has an in-built way of blocking any correct description that one may try to give it, quite simply because 'modernity' means 'that which is necessary if one wants to be contemporary to one's own history'.

Latour never stopped questioning this way of taking the modern at face value. The process of modernisation is no doubt a fact, but one that remains enigmatic. On the other hand, the notion of the necessity of modernisation, that it is a simple response to the intrinsic needs of the human soul or the inevitable necessities of 'development', is propaganda. This is not just normatively debatable, but above all descriptively unacceptable because it occludes an accurate description of the event which must be related to its *contingency*. We have never been modern means that it has never been necessary that we become modern.

Although it might not be found in that form in Latour's text, this is what I mean by the expression *relativising the moderns*. It means to describe precisely which choice defines modernity and to contrast it with other possible choices. These other possible choices may be consistent with each other, perhaps even capable of coexisting with the one that has been made. This is the sense in which we should understand his early work on the sciences. The great myth surrounding the invention of modern science consists in the basic notion that very intelligent and intellectually free people such as Galileo or Newton found a way to describe reality as it is without letting their prejudices or superstitions interfere with their thinking.

To practice an anthropology of science, as Latour proposed in his first book with Steve Woolgar, *Laboratory Life*, first published in English in 1979, requires that one set aside this myth in order to describe what scientists do at work.[2] Unsurprisingly, we do not find many people trying to get rid of their prejudices to confront a naked reality. On the contrary, what we see are people who employ a lot of ingenuity and energy to produce realities of a very particular kind: realities made up of scientific objects and facts. The molecular formula of the hormone that Professor Guillemin was trying to identify in the laboratory where Latour undertook his first ethnographic fieldwork about the moderns corresponds to an entity of a quite different sort from that of the bee spirits 'established' by the practices of the Amazonian shaman Davi Kopenawa.[3] This entity is not more real, but otherwise real. This difference certainly gives it an unparalleled grip on the world. It allows it to make alliances with a wider variety of interests and thus acquire power and authority, but not with all interests. Such a reality comes at the cost of a choice, of a selection, or sometimes, even often, a destruction.

Until the end of his life, I believe, Latour's whole question was to work out if these different realities could coexist. Beyond this, the question was of knowing if such a plurality of realities could help us establish a more just relationship with reality in general, by giving up our belief that there could be something other than this plural matrix. The properly *metaphysical* horizon of Latour's work thus lies in the sense that his work answers quite an old philosophical question: in what does *being* consist?[4]

The great misunderstanding regarding the expression 'to relativise' comes from believing that when one relativises something one is trying to take away part of its dignity, whereas one is simply trying to describe it more accurately, indeed, to define this very dignity with greater rigour by *contrasting* it with the alternatives. It is for love of the sciences and, in a certain manner, for love of the moderns that Latour has sought to relativise them: to show what about them was so singular, so original, so irreplaceable, without needing to think that all branches of knowledge should become scientific or that all forms of life should become 'modern'.

It should not be forgotten that Latour forged this intellectual project of an anthropology of modernity in Africa, or more precisely in the Ivory Coast following its final decolonisation. Cooperating with the authorities, he had been tasked with writing a report for ORSTOM on the difficulties that companies encountered in 'Ivorising' their personnel, and it was during this time that the central idea of this project emerged.[5]

This text involves a wide-ranging investigation into racism and the aporias of 'modernisation', showing the extent to which modernisation is inseparable from colonisation. To relativise the modern is also to grasp at what cost modernisation was implemented within the capillaries of the collective structure of empire, through what modes of translation, violence and misunderstanding it imposed itself as the only viable future for these societies. Latour often mentioned that he came up with his project of an anthropology of the moderns when he realised that one could turn the tools anthropologists use to describe 'non-modern' societies – their 'rituals', 'beliefs', and 'customs' – against the great institutions of modernity itself: science, technology, law, religion, politics, and so on. We could say that the fundamental presupposition of Latour's entire work (like that of Lévi-Strauss, with which it shares many features) is decolonisation – how to fully decolonise our modes of thinking.[6]

The colonial question is thus the first context to which the project of relativising modernity is applied. But Latour's work would not be what it is for us today had he not acknowledged very early on that a second context justifies the urgency of such an undertaking: the 'ecological' question, or more precisely the 'eco-planetary' question. It should be recalled here that it was in *We Have Never Been Modern*, published just after the fall of the Berlin Wall at the start of the 1990s, that Latour explained that global warming – whose reality was beginning to be accepted around the time of the international climate negotiations that would lead to the Rio Summit – constituted now an unavoidable aspect of any reflection on modernity. 'In Paris, London and Amsterdam, this same glorious year 1989 witnesses the first conferences on the global state of the planet: for some observers they symbolize the end of capitalism and its vain hopes of unlimited conquest and total dominion over nature.'[7] At the very moment when the world is no longer divided into two blocs and the Euro-American 'model' faces no more internal obstacles, an external frontier appears – what Latour would go on to call 'planetary limits'. The modern project comes up against a wall which does not separate two portions of the Earth, but which divides the Earth itself from its own fragility. It will later be said that it would take 5.2 planets for the American way of life to be extended to all of humanity. There is, in other words, no room for the 'modern' project.

In this way, the expression *relativising the moderns* changes its meaning. It is no longer a question of knowing what particular kinds of realities or arrangements of humans and non-humans as opposed to others the moderns produce. The question is no longer that of defining these beings in a more realistic manner. It is rather that of grasping what sort of *terrestrials* these beings are, in what ways such beings are linked into the terrestrial order so that they are able to construct a way of life. It is also about understanding what all of this does to the Earth, which is at once a condition and an effect of these forms of terrestrial habitation. It took several decades for Latour to arrive at a clear formulation of this problem, though one cannot say that this later version of his reflections on the subject are where he would have stopped had he been able to continue working. Nonetheless, there is little doubt that during the last 15 years of his life he devoted his intense intellectual energy to developing this problem as rigorously as possible, something he did in collaboration with a considerable number of people around him, as he always knew how to do. In the end, he developed a formula of this kind: the challenge of the present is to embed modern ways of life back within these terrestrial limits. To use an expression of my own, the moderns are deterrestrialised terrestrials who inhabit the Earth while forever ignoring, neglecting, their own terrestrial condition. The challenge of the present is to reterrestrialise them.

We must be careful, however, not to interpret this formula as if it implied that the Earth was a finite reality, with fixed boundaries like the unmovable walls of a house. The Earth, what Latour calls Gaia, is an active, dynamic, and historical entity, which reacts to the actions of the terrestrial beings who live on it and from it.[8] The point, therefore, is not to resign ourselves to these external limits, but rather to become more intensely and, precisely, more sensitive to our own terrestrial condition; that is to say, to the way in which we influence planetary dynamics by how we occupy the Earth, which we have made our terrestrial dwelling. The present situation is certainly distressing and full of present and future grief. Species are dying out, landscapes are changing faster than the living can cope with, forests are burning, war is once again knocking on our doors ... Yet this situation is also something of an opportunity and this ambivalence is itself typically *modern*.

For perhaps the first time in the history of humanity, we have the possibility of living in a closer, more intimate relationship with this planetary condition, a condition which is in fact ours, which has always been ours, and which has been so since there has been life on Earth. Latour, in fact, never missed an opportunity to remind us that it is the living who have created the Earth's climate, that it was bacteria that modified the terrestrial atmosphere so that other living beings could flourish there. This is the lesson he drew from James Lovelock and Lynn Margulis, from whom he borrowed the word 'Gaia' to designate precisely this feedback between the whole and its parts, the Earth and its terrestrial beings. We now know that by choosing a terrestrial dwelling for ourselves we choose an Earth. The question, then, is what kind of Earth?

There was a lot of confusion when Latour recently began to talk about a plurality of Earths, saying for example that Trump's Earth was different from ours.[9] Some responded in outrage: 'What! Isn't there only one planet? Isn't this an astronomical fact, the whole basis of the Earth System Sciences you claim to be so fond of? This is where your relativism leads us! We thought you'd calmed down with this nonsense but here you are again making absurd claims. There are no multiple realities, just as there are no multiple Earths. There's only one reality: scientific reality. And only one Earth: the one studied by the Earth sciences.' However, Latour was much closer to what these sciences teach when suggesting that the Earth should not be seen as locked in a fixed state that could be defined by certain biogeochemical parameters. Instead, it is a system that never achieves equilibrium and that is characterised by an irreducible historicity. Each of its states is best described as part of a set of alternative futures coexisting with one another as possibilities.

Of course, there is only one Earth, but this uniqueness is precisely one to which belong multiple alternative but coexisting futures, some of which may be incompatible with others. To be terrestrial is to have to choose one's territory (*terre*). We are still terraforming the Earth. The problem today is that we are terraforming it in reverse, or rather the problem is that the way we inhabit the Earth in the present destroys the possibility of other terrestrials envisioning other projects for its future, other lines of terraformation. The warming of the Earth by 3 or 4 degrees will not only destroy a very large number of terrestrial beings, human and non-human, but will also impose a particular condition of existence on many generations of terrestrials, for hundreds, even thousands or tens of thousands of years. Greenhouse gases in the atmosphere will take a long time to disappear, radioactive waste will in some cases remain for hundreds of thousands of years, synthetic molecules may substantially modify the chemical structures of the Earth in an irreversible way and with unpredictable consequences. The moderns have mortgaged the future of the Earth.

Landing the moderns means reopening the plurality of terrestrial projects. It is also to reflect on the conditions in which modernity could coexist on the same Earth with other forms of terrestrial dwelling, without eradicating or subjugating them. The uniqueness of the Earth would in this sense be a diplomatic uniqueness. The Earth would be precisely what a plurality of terrestrial projects must necessarily *share*. Bringing the moderns down to Earth means knowing what needs to be changed in their institutions so that they stop mortgaging the planet's entire space and future. This too is a way of *relativising* the moderns. They will learn what sort of terrestrials they are when they know in what conditions they can coexist, with their own difference or particularity and with other ways of being terrestrial. They will know themselves when they know *where* they are on Earth – that is to say, what sort of terrestrials they are able to be once they have stopped thinking that they can deterrestrialise themselves.

Such a landing (*atterrissage*), I repeat, should not be seen as a sad or frustrating enterprise. It will be difficult of course, but it also offers a unique opportunity to become more sensitive to a certain truth about our terrestrial condition. As they say in English, here is a 'once in a lifetime opportunity'. I think we could say that our contemporary eco-planetary catastrophe is a kind of 'once in a species-time opportunity'. It is a unique chance to get as close as possible to our own terrestrial condition. This can be understood in the general sense that nothing is more responsible for the earth's dynamics than the modern way of life which has 'awakened Gaia', with each particle of greenhouse gas we emit into the atmosphere contributing to accelerate warming, But it can also be understood in the specific sense that we will better understand the terrestrials we are by comparing ourselves with those with whom we coexist.

Re-embedding oneself within planetary limits does not at all mean limiting oneself, depriving oneself, but involves *gaining* something – gaining in truth, intensity, precision. By reappropriating our own terrestrial condition, we thus *add* to the world. Of course, all of this could go badly, and the odds ought to moderate our optimism. However, I believe it would be contrary to the spirit of Latour, at least to what I have gained from his texts and company, to rest satisfied with the anxieties and sadness that this situation legitimately arouses. This is something that should encourage us to read him. We must read Latour because he gives us tools to live better. In my opinion, no one more than Latour can be said to have fulfilled the great lesson of Spinoza: that there is no truth without joy. Latour is a joyful thinker.

He had a single project: an anthropology of the moderns that would relativise them. This project was unfolded through many investigations (on science, technology, law, religion, economics, politics, etc.), traversing many communities (the semiology of science, Science and Technology Studies (STS), Actor-Network Theory (ANT), pragmatic sociology, the ontological and anthropological turns, theories of Gaia … the list is too long), founding some of them before moving on to other pastures. He renewed modes of thinking everywhere he went, while always maintaining a coherent thread, which was outlined in his great work of 2012, *An Inquiry into Modes of Existence*. Nevertheless, this thread relates to two historical conditions that have both succeeded and added to each other – *decolonisation* and *ecologisation* – and which define the central stakes of his project. Or as Dipesh Chakrabarty would put it: globalisation and planetarisation. These two conditions, central to Latour's work, affect all social and political questions and oblige us to develop new tools to describe the relativity of the moderns.[10] This is how I propose to schematise Latour's intellectual trajectory in the hope that it will serve as a little portable map for anyone wishing to embark on it: it is an enormous enterprise that seeks to relativise modernity internally through a decolonial anthropology of modes of existence, on the one hand, and a diplomacy of the ways of being terrestrial, on the other.

Another important dimension must be added to this sketch: philosophy. Latour, in my view, seems to have always had an extremely nuanced relationship with philosophy. He would sometimes refuse to describe himself as a philosopher or he would present himself as an amateur philosopher, despite having been trained as a professional philosopher (agrégation, thesis, professorship). In fact, his true intellectual passion probably belonged to philosophy. In his later years, he seems to have made an effort to claim a clearer philosophical status for his work. His *Inquiry into Modes of Existence* should be understood in this light. Yet the fundamental originality of his philosophical approach is that it has always been *empirical* (depending on field investigations) and *pluralist* (refusing to *reduce* what he studied to anything other than what this object of study proposed as its horizon of reality). In this way, philosophy for him could no longer be seen to constitute a separate field. It exists only within anthropological, sociological, historical and artistic investigations. And yet philosophy is everywhere in his work. He himself ended up recognising that his project is fully grounded in it.

I am firmly convinced that we are yet to grasp the importance of his contribution to philosophy. I mean not just from the point of view of its contents, the theses that we may find in it, but also in terms of how he puts at stake the very status of philosophy as a discipline. Such is the centrality of philosophy in his work that one cannot philosophise in the same manner after Latour.

In any case, I cannot end this text without pointing out that while his work has clearly been *interrupted*, it is by no means finished. This singular force of action named Bruno Latour is now dispersed in his books, words, images, in the memories we have of him, in the inspiration he leaves to those he put to work and whose numbers will continue to grow. But although Bruno Latour continues to exist among us in a certain way, because of his death something is lost that is irreplaceable, something lost to all his contemporaries, who, through this very loss, become all the more contemporary with respect to each other.

One striking aspect of Bruno Latour's company and work was its unpredictability. It was enough to meet him after a month of absence to discover new ideas, unknown fields of research whose significance for one's own work would hit you out of the blue. You left with lots of books to read and things to discover. Some thoughts seem to lose their relevance with time. This was not the case with Latour. If there is mourning to be done, if there is reason to be sad, it is because there are many things we will never know because only Latour would have allowed us to discover them. He had an extremely rare ability to delve into the blind spots of our thinking and existence, to make us catch sight of a new perspective that would shift our horizons and simplify our questions, even as these would multiply, helping to awaken in us the desire, the courage to think and to act. The typical joy of Latour's thinking lay in this: you would always leave his company feeling that something in you had *increased*.

Without Latour, our collective sight gets a little blurrier, and with him we are losing a great optical device. He said recently that the great event of the year for him had been the launch of the James Webb Telescope. Latour was like a James Webb Telescope turned towards humanity. His death is like the crash of such a formidable instrument.

There is no better way to honour his memory than to continue working with joy, commitment, enthusiasm, passion, rigour, humour, creativity, solidarity, and sorority. If one could somehow compensate for this loss, it might be by taking inspiration from what he left us, helping us surmise what he could still have given us. Such discomfort, between mourning and gratitude, loneliness and the need to go on, between an awareness of our blind spots and a determination to open up our horizons, seems to me in the end quite an accurate way to characterise our present. We are and we remain in a *Latourian moment*.

Translated by Giovanni Menegalle

Notes

1. Bruno Latour, *An Inquiry into Modes of Existence: An Anthropology of the Moderns*, trans. Catherine Porter (Cambridge, MA: Harvard University Press, 2013).

2. Bruno Latour and Steve Woolgar, *Laboratory Life: The Construction of Scientific Facts* (Princeton: Princeton University Press, 1986). Latour provides a synthesis of his work on science and technology understood as *practices* in *Science in Action: How to Follow Scientists and Engineers through Society* (Cambridge, MA: Harvard University Press, 1987).

3. Davi Kopenawa and Bruce Albert, *The Falling Sky: Words of a Yanomami Shaman*, trans. Nicholas Elliott and Alison Dundy (Cambridge, MA: Harvard University Press, 2013).

4. This is the central theme of *An Inquiry into Modes of Existence*, cited above, and of the text co-written with Isabelle Stengers as a preface to Étienne Souriau's *Les Différents modes d'existence* (Paris: Presses Universitaires de France, 2009).

5. Bruno Latour, 'Les Idéologies de la compétence en milieu industriel à Abidjan' (1974), online at: http://www.bruno-latour.fr/sites/default/files/02-IDEOLOGIES-DE-COMPETENCE-FR.pdf.

6. On this notion of a 'permanent decolonisation of thought' as a way of characterising anthropology, see the works of Edouardo Batalha Viveiros de Castro, especially his book *Cannibal Metaphysics: For a Post-Structural Anthropology* (Minneapolis: Univocal, 2014). This can in many ways be read in parallel with Latour's work.

7. Latour, *We Have Never Been Modern*, 8.

8. On this point, see his book *Facing Gaia: Eight Lectures on the New Climatic Regime*, trans. Catherine Porter (Cambridge: Polity, 2017), where he offers his own interpretation of the term first coined by James Lovelock and Lynn Margulis.

9. He develops this particular idea in *Down to Earth: Politics in the New Climatic Regime*, trans. Catherine Porter (Cambridge: Polity, 2018).

10. See Dipesh Chakrabarty's recently published *The Climate of History in a Planetary Age* (Chicago: University of Chicago Press, 2021). For a French introduction to this work, see Jeanne Etelain et Patrice Maniglier, 'Ramener la critique sur Terre: le tournant planétaire de Dispeh Chakrabarty', *Critique* 903-904 (2022).

Maria Mies, 1931-2023
Fighting housewifisation and reclaiming our planet
Alessandra Mezzadri

When Maria Mies died, on 15 May 2023, I was re-reading her work on India, to reflect on its contemporary relevance for analyses of the world of work. I am profoundly saddened that the first way in which I will use my notes are to write this obituary. Yet, I am also profoundly honoured to celebrate Maria Mies' massive contribution to scholarship and activism. A towering figure in the fields of development sociology, feminist and ecofeminist theory and politics, a life-long activist and vocal ally of anti-imperialist movements everywhere, it is virtually impossible to acknowledge all of Mies' contributions in a short tribute. Here, far more humbly and still feeling the intellectual and emotional pain of her loss – I met her only once in 2018, in Cologne alongside her partner, eco-socialist writer and activist Saral Sarkar, and remember our encounter with great fondness – I shall limit myself to highlighting three key tropes in her intellectual and political life journey that spoke and still speak to me. I consider these tropes as gifts that she has left us, to further nurture and develop, with that form of highly political care labour that shaped Mies' aspirations towards a collectively envisioned *'good life'*.[1]

The first gift that Maria Mies leaves us is her understanding of capitalism as a global system reorganising life and production at once, experienced differently across the world economy, and centred on the home as the key patriarchal site of labour-surplus extraction and struggle. Mies is globally renowned for her book *Patriarchy and Accumulation on a Global Scale: Women in the International Division of Labour*, originally published by Zed in 1986,[2] and for proposing, in the words of Silvia Federici, who wrote the forward to the latest 2014 edition, 'a vision of world history centred on the "production of life" and the struggles against its exploitation'. Central to Mies' thinking is the concept of *housewifisation*, that concerns the ways in which capitalism structures patriarchy by constructing women as housewives, homemakers and/or subordinate reproductive labourers, eventually projecting this disadvantage onto the labour market.[3]

Whilst *Patriarchy and Accumulation* is undoubtedly her masterpiece, Mies started developing some of the key analytical categories that would shape her thought a few years earlier, when she completed a shorter and far more empirically grounded book published in 1982, titled *The Lacemakers of Narsapur: Indian Housewives Produce for the World Market*.[4] The work at the basis of this early book was funded by the International Labour Organization (ILO) in the context of its World Employment Programme (WEP), which started in 1969 with the aim of mapping the world of supposed unemployment in what was then referred to as the 'Third World', now renamed – a definition also marred by its own analytical and political problems – the 'Global South'.[5] The main contribution of the WEP is the 'discovery' of the informal sector; a segment of the economy not characterised by unemployment, as per the initial hypothesis by the ILO, but by the underemployment of a large pool of people labelled in Keith Hart's famous Kenya report as its 'working poor', which would become a key subject of development interventions and remains so to date.[6] Yet, while far less acknowledged in the development studies literature, *The Lacemakers* was a groundbreaking contribution. In Narsapur, a small town in Andhra Pradesh, one could say that Mies discovered how the whole world works.

In Narsapur, Mies understood that labour could be organised in life spaces in ways that regenerated an invisible assembly line running across the reproductive economy; a way of perfecting and fine-tuning the colonial putting-out system that infiltrated the home and turned it into both a unit of subsistence and a manufacturing production unit.[7] The system relied entirely on the extraction and appropriation of women's labour at cheap rates, as lacemaking was a woman's preserve learnt during the colonial period. Yet the whole decentralised system of production was dominated by men, with merchants towering over the top of the lace-making chain and organising a complex spiderweb of contractors under them. This homes-centred 'diffuse factory' was caste-bound and classed, besides being gendered, with the original Christian former low-caste women lace-makers being progressively pushed out of the industry during the export boom to be replaced with a larger pool of impoverished women from a variety of communities including upper-caste ones.[8] In short, as Keith Hart was coining what became the key definitions and actors of the informal sector or economy, Maria Mies was mapping its internal mechanisms of exploitation, and its most invisibilised gendered and racial aspects.

The domestication – or semi-domestication – of the lacemakers of Narsapur was based on their representation as housewives and the representation of their labour as housework, a key insight that Mies develops in the conclusion – and in the last endnotes – of *The Lacemakers*. It is here that she deploys the term 'housewifisation' for the first time, a key concept that she then developed more fully in *Patriarchy and Accumulation*. 'Housewifisation', Mies writes, 'expresses more concretely the specifically modern form of control over women occurring in this case than does the term domestication. I define housewifisation as a process by which women are socially defined as housewives, dependent for their sustenance on the income of the husband, irrespective of whether they are de facto housewives or not ... It leads to defining the bulk of women's subsistence work as non-work and hence open to unrestricted exploitation'[9].

Half a century on, housewifisation still defines the lives of millions of women across the globe. In fact, it has further extended its reach and role within contemporary capitalist accumulation, as I and others have shown.[10] First, in India, as elsewhere across the world economy, the bulk of women's employment continues being statistically mischaracterised as 'housework' and excluded from the computation of what represents employment proper.[11] Secondly, the regeneration of homeworking within the world system – which was never to be a transitory form of work eventually leading to 'free' wage labour, as Mies wrote very clearly in *The Lacemakers*[12] – has also extended the analytical reach of *housewifisation* to men too. Those performing 'homework', often situated at the margins of increasingly globalised supply chains, also see their labour devalued and represented as lying outside the 'proper' wage relation – indeed, a declination of women's work. Maria Mies' work speaks to the organisation of manufacturing in neoliberal times, and to the many 'forms of exploitation' – to deploy an expression by Jairus Banaji – that characterise it.[13]

The second trope in Maria Mies' work concerns her commitment to nature and the planet, by denouncing and fighting the commodification, extraction and depletion of human and natural resources imposed by capitalism. In fact, intersectional concerns on the ways in which capitalism subjugates both women and nature were already central to *Patriarchy and Accumulation*. Yet, it is in the book *Ecofemism*, written with Vandana Shiva, that they are more carefully spelt out. Mies' and Shiva's *Ecofeminism* is aligned with the work of other feminist scholars concerned with the environment, like Françoise d'Eaubonne – who coined the term *Ecofeminism* in the first instance – as well as Carolyn Merchant,[14] Wangari Mathaai,[15] Veronika Bennholdt-Thomsen,[16] Ariel Salleh,[17] Ana Isla,[18] Mary Mellor,[19] as well as many feminist Indigenous collectives across our planet, who constantly write *Ecofeminism* by doing.[20] It is another ground-breaking text and political manifesto denouncing the interwoven socially depleting, ecocidal features of capitalism. Across the twenty essays of this text, the authors connect patriarchal accumulation to the expropriation and plunder of our ecosystems, representing women and nature as 'the last colony'.[21] Intrinsic to Mies' thought, here, is the immanent critique of modernity and its simplistic dichotomies, which nevertheless shape reality as we know it so that:

> [M]odern civilisation is based on a cosmology and anthropology that structurally dichotomizes reality, and hierarchically opposes the two parts to each other: the one always considered superior, always *thriving*, and progressing at the expense of the other. Thus, nature is subordinated to man; woman to man, consumption to production and the local to the global, and so on.[22]

At times wrongly trivialised as an analysis comparing *ad litteram* the exploitation of women and that of the environment – and a text that must be approached with some sense of history[23] – *Ecofeminism* is better read as a pioneering analysis of the interconnections between the social and ecological destruction caused by unbridled capitalism. *Ecofeminism* provides an analysis of global capitalist production that systematically cheapens the work and lives of some communities (women, many of whom are Indigenous, colonised and racialised people), and also devalues the 'fruits' of nature, which are appropriated through processes of brutal plunder and enclosure often enforced against those same communities. Here, the trope of a continuous, ongoing process of primitive accumulation – which Mies already mentioned in 1982 in *The Lacemakers*, well before the systematic analysis developed by David Harvey on processes of accumulation by dispossession[24] – as affecting some people and some lands is more carefully developed. One of the most compelling contemporary avatars of Mies and Shiva's ecofeminist analysis is developed by Stefania Barca's *Forces of Reproduction* (2020), which illustrates the interconnections between patriarchy, violence against Indigenous communities and activists and ecocide.[25]

Given the ongoing, mounting violence against women, people of colour and our planet, and in the age of global pandemics like the one we are still battling, many of the insights from *Ecofeminism* could not remain more compelling to contemporary decolonial debates and degrowth arguments. Indeed, in later work with Veronika Bennholdt-Thomsen, and drawing on decolonial and anticolonial collective, anti-capitalist practices across the world, Mies wrote the key elements of their book *The Subsistence Perspective: Beyond the Globalised Economy*, a utopian, radical alternative to the free-market industrial system which must be dismantled.[26] As signalled by Ariel Salleh in her forward to the 2013 edition of *Ecofeminism*, '[t]he call is for degrowth, commoning and *Buen Vivir*'.

Finally, a third trope in Maria Mies' work we need to carry with us is her unflinching commitment to anti-colonial and anti-imperialist struggles and her prompt denunciation of the neocolonial violence imposed by international financial institutions on vast parts of the world. Examples of her activism and allyship are numerous, and choosing one to reflect on does feel arbitrary. Yet, inspired by the desire to illustrate the contemporary impact and significance of Mies' work and political commitments, I will do so. My choice speaks to the picture chosen for this obituary, of Maria standing in front of an anti-International Monetary Fund and anti-World Bank banner. Mies started writing against International Financial and Trade Institutions (IFTIs) already in the early 1970s, denouncing the neocolonial trade policies and corporate logics promoted by the then General Agreement on Tariffs and Trade (GATT), now World Trade Organization (WTO), the agrarian knowledge hegemony exercised by agencies like the Food and Agricultural Organisation (FAO), and the financial plunder orchestrated by the IMF and the World Bank.[27] Today, as feminist and ecological justice organisations worldwide continue mobilising against IFTIs-imposed conditionalities and debt and its repercussions on societies' gendered fabric,[28] or against global corporate socio-ecological plunder often involving the target-killing of Indigenous activists,[29] Maria Mies' analyses and activism could not appear more relevant. They are intergenerational, intellectual and political gifts that we need to carry with us and nurture – for *our* life, *our* times.

Rest in Power, Maria Mies. You are now the seed.

Notes

1. See Mies' own biography *The Village and the World: My Life, Our Times* (Australia: Spinifex Press, 2010).
2. Maria Mies, *Patriarchy and Accumulation on a Global Scale: Women in the International Division of Labour*, (London: Zed Books, 1986).
3. Yet, patriarchal relations may vary massively based on the type of labour subordination to capital. On this point, in *Patriarchy and Accumulation*, Mies relies significantly on Rhoda Reddock's insights in relation to slavery. See Rhoda Reddock, 'Women's Liberation and National Lib-

eration' in Mies and Reddock, eds., *National Liberation and Women's Liberation* (The Hague: Institute of Social Studies, 1982).

4. Maria Mies, *The Lacemakers of Narsapur: Indian Housewives Produce for the World Market* (Geneva: ILO, 1982).

5. On this issue, see A. Sajed 'From the Third World to the Global South' *E- International Relations* (2020), https://www.e-ir.info/2020/07/27/from-the-third-world-to-the-global-south/

6. K. Hart, *Kenya Report* (Geneva: ILO 1973), in C.O.N. Moser, 'Informal sector or petty commodity production: Dualism or dependence in urban development?', *World Development* 6:9-10 (1978), 1041–1064.

7. Mies, *The Lacemakers*, 57.

8. Ibid., 58.

9. Ibid., 180.

10. See Alessandra Mezzadri, *The Sweatshop Regime: Labouring Bodies, Exploitation, and Garments Made in India* (Cambridge University Press, 2016).

11. The reader can refer to S. Naidu and L. Ossome, 'Social Reproduction and the Agrarian Question of Women's Labour in India', *Agrarian South: Journal of Political Economy* 5:1 (2016), 50–76.

12. Mies, *The Lacemakers*, 4.

13. J. Banaji, *Theory as History: Essays on Modes of Production and Exploitation* (London: Brill, 2010).

14. See C. Merchant, *The Death of Nature: Women, Ecology and the Scientific Revolution* (San Francisco: Harper & Row, 1980); *Earthcare: Women and the Environment* (New York: Routledge, 1996).

15. W. Mathaai, *Green Belt Movement: Sharing the Approach and the Experience* (New York: Lanterns Book, 1985).

16. Co-authored with Mies *The Subsistence Perspective*, introduced later.

17. See A. Salleh, *Ecofeminism as Politics: Nature, Marx and the Postmodern* (London: Zed Books, 1997). Here, ecofeminism is understood as the political synthesis of four revolutions: the environmental justice movement, feminism, socialism, and post-colonial struggle.

18. A. Isla, *The "Greening" of Costa Rica: Women, Peasants, Indigenous People and the Remaking of Nature* (Toronto: University of Toronto Press, 2015); *Climate Chaos: Ecofeminism and the Land Question* (Toronto: Inanna Publications, 2019).

19. M. Mellor, *Feminism and Ecology* (New York: New York University Press, 1997).

20. For her dedication to environmental conservation and women's rights, Mathaai was awarded the 2004 Nobel Peace Prize for her 'contribution to sustainable development, democracy and peace'.

21. See also M. Mies, V. Bennholdt-Thomsen and C. von Werlhof, *Women, the Last Colony* (London: Zed, 1988).

22. Maria Mies and Vandana Shiva, *Ecofeminism* (Fernwood, 1993), 5.

23. For instance, the debate on reproductive technologies is clearly marred by gender essentialism.

24. David Harvey, 'The "New" Imperialism: Accumulation by Dispossession', *Socialist Register* 40 (2004), 63–87.

25. S. Barca, *Forces of Reproduction: Notes for a Counter-Hegemonic Anthropocene* (Cambridge: Cambridge University Press: 2020).

26. M. Mies and V. Bennholdt-Thomsen, *The Subsistence Perspective: Beyond the Globalised Economy* (London: Zed Books, 1999).

27. She wrote of these experiences in *The Village and the World*.

28. See, for instance, Veronica Gago's and Luci Caballero's analysis in the book *A Feminist Reading of Debt* (Pluto Press, 2020), illustrating the interconnections between debt as a macroeconomic relation and patriarchal violence in Argentinian households and streets.

29. Over two hundred people are killed each year whilst defending their land and environment. See updated estimates (last update May 2013) at https://www.globalwitness.org/en/campaigns/environmental-activists/decade-defiance/

www.ingramcontent.com/pod-product-compliance
Lightning Source LLC
Chambersburg PA
CBHW082009090526
44590CB00020B/3411